CAR MANIA

CAR MANIA

A Critical History of Transport

WINFRIED WOLF

Translated by Gus Fagan

PLUTO  PRESS
LONDON • CHICAGO, IL

First published in German as
Eisenbahn und Autowahn
by Rash und Röhring

Revised English edition published 1996 by
PLUTO PRESS
345 Archway Road, London N6 5AA
and 1436 West Randolph, Chicago, Illinois 60607, USA

British Library Cataloguing in Publication Data
A catalogue record for this book is available from
the British Library

ISBN 0 7453 0970 4 hbk

Library of Congress Cataloging in Publication Data
Wolf Winfried.
[Eisenbahn und Autowahn. English]
Car mania: a critical history of transport. / Winfried
Wolf. — 1st English ed.
    p.   cm.
Includes bibliographical references and index.
ISBN 0–7453–0970–4 (hbk)
1. Transportation—History. 2. Railroads—History.
3. Transportation, Automotive—History. I. Title.
HE151.W5813 1996
388'.09—dc20   95–49684
                                                        CIP

Designed, typeset and produced for Pluto Press by
Chase Production Services, Chipping Norton, OX7 5QR
Printed in the EC by T.J. Press, Padstow

Contents

Part III
The Car Society: Myth, Mania and Machismo

Lists of Tables, Figures and Maps

Tables

Figures

Maps

Preface

Hey Mitsubishi and Toyota
Who said that the war was over?
The city streets are full of hate
the lights are red, it's all too late.
How much can a poor man take?

Ray Davies (for The Kinks)
'Aggravation'

In 1989 Margaret Thatcher praised the 'great car economy'. By 1998, at the latest, Britain will have achieved that goal, with one car for every two persons. Such a level of car density, already surpassed in the US, Italy and Germany, was previously considered to be unacceptably high. Perhaps one could make a virtue of necessity: since the entire population of the United Kingdom, including children and the elderly, could fit into the front seats of these cars, there should be no difficulty in finding homes for the homeless and the refugees. The living space per person in the car is above the average to be found in the Third World.

But this is not what is happening: as the number of cars increases, so does the number of homeless and refugees. In the 'great car economy' of Britain and the US there are today hundreds of thousands living in that hybrid product of the car society, the caravan. It is the view of *The Times* that caravan sites are 'a blight without parallel since planning was introduced to stop the spread of ribbon suburbs in the 1930s ... These are the new squatter settlements ...' (7 August 1993). The 'great car economy' has become a car mania.

This is the third time that I have set about re-writing the present book and each re-write has been accompanied not just by new insights but also by changes in my own personal approach to mobility. The first German edition, 560 pages in length, was published in 1986 with the title *Eisenbahn und Autowahn* (*The Railway and Car Mania*). After nineteen years behind the wheel, I declared myself a private car-free zone and discovered *en passant* what a pleasant change it made to the quality of life. In 1992, with two editions now out of print, I decided to re-write the book. My publisher's concern that the book had now grown to over 840 pages was soon overcome when the book sold well. During the second writing I re-discovered cycling, a pleasant alternative to the fitness studio, another business spawned by the great car economy.

When my British publisher, Roger van Zwanenberg, agreed in 1994 to an English language edition, I decided once again to re-write the whole work. I was prompted in this also by Pluto Press's suggestion that the existing book should be shortened by at least 300 pages and published as two separate volumes. The result was not just an updated work but in many respects an entirely new one. Its theme is now the *international* car society.

Car Mania describes the history of the railways and canals, the resistible rise of the car and the forced decline of the railways, and the modern car society with its myths, mania and machismo. The companion volume, published as a separate title, is the logical continuation of *Car Mania*. It looks at the ecological and economic balance sheet of road transport; the international character of the 'great car economy', in particular its destructive effect in the Third World; the destruction through privatisation of the remaining rail networks; the resistance to the car society, and the alternatives available.

Preparing this book for the first English language edition has also made me more critical of the belief in the blessings that are meant to accompany the development of human productive forces, a belief that also finds expression in Marxism. And while travelling in a narrowboat on the Pontcysyllte Aqueduct and along the Llangollen Canal I discovered the pleasures of slowness. I am also probably the only member of the German parliament to refuse internal flights and to travel around Germany only by train.

For their help in the preparation of the present volume I am indebted to the team at Pluto Press, in particular to Roger van Zwanenberg and Robert Webb. I would also like to express my thanks to Philip Bagwell, the railway historian and trade unionist, whose expert advice was so freely given and so gratefully received. I would also like to thank Transport 2000, the Rail, Maritime and Transport Union (RMT), and the International Transport Federation (ITF) for their information and advice. My special thanks goes to Gus Fagan, who has been more than a translator and without whose help this new edition would not have been possible.

The present English language edition will also be the basis for a new edition in German and in Spanish. The fourth German edition will have benefited greatly from its travels in other countries and other languages.

Winfried Wolf,
Cologne, April 1996

Part I

The Eighteenth and Nineteenth Centuries: Railways and Canals

The railways are the product of capitalist industry and, at the same time, the most visible measure of the development of world trade and of bourgeois democratic civilisation.

V. I. Lenin

Marxist and non-Marxist historians alike take for granted that the railway was the principal means of transport at the beginning of the industrial revolution. Canals receive scant mention although it was the canal network that actually provided transport for the early industrial age. This was true especially of Britain, the birthplace of the industrial revolution, and of the United States, the most powerful capitalist economic power from the end of the nineteenth century.

The Stockton–Darlington line in the industrial heart of England, opened in 1825, is generally considered to be the first rail link in the world. But this is only partly true. It was indeed the first public passenger link and it was the first steam-powered locomotive, but horse-drawn rail transport had already been in existence for quite some time. The steam engine was already in use in manufacturing at the beginning of the nineteenth century.

The 150th anniversary of rail transport, celebrated in Britain in 1975 and in Germany in 1985, gave a rather false impression of the early development and primary purpose of this novel transport technology. The first German rail link, that between Nürnberg and Fürth in 1835, as well as the first Russian link, established two years later between St Petersburg

and the Tsar's summer residence in Tsarskoye Selo, were a
kind of pilot project in passenger transport. With the carriage
of passengers on these two lines, the transport of tomorrow
was tactically kowtowing to the continental rulers of yesterday.
It was the transport of goods and the demands of developing
capitalist industry, rather than the 'unproductive transport' of
people, that determined the early development of the railways.
The nostalgic images accompanying the anniversary celebra-
tions gave a false picture in other respects as well: the railway
was not a mode of transport for the rich and poor alike; it was
also not a form of public transport, remaining for over three-
quarters of a century in private hands. The peaceful images of
the train likewise belie the fact that, from the second half of
the century, and especially during the First World War, the
railways were a key element in military strategy.

With the advent of the railway, the previous means of
transport on canals and inland waterways rapidly became obso-
lete; its existence and its advantages soon formed no part of
public awareness. Transport history now appears to be repeating itself. The modern car society has had a similar effect on
the public awareness of rail travel and its advantages. The
railways have become 'old iron' and nostalgic images of the old
steam locomotive appear alongside those of the horse-drawn
carriage in British and American period-costume dramas. In
Part I, I want to look behind some of the myths and legends
that have drawn a veil over much of transport history.

1

Canal Mania, or Marx's Mistake

Too long. Morse nodded to himself – he was beginning to get the picture. ... Far quicker by rail, of course! And the fare she'd paid, 16s 11d, seemed on the face of it somewhat on the steep side for a trip as a passenger on a working-boat. In 1859? Surely so! What would the rail fare have been then? Morse had no idea. ... He could still see in his mind's eye the painting on the cabin in which he'd travelled, with its lake, its castle, its sailing boat, and range of mountains – all the traditional colours of red, yellow, green. But what was it like to live in such boats? Boats that in the nineteenth century had been crewed by assortments of men from all over the place: from the Black Country; from the colliery villages around Coventry and Derby and Nottingham; from the terraced cottages in Upper Fisher Row by the terminus in Oxford – carrying their cargoes of coal, salt, china, agricultural products ... other things. What other things?

Colin Dexter, *The Wench is Dead*

According to Karl Marx, the speculative appetite of manufacturers and merchants first found satisfaction in the construction of the railways. It was Lenin's view that the railway was the measure of development of world trade and bourgeois democratic civilisation. The German economist, Werner Sombart, described the construction of the railways as 'the greatest productive act ... of all history'. This is a view that has been shared by many.[1] The famous sentence of Marx according to which 'being determines consciousness' applies to Marx himself and to the other economists just quoted. In the rail epoch, they attributed all great and good things to the railway, completely ignoring the transport technology of the previous epoch.

The World of Canals: Britain, France, Italy and the US

The rail epoch was preceded by the epoch of canal construction and inland transport on canals and rivers. Almost all of the features attributed to the era of rail construction and rail travel were to be found in the previous era of canal construction and waterway travel in England, Ireland, France, Holland, Belgium, Germany and the US. The British magazine, Country Life, drew attention to this fact in one of its articles in 1993. In that year, British Waterways celebrated 'Canals 200', commemorating the fact that 62 different canals, more than half of the system, were being built or planned in 1793. The magazine described the canals as 'the motorway system of their day' and the 140-mile Grand Union Canal as 'the spine of the system which runs north–south through the Watford Gap like an aquatic M1'.[2]

Canal construction and inland waterway transport involved investment on a scale unmatched in previous human history. These investments had an economic use that was to last for over a century; they changed the landscape forever and revolutionised transport costs and the whole economy. Canal construction and inland waterway transport left their mark on a century of economic history – from the middle of the eighteenth to the middle of the nineteenth century. In Britain, this corresponded exactly with the period of the industrial revolution. Three-quarters of a century of industrialisation was to pass before the railway began to make its impact. It was not until a full century after the beginning of the industrial revolution that the railways began to replace the canals and inland waterways, the arteries of the industrial revolution in England and Wales.

Marx was wrong when he asserted that joint stock companies had their beginning with the railways; these had already existed during the period of canal construction. Banks developed during the same period and speculation was rife. England, at the end of the eighteenth and in the early part of the nineteenth century, was gripped by a canal mania. Philip

S. Bagwell reports, in his book *The Transport Revolution from 1770*, that in the four years between 1791 and 1794, '42 new canals with a total capital of £6.5 million – approximately one-third of all capital expended on canals up to 1830 – were successfully launched'.[3] Even after the advent of the railway, inland waterway transport remained competitive in England up to the beginning of the twentieth century and, on some routes, until after the Second World War.

It was said of England in the middle of the nineteenth century that no important town was more than twelve miles from a canal or inland waterway. Before the building of the first canal, Britain had around 1,500 kilometres of navigable inland waterway. One hundred years later, in 1850, the inland waterway system, excluding Ireland, stretched over some 7,000 kilometres. Engels, in his *Condition of the Working Class in England*, estimated that England (without Wales or Scotland) had 2,200 miles of canals and 1,800 miles of navigable rivers. The overall length of the English inland waterway system in 1850 corresponded to that achieved by the West German railway system 140 years later. Two major waterways crossed the island: the first, begun in 1766, was the Grand Trunk Canal which, by linking the Trent and the Mersey, created a water route through central England from the Irish Sea to the North Sea; the second was the Caledonian Canal that crossed Scotland, passing through Loch Ness.

The British canal network was not an exception in Europe. A similar network existed in France. A British text on the Leeds to Liverpool Canal mentions the Canal du Midi in France, completed in 1681 and linking the Mediterranean and the Atlantic, and raised the following problem:

> With the head start provided by the Canal du Midi, it is perhaps surprising that France did not beat Britain to it, but perhaps they lacked the drive of folk like the Duke of Bridgewater, who is rightly regarded as the father of the canal age.[4]

The solution suggested by the authors, France's lack of men like Bridgewater, is not really convincing.

The canal network of northern Italy was created even earlier. It was not only in Venice, with its canal system that

extended 100 kilometres inland, that water transport played
a major role. Milan, the main city of northern Italy, was
criss-crossed with canals and was part of a canal system that
linked this city to the Mediterranean. Leonardo da Vinci was
chief engineer of the city of Milan; he was responsible for
canal construction and invented a particular type of canal
lock.

Mark Twain was born in 1835 in the US, the leading
railway country of the mid-nineteenth century. But what
Mark Twain described in his novels was the principal form
of transport for goods and people in that country, namely the
steamship. Canal boats and river boats were so dominant in
the transport sector of the US at that time that they even
influenced the design of railway carriages.

Working Conditions in Canal Construction and Operation

The canals also formed a major chapter in the history of
labour. We do not have a great deal of information; the
standard literature tends to stress the achievements of the
'great builders', men like James Brindley, the architect of the
Duke of Bridgewater Canal, or Thomas Telford, builder of
the Shropshire Union Canal. The bookkeeper of the Leeds to
Liverpool Canal has also been praised: 'No one gave more to
the canal than Joseph Priestly.'[5] Undoubtedly, the canal engi-
neers achieved great feats. They built thousands of locks
with a great variety of designs, even ones that were able to
take account of the tides; they constructed a great number of
moveable bridges over the canals, as well as canal tunnels,
aqueducts, watergates, boat-weighing machines and canal
intersections. Ice-breakers had to keep the water free in winter; canals went into mines to carry out coal. There were
canal harbours, where goods were transferred between waterways and railways. According to Philip Bagwell, the Duke of
Bridgewater employed the 'self-educated genius', James Brindley, to build a canal which would

> link the extensive coalfields on his estate to the rapidly
> growing markets in Manchester and Liverpool. Under the
> two acts of 1759 and 1760 the first ten-mile stretch of

the Bridgewater Canal was opened between the coal mines at Worsley and Stretford in the suburbs of Manchester on 17 July 1761. The opening of this canal was as dramatic a turning point in the history of British transport as was the opening of the Liverpool and Manchester Railway on 15 September 1830. The famous Barton aqueduct which carried the new canal 38 feet above the river Irwell; the successful crossing of the boggy Trafford Moss and the cutting of an elaborate system of tunnels to the coal workings at Worsley all revealed that inland water transport could be far more extensively used than had been previously thought possible.[6]

Great as the engineering feats may have been, Brecht's *Questions of a Reading Worker* is still relevant: 'Who built Thebes with its seven gates? In the books we find the names of kings. Did the kings carry the stones?'[7] Historians have noted that 'the workers who built the canals didn't have the right to strike, nor could they join together in trade unions'.[8] Canal construction in Britain was regulated by special legislation. Labour was militarised and conditions were very similar to those that existed in railway construction in the middle of the nineteenth century.

The 'human material' used in canal construction came largely from Britain's Irish colony: thousands of young men and boys went to their deaths in building the canals of England. In the construction of the Leeds to Liverpool Canal, for example, the builders decided not to use a special machine to move the earth 'in view of the cheapness of labour'.

The barges, until the end of the nineteenth century, were drawn by horses, and the growth in productive resources that this brought was enormous: on land a horse could transport between 600 and 700 kilograms, but a single canal horse could move loads of up to 50 tons. Transport costs sank to a third of their previous level. Horses were more valuable than workers. In 1903 'a boat captain, his brother and his mate on boat no. 186 were sentenced to one month hard labour because they had overloaded and badly treated the company mare no. 111'. Later, horses were replaced by steam and, in the twentieth century, by diesel engines.

Map 1: English Canals, Showing Railway Ownership 1872
(Source: P. Bagwell, *The Transport Revolution*)

A large workforce lived and worked on the canals. According to Bagwell:

> More than 25,000 barges were being used on Britain's inland waterways in the middle decades of the nineteenth century. Living on board these boats was a floating population of no less than 50,000 persons, more than a third of whom were directly employed by the canal companies or the carriers. Of all the sizeable groups of wage earners in Victorian Britain this is almost certainly the one about which least was known by their contemporaries.[9]

The average crew on a canal boat was two men, a boatsman and his mate. As competition from the railways grew after 1835, the two-man crew became too expensive. The solution was the family crew – the boatsman with his wife and children. A small cabin at one end (two metres by three metres) housed the couple, while a smaller cabin at the other end served the children. Summer and winter, this was home for tens of thousands of boat people. Overcrowding, poor sanitary conditions and lack of educational provision for the children were growing problems. Although the Canal Boats Act of 1877 and the Canal Boats (Amendment) Act of 1884 introduced regulations on registration and sanitation, there was little or no enforcement. It would be truer to say, as Bagwell wrote, that the problem 'disappeared in the fulness of time rather than that it was solved by the intervention of parliament'.[10]

Canal work in the eighteenth and nineteenth centuries was hard and it became even harder with the advance of the industrial revolution. Legging was just one example of the difficult and often inhuman tasks that the canal workers had to endure. The horses were not able to pull the canal boats through the tunnels, so the horses were walked overland while specialised workers had to move the boat through. To do this, two workers had to lie on the boat, shoulder to shoulder, and push the boat through with their feet against the tunnel wall. The boatsmen also had to load and unload the boat, which was backbreaking work since the cargo was generally coal, iron or limestone. The reality of work on the canals was a stark contrast to the popular idyll of water gypsy life.

As late as the Second World War, the canal boatsmen were used as a reserve for the British Royal Navy, which meant that the wives took over the running of the boats. During the war the canals played a strategic and increasing role in the transport of goods. The German *Wehrmacht* was aware of this and bombed the canals.

The most important and most profitable canal in Britain was the Leeds and Liverpool Canal, 116 miles long, built between 1770 and 1790 at a cost of exactly £877,616. The Canal was a bonanza. The joint stock company that ran the Canal never failed to make a profit between 1786 and 1919; in this period of over 130 years its yearly profit was generally between 15 and 20 per cent.[11] Philip Bagwell describes the more prosperous canals in Britain before the arrival of the railways as 'veritable gold mines'. A list of share prices and dividends published in 1830 showed that the seven most prosperous canals all paid dividends in excess of 25 per cent.[12] Between 1851 and 1874 the Leeds and Liverpool Canal was leased to its competitor on the same route, the railway company. For a quarter of a century the Canal owners collected the yearly rent from the railway company. The railway company, which had a duty to maintain the Canal, did its best to undermine its main competitor. But when the Canal owners took possession again in 1874, the Leeds–Liverpool waterway revived completely. The extent to which canal transport remained competitive, at least in Britain, is attested by the fact that the Grand Union Canal was extended as late as 1930.

Germany

The development of the transport sector in Germany was different in many respects. Germany's late development meant that the period of the industrial revolution there coincided with the age of the railway. At the time when the Prussian state abandoned internal customs duties, creating a unified market of 10.5 million people, the Merthyr Tydfil plant in South Wales had already produced its first steam-powered locomotive, built by Richard Trevithick.

However, in at least the more important regions of Germany, water transport had preceded rail and had brought about a first price revolution. In the words of one history textbook:

The mass of consumer goods could be transported more cheaply on water. Water transport through the Öresund (the strait between the southwest of Sweden and Zealand) increased dramatically. At the beginning of the 16th century, 1,300 ships were registered; at the end of the century the number had reached 5,000. German coastal towns experienced an unprecedented boom in shipping.[13]

Canals were built in and around the coastal towns. When the first railways were built in Germany, they could not compete with the canals on the same routes.

The first railways in the vicinity of navigable rivers were built mainly to provide access to the waterways, for instance, the lines in the Rhine region between Mannheim and Heidelberg (1840), between Düsseldorf and Elberfeld (1841), between Köln and Aachen (1841), and between Deutz and Minden (1845). With water transport being as cheap as it was, the construction of rail lines alongside waterways was seen as fruitless speculation.[14]

Even in the last quarter of the nineteenth century, following the creation of the Empire and in the midst of a railway-building fever, the rate of growth of inland waterway transport equalled that of the railways in Germany. In 1875 transport on German inland waterways reached 2,900 ton-kilometres (one ton-kilometre (ton-km) is one ton carried one kilometre); in 1900 the figure was 11,500 ton-km, an increase of almost 400 per cent. The volume of rail transport was three times higher than water in 1875, at 10,900 ton-km, rising to 36,900 ton-km in 1900, an increase of 338.5 per cent, lower than the increase on the waterways.[15]

Parallels in the Decline of Canals and Railways

The decline of the canals and of inland water transport resembles, in many ways, the later decline of the railways. A fierce competition developed between railways and waterways from the middle of the nineteenth century. In Britain the railway companies deliberately laid railway lines along the canal routes. A price war began which meant a steady increase in the intensity of labour for workers in both sectors.

In the US rail owners made large-scale use of bribery to destroy competition from the canals. The Erie Canal was destroyed by the prominent rail magnate, Vanderbilt, and the rail owners Garret and Hopkins were able to bribe the members of the state legislature of Maryland to close the Chesapeake and Ohio Canal. In both cases these canals had been built on the basis of massive public investment. The Chesapeake and Ohio Canal was run by the state of Maryland. This destruction and waste of public property and public investment, on the one hand, and private enrichment, on the other, is something we will meet many times in the history of railway destruction as well.

Although the trains were faster than the canal boats, improvements in canal transport as well as the fact that the big industrial centres, factories, and mines were often built beside the canals, meant that the canals were able to collect and deliver directly. Transport by rail, on the other hand, often involved a transfer of load from boat to train or from train to road. This helped to offset rail's speed advantage. In addition, the canal companies introduced 'flying boats' which were capable of greater speed, travelled day and night and had priority at locks.

In the middle of the nineteenth century the rail companies in England and in the US grew to become one of the most powerful groups of owners of capital. They were a forceful lobby against the canal companies and they were able to bring about changes in the law which disadvantaged the canals. Finally, many of the canal companies were bought out by the railways. General Motors and Ford were to use the same tactics three-quarters of a century later when they bought the railways in the US.

In the mid-nineteenth century large investments were needed to maintain the waterway infrastructure but the necessary capital was either not available or had been invested elsewhere by the canal companies. Philip Bagwell agrees that:

There is some substance in the charge that the shareholders of the most prosperous concerns were content, year after year, to draw monopoly profits, and that the public, and possibly they themselves, would have been better served in the long run if they had shown a greater far-sightedness and less avarice in re-investing their money in the widening and deepening of the canals, the enlargement and standardisation of locks and other equipment and the development of commercial arrangements for through traffic. Their properties would have been in a better state to meet the competition of the railways.[16]

A similar pattern was to repeat itself a century later for the railways. The result was an accelerated decline of the canal network and the canal boat stock.

The canals were hit particularly hard by changes in energy use. Coal was one of the principal items of freight on the canals; the basis of steam power, it was the energy source that drove the industrial revolution. In fact, the canals were often built for precisely this purpose, many of them leading directly to the coal face. Factories were built alongside the canals to facilitate coal delivery. But at the turn of the century oil began to replace coal as the diesel- or petrol-driven engine became the standard. The railways profited from the change. It was this new energy source, however, which was later to fuel the massive rise in road transport and contribute to the decline of the railway. A report on the Brecon–Abergavenney Canal in Wales (written in 1963) records this ironic twist in transport history: 'The railway between Abergavenny and Merthyr that killed the canal as a commercial enterprise in 1870 ran its last service last year. While its rails grow rusty, the canal it superseded takes on new life (for tourist purposes).'

Like railway construction over a century later, the construction of the canal network brought massive changes to the environment and to demographic patterns. Factories, which earlier had been situated on high land to take advantage of the energy from wind and water, moved into the valleys along the waterway routes and used the coal-powered steam engine. Worker settlements grew around the factories and gave rise to the big urban centres of the industrial revolution: Manchester, Leeds, Liverpool and Birmingham. During the canal era, according to Ron Freethy and Catherine Woods: 'The rich then took to living in the hills above the smog-laden working areas.'[17]

In the twentieth century, of course, the rich left the valleys *and* the hills of central England and Wales. This one-time centre of the industrial revolution, with its dense network of canals and railways, is today an example of unparalleled decline in which whole regions have become museums of industrial and transport history. The big profits today are to be made in the City of London, where the yuppies and the financial sharks have built a modern Babylon close to what was once the heart of London's docklands.

2

The Rail Revolution

The railway kills space; what we are left with is time. For me, it is as if the mountains and forests of all countries have moved closer to Paris. I can smell the perfume of the German lime trees; the North Sea is splashing in front of my door.

Heinrich Heine

A dense network of rail lines developed in the coal fields of England during the second half of the eighteenth century, especially in the area around Newcastle. The first steam-powered train in the world travelled on the line of the Merthyr Tydfil iron works in South Wales in 1804. Although George Stephenson is today celebrated as the inventor of the steam locomotive, Philip Bagwell is right when he writes that it was Richard Trevithick (1771–1833) 'who made the greatest contribution to the adaptation of the steam engine for tractive purposes'.[18]

In 1803–4 Trevithick designed a locomotive for the Penydern ironworks. On 13 February 1804 he reported to his friend, Davies Giddy: 'The locomotive worked very well and ran uphill and downhill with great ease.' The locomotive hauled ten tons of iron, five wagons and 70 people riding on them for the whole of the journey, nine miles in four hours and five minutes, using 102 kg of coal.[19]

Trevithick and Stephenson were quite different characters. Trevithick was the inventor not only of the railway but also of the steamer, the high-pressure steam engine, the steam-powered canal boat and the steam-powered Thames dredger. He rushed from one invention and place to another, finally ruining his livelihood and his health when he attempted to apply steam power in the silver mines of Peru. This genius who was 'born before his time' had only limited success in putting his ideas into effect because he could not find the capital or the entrepreneurial interest that he needed. In the case of the railway, he had to make do with cast iron rails instead of the stronger steel rails that came later.

George Stephenson made industrial use of Trevithick's invention, the steam locomotive. Having achieved success as a locomotive manufacturer, he left his locomotive works to his son, Robert. Under Robert Stephenson's direction, the firm enjoyed a virtual monopoly in Britain for some decades (and for a shorter period of about 15 years in continental Europe). George Stephenson devoted himself to railway construction and was builder and engineer on the first big railway lines (including passenger lines) that were built during the great rail-building boom that began in Britain in the 1830s and on the Continent around the middle of the century. George Stephenson personified the industrial revolution in the motherland of modern capitalism. His fame is still celebrated today. Richard Trevithick was forgotten: he was buried in 1833 in a pauper's grave in Dartford in Kent.

But it was not just the combination of invention and entrepreneurial spirit that gave the impetus to rail travel. Rail was also attractive because of costs: it was cheaper to maintain a steam locomotive than it was to maintain a team of horses for carriages or for waterway transport. In the cost comparison – grain prices plus the cost of replacing horses versus coal prices plus the cost of replacing locomotives – it was the horse-drawn wagons and coaches that were increasingly disadvantageous. Thomas Gray, one of the major rail promoters of the period, complained in his *Observations on a General Iron Railway*, in 1820: 'The exaggerated prices that the public has to pay for the transport of goods and persons in horse-drawn wagons and coaches is ... essentially due to the incredible cost of maintaining and replacing the stock of horses.' He emphasised that 'no animal strength will be able to give that uniform and regular acceleration to our commercial intercourse which may be accomplished by the railway'. The cost comparison favoured a turn to mechanised transport, initially in the coal-mining areas, but within a decade of the first steam railway the transition to rail was universal.

According to Wolfgang Schivelbusch, in his interesting book on the history of rail travel: 'After 1815 the advantage of cheap coal over expensive animal fodder applied to the whole of England. In that year the British parliament, dominated by landed interests, passed the Corn Law which imposed a tax on imported grain and drove up the price of grain.' Under those circumstances, 'the artificially high grain prices gave a stimulus to the replacement of animal by mechanised power' just as, in eighteenth-century Europe, 'the general scarcity of wood gave a stimulus to the development of the coal industry'.[20] The increase in rail transport was also promoted by the elimination of competition from the canals, as described earlier.

The First Steam Railways

Steam railways soon acquired a large share of goods transport. In 1825 the first line that carried passengers as well was opened between Stockton and Darlington. But, in this case also, it was industrial interests that were predominant: coal transport in South Durham. The Act to establish the line was obtained in 1821 by the Society of Friends (Quakers) in Durham. The Act was 'For the passage of wagons and other carriages from Stockton to Witton Park Colliery in Durham'. It was originally projected as a tram road but George Stephenson convinced them to use locomotive engines rather than horses. Stephenson became the engineer and the Stockton & Darlington – or Quakers' Line – opened on Tuesday, 27 September 1825. The original projector of the line was Edward Pease. Rodney Dale has given us the following report:

> The procession moved off, the train moved on, preceded by a man on a horse, reaching a speed of eight miles an hour. Number One was driven by Stephenson himself. It pulled six loaded wagons, a passenger coach, 21 coal wagons crammed with passengers, and six more filled with coal – a considerable load ... All along the road and embankment were crowds – rushing, running, cheering, galloping along, in sight of the train till Stephenson, telling the horse pilot to get out of the road, put on steam and soon left the excited multitudes panting in the rear.[21]

The line was used at first only for merchandise and coal traffic. Industrial interests were also decisive in the Liverpool to Manchester line, opened on 15 September 1830. This line represented the arrival of modern rail transport for goods and passengers: locomotive-driven, two tracks, stations with siding and shunting line, a tunnel, viaducts, a large number of trains and a timetable. On the Stockton & Darlington line at that time the greater part of the haulage was still being done by horses.

The horse, indeed, continued to compete with the steam locomotive: horse-drawn freight wagons and coaches, horse-drawn railways and canal boats. Some decades after the opening of the Stockton–Darlington line there were still horse-drawn railways in England; in urban transport they were still in use at the beginning of the twentieth century. Canal transport, driven by horse, steam or diesel power, survived to the beginning of the car era.

During this period in the United States, a number of people were planning railways from New York to Philadelphia, from Baltimore to the West, from Albany to Lake Erie, and from Charleston, South Carolina, to the West. But, according to Dee Brown,

> in most cases, the planning did not include the use of steam power; the cars would be pulled by horses, as was done on the short lines that ran from coal mines to canals or rivers. In 1825, Colonel John Stevens demonstrated a one-cylinder steam-powered locomotive on a circular track on the grounds of his estate in Hoboken, New Jersey, but the public viewed it as an amazing toy. Not until 1828 did a trained engineer travel to England to examine the marvellous Iron Horse at work.

The name of the engineer was Horatio Allen and he was so impressed by what he saw that he ordered four 'Iron Horses'. The first one, built in Stourbridge, England, arrived in New York City on 13 May 1829. It was shipped by river and canal to Honesdale, Pennsylvania, where it made its first run on 8 August 1829. One year later, Peter Cooper took the first locomotive built in the US on a trial run on the Baltimore and Ohio's recently completed 13 miles of track between Baltimore and Ellicott's Mills in Maryland. The locomotive was named Tom Thumb and it carried its first passengers, in a car that resembled an open boat, on 28 August 1830, at a speed of between 15 and 18 miles per hour. This first run was also a race with a horse-drawn rail car. The blower belt slipped on the engine and the horse beat the machine. The Baltimore and Ohio, however, opted for Peter Cooper's 'Iron Horse'.[22]

In 1834 the Belgian government had George Stephenson design a rail network, with the main junction situated in Mechlin. This network would not just link the main cities of Belgium, but also France and Germany. On 5 May 1835, the Brussels to Mechlin section was opened, the first public Continental steam railway and the first state-owned railway in the world. Six months later the first German line was opened, the Ludwigsbahn (Ludwig Line) between Nürnberg and Fürth. The 'Adler' locomotive came from Stephenson's factory and even the driver had to be imported from Britain. Two decades after the steam locomotive first travelled this line, horses were still being used on the same stretch of rail.

On 4 March 1836 the Rothschild banking concern was granted the 'exclusive concession' to run a railway line between Vienna and Cracow. This locomotive-powered line was meant to open up the coal-producing region of Galicia (today in Poland). The best known Austrian defender of rail transport at the time, Franz Xaver Riepl, travelled twice to England, at Rothschild's expense, to study railway construction there and to be advised by George Stephenson. The first steam railway in Austria was the line between Florisdorf (near Vienna) and Wagram.

The first railway in the Netherlands was the 'Lustbahn' (Fun Line) between Amsterdam and Harlem, opened in 1839. In Italy the first steam train travelled between Naples and Portici on 3 October 1839. On 9 August 1847 the Swiss opened their first steam railway between Zürich and Baden.

The new technology not only revolutionised the whole economy in the transport sector, it also had a major effect on the lives of ordinary people. In his novel, *One Hundred Years of Solitude*, Gabriel Garcia Marquez describes the coming of the railway to Macondo:

At the start of another winter, however, a woman who was washing clothes in the river during the hottest time of the day ran screaming down the main street in an alarming state of commotion. 'It's coming,' she finally explained. 'Something frightful, like a kitchen dragging a village behind it.' At that moment the village was shaken by a whistle with a fearful echo and a loud, panting respiration. ... When they recovered from the noise of the whistles and the snorting, all the inhabitants ran out into the street and saw Aureliano Triste waving from the loco-motive, and in a trance they saw the flower-bedecked train which was arriving for the first time eight months late. The innocent yellow train that was to bring so many ambiguities and certainties, so many pleasant and unpleasant moments, so many changes, calamities and feelings of nostalgia to Macondo. (p. 183)

The Industrial Revolution:
Transport Costs and the Railway Boom

For over two thousand years the speed of transport had hardly changed. The roads that Napoleon built were similar to those built by Caesar. Propulsive power for the transport of goods and people on land was provided by people and animals, on water by people, animals and wind. The indus-trial revolution gave rise to a massive increase in national and international trade. Between 1700 and 1800 the total tonnage shipped from English ports rose from 317,000 tons to 1,924,000 tons. In the decade between 1790 and 1800 the volume of export from Britain rose by 95 per cent.[23] The existing transport technology, according to Marx, constituted

> unbearable fetters on large-scale industry, given the fever-ish velocity with which it produces, its enormous extent, its constant flinging of capital and labour from one sphere of production into another and its newly created connec-tions with the world market.[24]

It was this contradiction rather that human inventiveness that led to the transport revolution. Already at the end of

the eighteenth century the construction of roads was qualitatively improved, first in England and France and later in
the rest of Europe. The first revolution in transport took
place with the construction of inland waterway systems in
England, the Netherlands, France, Italy and North America.
The second revolution occurred with the introduction of
the steam-powered railway. At the level of world trade this
revolution was signalled by the replacement of the sailing
ship by the ocean steamer. It was given further impetus by
the construction of the Suez Canal which (from 1869) cut
the travel time between Hamburg and Bombay by 24 days.

The way in which the new rail lines were routed pointed
to a qualitative shift in transport; as particular lines developed into a network, it became clear that the railways were
built for a rapid flow of transport. Unlike the existing roads
and highways, they did not link city centre to city centre.
The new train stations, except for the big termini in major
cities, were built outside cities or on their periphery. It was
not until the twentieth century that the road network broke
away from the centuries old tradition and followed the example of rail. The new super highways and motorways then
became part of a long-distance rapid-flow network, in many
instances running parallel to the existing railway lines. While
the routes of the inland waterways and the traditional roads
adapted generally to the natural environment, the new railways sought the shortest route from A to B. The result was
a massive increase in bridges and tunnels.

During the course of a few decades in the middle of the
nineteenth century, a rail network was established in the
leading industrial nations of Europe that extended over
200,000 kilometres (see Table 2.1). Until 1865 Britain led
the rest of Europe in rail transport, although France and
Germany were catching up after 1845. By the final decades
of the century, France and Germany had overtaken Britain.[25]

A comparison of the leading industrial nations (Britain,
France and Germany) and the less developed states of southern
Europe (Italy, Spain and Portugal) would demonstrate a close
link between industrialisation and railway construction. The
Iberian states and Italy, at the beginning of the twentieth century, had only a very modest rail network. The networks that
did exist in these countries were also concentrated in the

Map 2 The British Railway System in 1872
(Source: P. Bagwell, *The Transport Revolution*)

industrialised areas, with whole regions excluded from modern forms of transport.

The imperialist division of the world was also reflected in railway construction. Lenin described this phenomenon in his 1916 text, *Imperialism, the Highest Stage of Capitalism*. He pointed to the fact that, at the end of the nineteenth century, the development of the railways was more rapid in

Table 2.1 Size of Rail Networks 1835–1917 (km)

Country	1835	1845	1855	1865	1875
Britain*	471	3277	13411	21382	26803
France	176	883	5535	13562	21547
Germany	6	2315	8352	14762	28087
Italy	–	–	1500	2000	7500
Spain	–	–	475	4832	6134
Portugal	–	–	37	700	919

Country	1885	1895	1905	1917
Britain*	30843	33219	36447	38135
France	32491	39357	46466	51431
Germany	37572	44882	56477	64987
Italy	11000	12000	13600	–
Spain	8933	11435	14430	15350
Portugal	1529	2340	2571	2983

* including Ireland

the colonies than in the imperialist centres. Following the construction of dense rail networks in Europe and North America, the construction of rail networks in Africa and Asia reflected the growth of capitalism and finance capital in the world market. At the same time, ownership of these railways was becoming increasingly concentrated:

Thus, about 80 per cent of the total existing railways are concentrated in the hands of the five biggest powers. But the concentration of the ownership of these railways, the concentration of finance capital, is immeasurably greater since the French and British millionaires, for example, own an enormous amount of shares and bonds in American, Russian and other railways.[26]

Around the turn of the century a country with an articulated rail network was also a country that was part of the process of industrial revolution and shared in the general rise in productive resources. Countries without such a rail network stagnated at a pre-industrial level.

Wolfgang Schivelbusch describes one of the social changes in England that resulted from the advent of the railways: 'When the seaside resorts on the English south coast, once the reserve of the aristocracy, became accessible by rail, they were taken over by the middle classes. The aristocracy then withdrew to the less accessible resorts in Scotland, Ireland and the Lake District.'[27]

The English aristocracy's problem with rail travel was, however, an exception. For the bourgeoisie and the middle classes, the railway brought great advantages. Bourgeois economists, in particular, were enthusiastic about the economic advantages of the new transport technology. The German economist and rail investor, Friedrich List, claimed in 1837 that 'The inexpensive, fast, secure and regular transport of persons and goods is one of the most powerful levers of national welfare and civilisation.'[28] For the farmers, he argued, the transport of livestock on rails over longer distances, without the usual weight loss associated with traditional forms of transport, would certainly mean a much higher income. But it was industrialists that would benefit most from the railways: rail transport in Germany would overcome the distance between the reserves of coal and iron, offsetting England's natural advantage in this respect and increasing Germany's competitiveness.

The new transport technology did indeed bring about a price revolution, initially with the introduction of rail and later with the rationalisation that took place within the rail industry itself, with the large-scale production of rail stock and the expansion of national and international rail networks. Table 2.2 illustrates the sinking transport costs in Germany between 1840 and 1913 as well as the massive increase in the volume of transport.[29]

Although the expenditure on transport in German industry and agriculture increased in this period by a factor of 72, the volume transported increased by a factor of over 200.[30] If we compare these figures for transport volume with the

Table 2.2
Goods Transport on German Railways 1840–1913

Year	ton–km (mn)	price per tonne–km (pf)	total cost mn marks
1840	3	16.90	0.5
1850	302	10.20	30.8
1860	1675	7.90	132.3
1870	5875	5.60	329.0
1880	13039	4.40	573.7
1890	22237	3.90	867.2
1900	34699	3.70	1283.9
1910	51851	3.70	1918.5
1913	61744	3.60	2222.8

figures in Table 2.1 for the size of the rail networks, we see
that there was a constantly increasing rate of utilisation of
rail which was, in turn, an important factor in the lowering
of costs. The denser the rail network in a particular country,
the lower were relative transport costs. From the point of
view of price, the location of production became, in many
cases, less important, the price of a commodity near the site
of production being only marginally lower that elsewhere in
the national market. Manufacturing plants could now be
situated quite a distance from raw material suppliers without
this constituting a major competitive disadvantage.

The Workers in Railway Construction and Operation

Werner Sombart has described the construction of the railways as 'the greatest productive achievement not only of the
nineteenth century but in all of history'. He made the
following assessment of the labour that was invested in this
transport technology:

> Up to the end of 1910, the German railways have cost
> 17 billion marks. If we reckon the cost of wages to be
> about three quarters of this, we arrive at a figure of
> around 12 or 13 billion marks. If we assume an average
> yearly wage to be 500 to 600 marks (a rather high
> estimate) ... then we have a labour achievement of
> around 25 million labour years or 7½ billion labour
> days. In other words, 1 million slave labourers would
> have had to work for 25 years or 100,000 of them
> would have had to work for 2½ centuries to build this
> railway. If we make the reckoning for the actual histori-
> cal period we get the following: in the 70 working
> years, 100 million working days have been devoted
> annually to the construction of the railways; year for
> year, three quarters of a million workers have done
> nothing else but build the railway system and all of its
> component parts – stations, rolling stock and so on.[31]

Similar figures could be produced for Britain, France, and
the US.

Sombart's figures suggest the following question: how was bourgeois society able to manage this massive and long-term allocation of social labour without causing a collapse in other basic areas of social production, in the economy and in agriculture? There is a threefold answer to this question.

The first and most important factor was the general increase in productive forces that provided the foundation of the industrial revolution. It made possible a radical reduction in the number of workers engaged in the agricultural sector, while at the same time maintaining or actually increasing the level of agricultural production. Industrial manufacture also lowered the costs of the basic day-to-day products previously produced by the crafts. The labour force that was no longer employed in the production of these commodities was now available for industry in general and for railway construction in particular.

A second element, as Sombart himself pointed out, was the fact that a large part of the original capital that was invested in railway construction came from *external* sources. In the case of England and France, it was the exploitation of the colonies that provided most of the initial capital. In Germany, the railway boom of the 1870s was financed by the reparation payments that followed the German victory over France. As Sombart commented: 'One could say that France built our railway for us as reparation for the war.'[32]

Finally, this great construction feat was achieved on the basis of the extreme exploitation of the workers. The industrial revolution was accompanied by the destruction of numerous traditional occupations in the countryside, creating a mass of uprooted and property-less human beings in need of employment. For these workers there were only three alternatives: 'America, the railway, or the factory.'[33] The railway offered certain advantages over the factory, namely the low level of skill required and a wage slightly higher than for comparable unskilled labour elsewhere. There was an even greater number of disadvantages, however: the work site was situated far from home and workers were constantly on the move; work was heavily dependent on the weather and workers were not paid for idle days; there was a very high level of accidents and work-related illnesses in this sector; of all the sectors of the early capitalist labour market, this one was the

most regimented and legally controlled. For instance, the
identity papers of the rail workers were kept by local officials
to enable police authorities to maintain greater control. The
working day was between 12 and 13 hours, between 60 and
65 hours per week, often more in the summer months. Rail
workers normally had to live in barracks, where even leisure
time was subject to strict discipline. The working day began
and ended with a military-style roll call. A worker who
missed the morning roll call was not permitted to work on
that day. 'Drunkenness, fighting, rowdiness, ... demands for
higher wages, ... plans for any kind of social or political
demonstration' were punished with immediate dismissal.[34]

In Europe as well as in the US, the railway companies made
large-scale use of immigrant labour in railway construction. In
the case of England, the immigrant labour came largely from
Ireland. The use of cheaper immigrant labour meant that the
employers paid little attention to safety, and accidents were
numerous. Immigrant workers were used in particular where
working conditions were dangerous. In the building of the
Gotthard Tunnel in Switzerland during the 1870s, it was
mainly immigrant Italian workers that were employed. 'When
they travel to work at the beginning of the day, they say they
are going to "battaglia", to the battle. The work is like a daily
war with the elements; every day there are injuries and
deaths.'[35] When the workers rebelled and demanded a reduction in shift hours from eight to six, their demands were met
with bloody repression by the Swiss army.

The working conditions for the regular employees of the
railway companies differed only marginally from those of the
workers in construction. The idyll of the 'local station
master' did not correspond to the social reality. Until the
end of the nineteenth century there was very little job
security for rail employees. In the middle of the century, the
working week was 65 hours, falling to 60 hours in the
1890s. There were two free days in a month with no right to
annual holiday until 1894. Wages were kept very low. Investigations into train accidents generally found that rail
employees had reacted wrongly due to tiredness. During their
hours off, they usually had to work on a second job.

It was also on the railways in Europe that the attempt
was made for the first time to create artificial divisions

among the class of wage earners. There were the regular full-time workers, who usually worked in shifts, and the seasonally employed workers, who were taken on especially during harvest time. There were also the workers in the rail works who had a regular job but who, like the rail-building workers, were subject to rigorous discipline. Finally, after the nationalisation of the railways, there were the different levels of rail officials with their corresponding levels of security and privilege. The most important of these privileges was the pension that the official enjoyed after active service, or that went to his wife and dependants in the case of death. This pension was made available to all rail officials in Germany in the second half of the nineteenth century. Ordinary rail workers did not have pension rights until much later.

An almost military labour discipline was demanded of rail officials. This was intensified by the increasing employment of ex-soldiers and ex-junior officers. This was a deliberate policy of the German military once they realised the strategic importance of the railways in time of war. The employment of ex-military personnel was accompanied by a general prohibition of trade union membership or political activity. The German Social Democratic Party had almost no success in organising the railway workers right up to the end of the nineteenth century. Some of the other industrial countries witnessed major strikes on the railways in the second half of the nineteenth century. In the US there was a national rail strike in 1877, with weekly occupations and armed defence of strikers. For the first time in US history the Federal army was used against the strikers and there were 100 deaths. This was a milestone in the history of the US labour movement. There were no major strikes on the German railways until after the First World War.

3

Capitalism and the Railways: The Railway Industry, Private and Public Ownership, Class Society and the Railways

The shaking produced by driving in carriages and later by railway travel exercises such a fascinating effect upon older children that every boy has at one time or other in his life wanted to be an engine driver or a coachman. It is a puzzling fact that boys take such an extraordinarily intense interest in things connected with railways, and, at an age at which the production of phantasies is most active (shortly before puberty), use those things as the nucleus of a symbolism that is peculiarly sexual. A compulsive link of this kind between railway travel and sexuality is clearly derived from the pleasurable character of the sensations of movement.

Sigmund Freud, *Three Essays on Sexuality* (1905)

The train was not just the drawing horse of the industrial revolution; it was also, for a long time, a core sector of modern industry.

The Structural Weight of the Railway Industry

In their analysis of North American capitalism, Paul A. Baran and Paul M. Sweezy point out that during the last two decades of the nineteenth century, between 40 and 50 per

cent of private capital was invested in the railways.'[37] North
America was not a special case; the railways were a major
sector in the economy of all the leading industrial nations
during the industrial revolution.

The railway and rail-related industries enjoyed a dominant
position in *Britain* in the middle of the nineteenth century.
Having established his track width as standard for the industry, George Stephenson was able to establish a dominant position for his own company and for the British manufacturers of
locomotives, rolling stock, and rail track. These British manufacturers also enjoyed a dominant position in the European and
world markets. The Dowlais Iron Company in South Wales,
for instance, producers of iron for use in rail track, was considered at the time to be the biggest factory in the world. In 1845
it produced 58,000 tons of iron, about 4 per cent of all British
iron production. Three-quarters of Dowlais iron went into the
making of rail track. The volume of Dowlais production was
around 50 per cent of the entire Prussian production of iron at
that time. The biggest iron producer in continental Europe was
the Belgian firm, Cockerill, also mainly involved in the production of rail track. In 1845 it produced around 18,000 tons of
track. The biggest German producers at the time were the
Gutehoffnungshütte plant with a capacity of 6,500 tons and
Hoesch with a capacity of 9,000 tons.[38]

The growing weight of the rail industry in *Germany* is
indicated by the following comparative figures for investment
in rail, industry and the whole economy. In the 1850s
investment in rail was 75 per cent of the entire investment
in the rest of industry. In the period 1865 to 1880 investment in rail was higher than investment in the rest of
industry. In the period 1875 to 1879, investment in rail was
over 25 per cent of the investment figure for the whole
economy.[39]

The first German train between Nürnberg and Fürth was
drawn by a Stephenson locomotive. The first train manufactured in Germany, the Saxonia, which began to operate on
the Dresden to Leipzig line in 1839, was also drawn by a
British locomotive. By mid-century, however, there was
strong competition in Germany between German, British and
Belgian locomotives. In 1840, 92 per cent of the locomotives
on the Prussian railway were British. Five years later, the

majority of locomotives on the Germany railway were manufactured in Germany; the British share had dropped to 42 per
cent. From the 1850s the Prussian market in locomotives
was totally dominated by Prussian manufacturers.[40] State
assistance in the form of tariffs on imported rail stock played
an important role in the advance of German manufacture.
Soon German rail manufacturers were capturing a growing
proportion of the world market, an indication of the increasing competitive strength of German industry.

The locomotive manufacturers were the first big industrial
enterprises on German soil. In many instances, the big industrial concerns of the twentieth century had their beginnings in
the nineteenth-century rail industry. The modern firm of
Thyssen is an example: it began as the Egestorff firm in Hannover, enjoyed the boom after 1868 under the leadership of
Germany's rail king, Bethel Henry Strousberg, then went into
crisis and was restructured to become the Hannoversche
Maschinenbau AG (Hanomag). Eventually it was taken over by
the leading locomotive manufacturer of the 1880s, Henschel,
today Thyssen. The same was true of other major rail enterprises, for instance, Krauss and Maffei, Borsig (today Babcock),
Siemens and Krupp.

B. H. Strousberg employed 100,000 workers at his Egestorff
locomotive plant in Hannover. The Hannover plant was
expanded so that it produced one locomotive every day. It was
also under his direction that the Dortmund ironworks was
expanded, with most of its materials delivered from Spain.
Strousberg was also an example of the enlightened bourgeois
who understood the importance of working environment as a
productive factor. In a letter to Marx in 1869, Engels wrote:

> Strousberg is absolutely the biggest man in Germany. The
> fellow will soon be German kaiser. Where-ever you go,
> everyone is talking about Strousberg. And he's not such a
> bad fellow either. My brother, who had some dealings
> with him recently, gave a very lively description of him.
> He has a good sense of humour and some very genial
> features; he is certainly infinitely superior to (England's)
> railway king, Hudson. He is currently buying up all pos-
> sible industrial establishments and reducing working time
> everywhere to ten hours, without cutting wages.[41]

Strousberg also built exemplary housing for his employees in Linden (Hannover). There were workplace nurseries and a mid-day meal for all employees.

From the available data it is clear that the railway construction industry was a major economic sector in the economies of Europe and North America in the second half of the nineteenth century, with effects throughout the whole economy. Werner Sombart is right when he says that the decisive industrial sector of the German or any other national economy in the mid-nineteenth century, the coal-steel-mechanical engineering sector, owed its rise essentially to the railways.[42]

The Contradiction between Private Ownership and Social Needs

The arguments for a centralised direction of rail transport, for national if not international organisation and planning, are numerous and convincing. There is the need, first of all, for a national (or international) timetable. In the absence of such a plan, accidents and chaos are unavoidable. This requirement, however, contradicts the basic principle of capitalism – competition. A unified rail network excludes the 'free market'. Whereas product variety makes sense in a 'normal' capitalist economy, in the case of rail travel it is unproductive. The nature of rail transport requires a standardisation of track width, carriage type, locomotive, and method of propulsion (steam, diesel, electric).

Rail transport played a decisive role in the creation of a domestic market and indeed in the creation of the nation state as the framework for such a market. The even distribution of the rail network, diminishing the significance of the conjunctural or sectoral element, promotes the development of a unified, equal and free market: location advantage tends to disappear, enabling commodities (including the commodity labour power) to be offered at similar prices over the whole of the domestic market. A private regime of rail transport would work against this tendency, aiming instead at maximising its own transport load and its own short-term profit. Military considerations also favoured a national network, particularly in the second half of the nineteenth century leading up to the First World War.

The time element also favoured a national network. It was rail which, for the first time, brought regions, towns and cities in such close contact that they had to have a 'common' time. Wolfgang Schivelbusch describes the change:

Isolated from one another, each had its own individual time. London time was 4 minutes earlier than Reading, 7½ minutes earlier than Cirencester, and 14 minutes earlier than Bridgewater. These time variations were not a problem as long as travel between the regions was so slow. The railway's shortening of travel time confronted not only regions with each other but also their local times. Under such circumstances, a supra-regional timetable was an impossibility. ... Regular rail travel demanded a unified time, just as the technical standardisation of tracks and carriages favoured a transport monopoly.[43]

For over half a century, however, these rational requirements were ignored. The state was allowed to intervene only when the private railway companies crashed, as hundreds of them did in the world economic crisis of 1873. In the latter half of the nineteenth century rail travel was organised by competing companies, sometimes even on the same stretch of rail. Fourteen years after the opening of the first public steam railway, the British parliament had to introduce a law prohibiting competing locomotives on the same line. Until the 1860s, four decades after the opening of the Stockton–Darlington line, there was no unified network linking London with the north of England. England had at that time over 300 competing railway companies. In 1870 there were 11 large rail companies that covered between them a network of around 14,000 km; the remaining 10,000 km were owned by a large number of small companies.

Until the end of the nineteenth century there was no standardisation of rail transport. The track width of 1,435 millimetres dominated and became the norm by the end of the century. This was largely due, however, to George Stephenson's and Britain's monopoly position in production.

George Stephenson's leading position was challenged by the English engineer, Isambard Kingdom Brunel (1806–1859), who inherited a famous name and authority from his father, the pioneer builder of the tunnel under the Thames. Brunel had no intention of following Stephenson's diktat on the question of track width. At the age of 27 he was given the job of constructing the Great Western Railway between London and Bristol. He used a new track width of 7 feet (2134 millimetres). Brunel wanted a faster train and he thought this would only be possible on a wider track. Eventually, the unavoidable happened: the rail networks expanded and met. A famous example of this muddle was the train station at Crewe, where three rail networks met, each with a different track width. In Ireland, where two track widths existed side by side, officials imposed an average width of 1600 millimetres.

This turmoil on the tracks led eventually to state intervention. A government commission proposed that all new railways should be built according to the Stephenson standard. The bill was passed in the House of Commons on 12 August 1846. The Great Western Railway was allowed to maintain its 7-foot gauge but eventually it too had to conform. The Brunel rebellion against Stephenson was an expensive experiment for Great Western. The rebuilding work took a long time and it wasn't until 1890 that 5,000 workers finished the final stretch between Exeter and Bristol.[44]

There is still no continental European standard. The standard gauge is used in central Europe but wide gauges are used in Spain, Portugal and eastern Europe. The European Union's proposal, in 1995, for Trans-European Networks that would establish a small number of high-speed links, for instance, between Paris and Lisbon (via Madrid), does not aim to introduce the standard gauge to the Iberian Peninsula. As in the nineteenth century, the two gauges will remain. There were six different track widths in the US in 1865; it was the Civil War which provided the impetus to standardisation.

Rational criteria were also ignored in the selection of routes. In Germany, regional interests and short-term profit motives dominated. The governments of the various states that established a common customs union in the German Bund wanted to concentrate as much railway line on their own territory as possible in order to maximise income from freight and customs duties. The Black Forest line, the line between Munich and Lindau, the Braunschweig-Wolfenbüttel line and many others did not run on the shortest route or the easiest terrain but along the state borders. The lines were unnecessarily long, the construction costs were greater and the transport costs were higher.

The Prussian state railway is often praised as a model of public enterprise. From the standpoint of rational transport policy, the routes chosen, always in pursuit of particularistic Prussian interests, were downright ridiculous. Rather than a direct route from Berlin to Rhineland-Westphalia that went over Magdeburg, Braunschweig, Hannover and Hamm, the authorities chose a route through Halle, Eisenach, Erfurt and Bebra. The only reason for this diversion was that it avoided the national territory of Hannover.

It was not until half a century after the dawning of the rail era that the problem of time was resolved. In the 1840s in Britain, each railway line had its own time. A unified time, Greenwich Time, was established in mid-century. Until the end of the century, however, this was used only for rail travel; different local times continued. An international conference in Washington in 1844 established four world time zones. Different local times were abolished in Germany in 1893 and official zone time was introduced. In the US, there were as many different times in 1883 as there were railway companies. 'In train stations with different railway companies, the clocks showed different times. In Buffalo, for instance, there were three, in Pittsburgh six.'[45]

The only European country in which the railway was nationalised from the beginning was *Belgium*. The results were impressive: although Belgium began with railway construction a full decade after Britain and around the same time as Germany, 'it had in 1890 the most dense rail network in the world, with 18 km of rail per square km and 5263 km of rail line altogether'.[46]

The contradiction between private capitalist interests and the objective need for a centrally organised network and national (or continental) planning led to increasing public demand for nationalisation of the railways. The result was an unevenness and lack of consistency in public transport policy.

Austria was a classic example of this problem. In 1854 around 1,000 km of rail line, 70 per cent of the entire network, was under the control of the Austrian state. The Habsburg state had financed the building of the railways, especially the more costly projects such as the Semmering Tunnel, as a response to the demands of the 1848 revolution for more job-creating measures. After 1855, in order to resolve some of its own financial problems, the Austrian state began to sell off sections of the network. The buyers were private entrepreneurs, mainly French. The economic balance sheet is an interesting one: up to 1854, the state had spent 336 million gulden in the construction of the railways. The returns on privatisation were exactly half this amount – 169 million gulden. The private owners then demanded subsidies from the state. These increased to such an extent that by the mid-1860s they made up 5 per cent of the total state budget. The Austrian government then decided to purchase back the privatised railways. The main lines were again in public ownership by 1909.[47]

Developments in other countries were essentially similar. The *Italian* government decided in 1870 to nationalise the biggest private rail company, the Alta Italia. The state, however, had difficulties in financing its rail-building programme and the railway was once again sold into private hands. Nationalisation was introduced once again in 1905, with the formation of the Ferrovie dello Stato (FS). One-third of the railways remained in private ownership. In *France*, a concentration of ownership in the mid-nineteenth century resulted in six private rail companies. The state subsidised the construction and running of the railways through tax concessions but it had no control over the transport system. In 1837 the SNCF (Société Nationale des Chemins de Fer Français) was established, which linked the private rail companies in 'régions'. Rail was nationalised after the Second World War. In *Britain* the railways were brought under public administration during the First World War, but private owners were once again in control from 1921. During the Second World War the railways were once again under public control and nationalisation followed in 1947, 122 years after the opening of the first rail line. In *Russia*, according to Ralf Roman Rossberg: 'when the balance sheet was drawn up at the turn if the century, it was discovered that although the state financed 90 per cent of the railway, it exercised some kind of control over just 10 per cent'.[48]

The *Swiss* railways remained under private control until the end of the century although there had been a number of attempts to establish a state network. The people voted for nationalisation in a referendum in 1898 and the state-owned SBB (Schweizerische Bundesbahn) was established in 1902. State regulation of the *Netherlands'* two private railways was already quite advanced in the 1860s but full nationalisation did not happen until 1937. In 1930 around 85 per cent of *Spain's* rail networks were in private hands but the Civil War and the reconstruction that followed led to the establishment of the national network, the RENFE (Red Nacional de los Ferrocarriles Espanoles). *Portuguese* rail was nationalised in 1947. In *Sweden*, 15,000 km of network were nationalised in 1950, with 1,265 km remaining in private hands. *Japan's* first railway was opened in 1872; it was built by the state and then privatised. Thereafter Japanese railways were run by private companies with government subsidy. Nationalisation followed in the aftermath of the Russo–Japanese War of 1905.

In the *United States*, railways were owned by a number of private companies until the 1970s. At the turn of the century there had been as many as 752 private rail companies. They were taken under state control during the First World War but, under pressure from owners and shareholders, they were privatised again in 1920. Since the Second World War there have been quite a few bankruptcies and a rapid process of concentration of ownership. In 1976 the remaining companies were fused to form Conrail, a private company with a massive state subsidy (in the period 1976 to 1984 it received $7 billion). After a brief period of state administration, Conrail was again privatised by the Reagan administration in 1985. The German weekly, *Wirtschaftswoche*, drew a very negative balance sheet of what had once been the biggest and most efficient railway in the world: 'After around 140 years of private rail transport, the railway companies threw in the towel in the 1950s and early 1960s and left to the state a run down and desolate railway.'[49]

The *German* railway was no exception to this general pattern of development. The state was involved in railway

construction at an early stage, for instance, the Braunschweig–Wolfenbüttel line, opened in 1838. However, during
periods of economic upswing and on routes that offered low
construction costs and high profits, it was always private
interests that had the upper hand. Between 1863 and 1873
there was a private rail boom in Prussia which ended with
the economic crisis of 1873. During the 1880s and 1890s,
the policy of a state-run network was generally accepted but
it was not until the Weimar constitution of 1919 and the
creation of the Deutsche Reichsbahn in 1920 that this was
finally achieved.

Joseph Schumpeter was right, however, when he claimed
that 'the creation of the German railway system was essentially the work of private entrepreneurs'.[50] The traditional view
of the railways as 'classic state technology' and Germany (Prussia) as 'the classic country of the state owned railway' does not
stand up to close examination. What is correct is that the
state, in Germany and elsewhere, always had to come to the
aid of the private railway companies when profit margins were
too low. Losses were always socialised (through subsidies or the
purchase of bankrupt lines). The privatisation of rail once
again at the end of the twentieth century is a repetition of the
same game, one that has always cost society dear.

Railways and Capitalist Anarchy

The classic forms of private enterprise proved inadequate in
the case of rail technology. The scale of the undertaking was
such that it could not be mastered by the existing type of
private enterprise. Even the construction of a relatively short
line required the investment of hundreds of 'normal' capitalist entrepreneurs. Joint stock companies were given enhanced
importance in response to the new technology and as an
alternative to the state. This new form combined two essential elements of the capitalist mode of production: private
rights of disposal remained, at least for the decisive group of
big shareholders; individual small shareholders, however,
sank into the 'anonymity' of the big corporation.[51] This new
form of enterprise expressed the anarchy of the capitalist
mode of production at a higher level.

According to Marx, this new form of capital made possible

> an enormous expansion of the scale of production and of
> enterprises, that was impossible for individual capitals. ...
> This is the abolition of the capitalist mode of production
> within the capitalist mode of production itself, and hence a
> self-dissolving contradiction, which prima facie represents a
> mere phase of transition to a new form of production. ... It
> establishes a monopoly in certain spheres and thereby
> requires state interference.[52]

The private railway companies were mainly large joint stock
companies that established themselves in the second half of
the nineteenth century. Initially they took the form of joint
ventures involving a number of individual firms that exercised a form of collective control. In the early phase, these
shareholders, like private entrepreneurs, had unlimited liability for the whole undertaking. In the second half of the
nineteenth century, at the beginning of the railway boom in
central Europe and North America, liability was increasingly
limited until eventually shareholders were liable only for
their own share value.

In a very short time, it became much easier to attract capital. Entrepreneurs with only modest capital, and speculators
with none at all, were soon establishing joint stock companies.
They appealed for investments for a particular project, for
instance, the construction of a railway line, initially to private
individuals, then through the banks, and eventually through
the stock exchange which was created, to a large extent, by the
railway companies. State concessions for the construction of a
rail line, and the monopoly it entailed, lent credibility to such
projects and made it easier for them to attract capital. Having
acquired the starting capital in this manner, the banks then
usually stepped in with credit. It was through their links with
railway construction and with these joint stock companies that
the banking system developed to what it has become in the
twentieth century. The banks acted as creditors for the share
companies and took responsibility for the financing of the decisive initial phase of construction. They often had their own
shares and, at a later stage, as representatives of numerous
small investors, exercised de facto majority control. In France

and Germany in the mid-nineteenth century there were about a dozen such banks involved in railway construction. German banks had 2.5 billion marks invested in railway companies in 1865, generally in the form of credits. In 1870 this reached 4 billion and, in 1880, 9 billion marks.

The necessary foundation was thus established for major projects – or large-scale bankruptcies. The railway boom experienced both. Where railway companies were established during a period of economic revival, they generally had their trains rolling within a few years, paid high dividends to their shareholders and paid off their creditors. The absence of competition, however, was an important factor. Where companies competed for investments and credit and where shares were often over-valued, a cyclical downturn in the economy usually meant bankruptcy. There were many such bankruptcies in Britain in 1847 and in Germany in 1873. The collapse of such a major project had nothing in common with the traditional bankruptcy of a small capitalist firm. The losses involved in such bankruptcies were not paid by the 'anonymous' investors but by society itself: the thousands of building workers whose wages were not paid and who found themselves overnight on the streets; the hundreds of small suppliers whose deliveries were not paid for and who now faced ruin; the state, which set up receiverships to partially reimburse the major creditors and generally had to take over the construction of the partially finished line, which it financed from state revenue.

This pattern of private enrichment and socialisation of losses in railway construction was accompanied by massive speculation in land. The railway companies and banks did not merely speculate, in the strict sense of buying and waiting; they were in a position to influence, by their own actions, the value of land. Often working very closely with urban authorities, the railway companies were able to make massive gains.[53] In North America, farmers wanting to buy land often found the best land already in the hands of the railway companies.[54]

The list of major railway bankruptcies is a long one. In many instances they were accompanied by political scandals, since state bureaucracies or even governments were frequently involved. In *Prussia*, the case of B. H. Strousberg is perhaps the best known. Born in modest circumstances in East Prussia, Strousberg became involved with the railways in 1855 with no capital whatever of his own. In the 1860s he became the 'railway king' of Germany. His career ended in 1878 with what was, at the time, the biggest bankruptcy in German history. When his affairs were wound up, the assets were enough to repay only 1 per cent of debts; 99 per cent were socialised in the manner already described.[55] It was the 'incorruptible' Prussian bureaucracy, the ruling parties and the government of Bismarck itself, so highly praised by Schumpeter, that had allowed the 'Strousberg system' to flourish, in contravention of existing law. But this was hardly surprising since they were direct participants and beneficiaries of the share swindle. 'A quarter of the *Reichstag* and Prussian *Landtag* deputies were board members of share companies, especially railway companies. ... The leaders of the liberal and conservative parties were founders' (of new railway joint stock companies). Bismarck himself bought shares in railway companies that he later nationalised, at great profit to himself.[56]

The Prussian railway scandal was not a specifically German phenomenon. Every leading industrial country in the nineteenth century had its own Strousberg. Some of the biggest of the railway companies went bankrupt, taking many others down with them. *Britain* had experienced its railway-building boom some three decades earlier than Germany. George Hudson, the builder of the Midland Railway in the mid-1840s, later became the 'railway king' of England and at the centre of a rush to establish new railway companies in what Marx describes as 'the first big railway fraud'. Almost the entire productive sector of the British economy limited investment in their own sector in the hope of high profits that were expected from railway construction. Nicholas Faith describes Hudson as 'the very archetype of the vulgar, swaggering adventurer bred world-wide by the railways'. He represented his native York in parliament and had his money in landed property and banks as well as in the railways. In the railway boom that erupted in 1845:

Parliament passed 225 Railway Bills, with a further 270 in the following session, providing for 4,540 miles of track, costing nearly £100 million. Members were not exactly impartial. In 1845, a total of 157 had their names on the registers of the new railway companies – one company boasted of being able to command a hundred votes in the House of Commons alone. ... The mania was universal. In a Yorkshire vicarage, Emily and Anne Bronte ignored the warning of their sister Charlotte and invested their meagre savings in the Yorkshire & Midland Railway.[57]

The crash that followed in 1847 inflicted severe losses on thousands of small investors. In a report from the House of Lords on the crisis of 1847, a report that was kept secret for a long time, it was stated that: 'In 1847 almost all merchant houses began to starve their own businesses by investing part of their capital in railways.' Hudson's collapse came two years after the great crash, as a result of a scandal in his management of the Eastern Counties railway. He controlled 1,450 of England's 5,000 miles of railway but his competitors built a direct line from York to London and undermined many of the routes he controlled between these two cities.

Two decades later in France the biggest railway company collapsed. This was the *Société Générale du Crédit Mobilier*, a finance corporation involved in railway construction and in speculation with railway company stocks. It had close links with the government of Napoleon III and was heavily involved in the construction of railways in Russia. Its biggest source of income was speculation in shares from railway companies established by itself. When it went bankrupt in 1867 it caused a major political crisis in France. In Russia the Tsarist government had to take over the construction of the unfinished railway lines. These same lines were of major strategic importance in the Russian–Turkish war of 1877–8.

There are interesting parallels in the character and in the rise and fall of the railway kings. Schumpeter gives us the following description of Hudson:

From the point of view of his background, he was an insignificant man. With no knowledge of technology, commerce, or of railway financing, he possessed only one ability, albeit an important one – he could bend the wills of his fellow men to his own goals. In a Bolshevik state, he would be invaluable as a member of the council of commissars. He knew how to get his way with parliament.[58]

Little is known about Strousberg's background. When he began his railway company in 1863, he had neither capital of his own nor technical knowledge. But he knew how to establish good relations with government figures and to get them involved in his venture. He also acquired his own newspaper, *Die Post*, which was very useful in promoting his own company and in enticing investments from the middle class. The issue of 2 May 1867 contained the following: 'Nature lovers in particular have the opportunity to enjoy the most beautiful spots in our romantic Spree Forest, made accessible to us now by the railway.'[59] It was Strousberg's railway, of course. Emile Zola gives us an interesting picture of railway speculation in his novel, *Money*. The main character in this novel, the finance and railway king, Saccard, is modelled on the French financial *jongleur*, Mirès, and his banking house has certain similarities to the Crédit Mobilier.

In *North America* a number of major railway companies collapsed in 1854. Three years later, 150 banks, many of them heavily involved with the railway companies, had to close. Two decades later, at the time of the international recession in 1873, there was a major bank crash in North America; the stock exchange was forced to close. Dozens of railway companies went bankrupt, among them the biggest, the Northern Pacific Railroad. The depression that followed and that lasted until 1877 was in many respects similar to the depression of 1929–32. Two decades later, in 1893, there was a renewed crisis among the railway companies. Ralf Roman Rossberg writes that 'in the black months of 1893 ... 74 railway companies, with a rail network of 47,273 km, and with a capital investment of 7 million gold marks' were in receivership. The value of the bankrupt American rail companies was higher at that time than the value of the entire German rail network. The state-appointed receivers, however, approved state subsidies for a renewed privatisation, this time as bigger, 'consolidated' companies'.[60]

The banking house, J. Pierpont Morgan, became involved in this 'reorganisation of the US railways', initially in alliance with the US railway king, Cornelius Vanderbilt, and by the end of the century he led the biggest financial and industrial group involved in running the US rail network. In the US, as in Britain, Germany and France, private interests, state bureaucracies and governments were involved in a network of speculation and corruption.

On 27 June 1970, the biggest transport company in the world, the Penn Central Railway, declared bankruptcy. Three billion dollars worth of short-term credits had to be met within hours to prevent this collapse from drawing down other banks and corporations with it. In the judgement of one representative of the US National Bank: 'It is no exaggeration when I say that we barely managed to avoid another 1933.'[61]

In the second volume of *Capital*, Marx considers why private capital is particularly unable to pursue the construction and maintenance of railways in the long term. A significant part of the capital invested in the railways is subject to a secular wear and tear that extends over many decades. This applies to rail track, bridges, viaducts, tunnels and dams. These have to be renewed only every 50 or 100 years. Marx quotes the British railway expert, Lardner, about

that wear and tear which, being due to the slow operation of time acting upon the more solid structures, produces an effect altogether insensible when observed through short periods, but which, after a long interval of time, such, for example, as centuries, must necessitate the reconstruction of some or all even of the most solid structures. ... The operation of time upon the more massive works of art upon the railway, such as the bridges, viaducts, tunnels, etc., afford the example of what may be termed secular wear and tear. ... For financial and economic purposes such an epoch is perhaps too remote to render it necessary to bring it into practical calculation ... .[62]

Marx did not draw any explicit conclusions. At the time when *Capital* was written, the big wave of railway bankruptcies had not yet happened. That point in time when, according to Lardner, secular wear and tear would require massive new capital investment would happen only around the turn of the century.

In traditional industry the capital advanced has to be replaced in the course of the industrial cycle. A private capitalist will set aside an annual amortisation fund so that after the wear and tear of seven or eight years the capital can be replaced. But with capital invested in the railways the situation is different. The only costs that enter the calculation are the normal running costs. The costs of 'secular wear and tear' are not replaced, let us say, at the rate of one hundredth or one fiftieth each year, so that at the end of the long period the entire capital could be replaced. No private capitalist firm makes its calculations over such a period. It is only society or the state controlled by society that can make such a calculation.

In such conditions, there are two possible courses of action: both actually happened in the railways and both conflict with the goal of an ongoing and expanding rail sector. The first possibility is that rail transport services are sold at their true value, in other words, the amortisation costs, the costs of secular wear and tear, are included in the price of transport. This may have happened in the early phase of the railways and in those cases where one particular railway company had a monopoly on a particular line. The railway company would then replace each year a fiftieth or a hundredth of the advanced capital needed for later renewal. After ten or twenty years this would be a considerable sum which the company could invest wherever maximum profit could be expected. Capital could be invested in extended railway construction or in some other sector of industrial production. During the boom of the early years of railway construction, a lot of this capital would be tempted into the financial sector and into speculation. In such cases, the replaced capital is not permanently set aside for secular investment and renewal in the railways.

The second possibility is that transport prices do not include the costs of secular wear and tear. This would happen particularly in cases where competition was strong, where parallel lines competed for business, where price competition was necessary to attract customers and maximise profit. In such cases the railway companies would operate according to the motto: 'after us the flood'. Short-term profits are privatised and nothing is set aside for medium-term, much less long-term renewal. Eventually the point is reached where the company goes bankrupt; the state or state-subsidised receivers carry the pre-programmed losses.

The abstract presentation of these two development possibilities demonstrates the heart of the problem. In the real history of the capitalist transport sector, elements of both solutions were mixed, as Marx himself was aware when he gave examples of the very different sums that the English railway companies wrote off annually for repairs and maintenance of the permanent line and buildings, where the differences had little to do with actual expenditure but with calculations of desirable dividends. In both cases described above, the law of value is temporarily set aside for the individual companies. It reappears, as it were, behind the backs of these companies, mediated through the bankruptcies, the subsequent nationalisations and the socialisation of the costs that had previously been taken out of these companies in the form of private profit.

The US railways are a classic example of this problem. They went through hundreds of bankruptcies and state-financed rescue operations. But through all of this they remained in private hands. Even in periods of crisis, investors drew a 'normal' profit. The Pennsylvania Railway Company, in the period between 1856 and 1969, a period of 113 years, paid an annual dividend of between 8 and 10 per cent (in 1931, 6.5 per cent). Civil wars, bank crashes, world economic crises, rise of the car industry, world wars – none of these had any effect on the big share holders. This inexhaustible treasure, from which they paid themselves year by year, was the result of a large-scale robbery of the invested capital; nothing was put aside for major renewal investment.

Schumpeter describes similar short-term calculations that were behind the US bankruptcies of 1907.[63] Hudson in England, Strousberg in Germany and the Crédit Mobilier in France carried out the same short-term manoeuvres in their time, with the same results – bankruptcies, state subsidies and socialised losses.[64]

Under these circumstances, the basic investment needed to ensure safety was also not forthcoming, which resulted in increasing accidents and deaths. According to US statistics there were, in 1900, 2,550 dead and 39,643 wounded railway workers (not counting civilian victims of rail accidents). In 1910 the number of dead was 3,382 and the number of wounded was 95,671. It was deaths and injuries like these that led to the founding of the railway unions, the first major concern of which was worker safety.[65]

Class Society on the Railways

The car in the twentieth century is linked with the idea of individual freedom. In the nineteenth century the train was identified with egalitarian tendencies, the freedom from classes and the freedom of the collective. The early socialist, Constantin Pecqueur, thought that technology would bring political equality: 'It is the same train, the same power, that carries big and small, rich and poor. The trains are a tireless instructor in equality and fraternity.'[66] Such sentiments must appear naive today. But looked at in the light of transport history, they made a great deal of sense. The dominant form of transport in Europe before the era of the train was the coach, an elite and costly means of travel. The train appeared to offer a means of transport available to everyone, to all classes of society. The lowering of prices that came with the train was another factor making it available to ordinary people.

But what the socialists and the people looked forward to was feared by the authorities and the elite. The Habsburg, Ferdinand Maximilian, later king of Mexico, saw in the railway 'the symbol of equality, the lever of an advancing socialism'.[67] And indeed the railways did transport the masses. In 1831 about one million people travelled by coach in the German Empire. In 1910 the number of train journeys was 1,514 million.[68]

The owners and managers of the railways, however, did everything they could to counteract the egalitarian tendencies of the new form of transport. Class society was to be reproduced on the railways. The clearest example of this was the introduction of the compartment car, a special form of coach designed for first- (and later second-) class passengers. This reproduced, in the train, the old (horse-drawn) coach, a nostalgic conservation of the old form within the new. Secure and separate from the rest of the passengers, the gentlemen could travel with their own kind. Any intrusion into this elitist seclusion was resented and feared. The strength of this resentment was manifest in the middle-class outrage over the first 'compartment murder' on 6 December 1860 in France, an outrage which was expressed throughout the whole of Europe.[69] The large number of fatal accidents among railway workers before this incident had failed to raise any public concern. The compartments, in the trains of the period, were accessible from the outside. Today's corridor is not an extension of the compartments but of the outside running board along which the conductors had to walk in the first decades of the train.

Numerous writers have written about the anachronistic character of the compartment car, the dominant coach form in Europe until the 1980s. One of them, Joseph Roth, complains: 'We continuously look at each other: when we peel an apple or an orange or eat sausage. Sometimes we squirt the juices of southern fruits in each other's eyes. When we open a window, the passengers with colds protest. I have to excuse myself six times when I want to leave the compartment.'[70]

Lower-class passengers were transported in coaches with a design similar to that of goods and animal cars. Indeed, in the beginning, lower-class passengers were carried in open animal cars, then in animal cars with wooden benches, finally in cars with seats and a central aisle. Until the 1840s, in England, lower-class passengers were not considered part of passenger transport but as an appendix to the transport of goods. Coaches for third- and fourth-class passengers were simply attached to goods trains. It was 17 years after the opening of the first public railway in Britain that a law was passed stipulating that these coaches had to be roofed (Gladstone Act 1844). The poor were not encouraged to travel unless it was in search of work. The Manchester and Leeds Railway decided in 1838 that there should be three classes of carriage:

First class: six inside – complete with everything which can conduce to comfort. Second Class: to carry twenty four passengers – divisions chair high – window in door but none in panels – and no cushions. Third Class: open boxes – no roofs, nor buffer springs.[71]

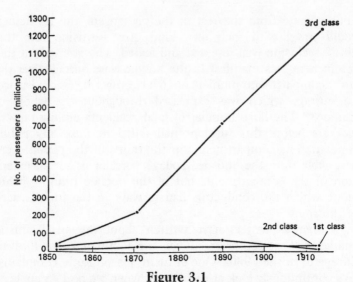

Figure 3.1
British Railways: Number of Passengers by Class

Robert Stephenson told a Select Committee on Railways in 1839 that there was 'a class of people who [had] not yet had the advantage from the railways which they ought, that is the labouring classes'.[72] The Midlands Counties Railway was typical of early railway companies: it carried third-class passengers in open carriages without seats. The open carriages carried 60 passengers and it was assumed, according to the Select Committee of 1839, that 'no one will go in it who can afford to go in others ... the passengers all stand, they are taken as the pigs are'.[73] The Gladstone Act stipulated that there should be third-class accommodation on at least one train a day in each direction at a maximum fare of one penny per mile. Thereafter the number of third-class passengers increased more rapidly than did the numbers in the other two classes. The total number of passengers carried on Britain's railways increased from 24.5 million in 1842 to nearly 73 million in 1850 and 507 million in 1875.[74] Third-class travel increased more rapidly after 1874 when the Midland Railway abolished the second class and improved the comfort of third-class passengers, an initiative which obliged other main line companies to follow suit. By 1890, over 70 per cent of revenue was coming from passengers who travelled third class.[75] See Figure 3.1.[76]

When rail travel increased among the lower classes, trains themselves were made into upper- or lower-class trains. In Germany the express train (*Fern-D-Zug*) was an exclusive first-class train until the Second World War, as was the legendary 'Flying Hamburger' that linked Berlin and Hamburg from 1933. After the war, the German Federal Railway (*Deutsche Bundesbahn*) took over this class tradition, with the introduction of the TEE trains for first-class passengers. The other European railways followed a similar pattern. The German Intercity trains, when they were first introduced in 1971, were for first-class passengers only. But they lost money and were opened to second-class passengers in 1979. Its slogan was 'Every Hour, Every Class'. In modern Intercity trains the restaurant car is the class divide. With the introduction of lower fares for first-class travel in the 1980s, there were frequent complaints from business travellers about the class of persons that were now allowed to travel in first-class accommodation.[77]

4

The US: Land of the Railroads

Good morning America, How are you?
Don't you know me, I'm your native son.
I'm the train they call the city of New Orleans.
I'll be gone five hundred miles when the day is done.

US folk song

'President Reagan wants to cut federal subsidies for Amtrak, the American rail company.' The United States will 'soon break another rail record. From October (1985) it could be the only industrial nation in the world without a rail passenger service.'[78] This was the report in the economics weekly, *Wirtschaftswoche*, in 1984. But it has not happened. Not yet.

North America was once *the* railroad continent. On this continent, more than on any other, the industrial revolution, the economic boom and the transport services that these required would have been unimaginable without the railroads. The structural weight of the industries that were dependent on rail was much greater in North America than in any country of Europe. This was dictated by the nature of American transport at the beginning of the industrial period. At the beginning of the nineteenth century the US did not have a developed road system. 'The riverboat was for the American train what the coach was for the European.'[79] The steam boat had its world-wide day of glory some two decades before the train. In 1812 there were over 50 such steam boats on US rivers. In 1819 the first ocean steamer, the Savannah, crossed the Atlantic; six years before the opening of the first railroad, the Savannah left Liverpool (US) and landed 25 days later in Liverpool (England), linking the old centre of capitalism with the new.[80]

This revolution in transport also had a lasting effect on the railroads. The railroad carriage of the 1840s in the US resembled the passenger quarters on a riverboat: a long car without compartments and with no resemblance to the horse-drawn coach. Carriages had four seats on each side of a central aisle and the seats could be turned to face either direction. For a long time there were no class divisions on the US railroads. Rossberg sees this as an expression of 'the democratic assumptions of the US citizens who considered everyone equal'.[81] Wolfgang Schivelbusch considers the 'spatial classless carriage as an economically, politically, psychologically and culturally appropriate vehicle of a democratic pioneer society, while the compartment was an expression of European social relations'.[82]

The introduction of the Pullman Car in 1859, a luxurious version of the standard railroad carriage, was actually closer to the class reality of American society; it was effectively a first-class car. The egalitarian tendencies were, in any case, restricted to American white society. The black population was by and large excluded from the railroads. For the native Indian population, the railroads were simply the transport of their destroyers. The more land the railroads opened up for the white colonisers, the more dead Indians there were and the more restricted was the space in which they could live. Buffalo Bill's great slaughter of 4,000 buffaloes in 18 months simply provided food for the workers of the Union Pacific Railroad Company, which completed the first trans-continental railroad in America in 1869.

The US also had its own Trevithick. His name was Oliver Evans and in 1797 he published a work on the advantages of travel by rail. In 1801 he built the first steam-mobile and in 1804 another, designed to travel on the streets of Philadelphia as well as on the canals. His plans, however, met with no enthusiastic response and no offers of capital. In American textbooks he is quoted as saying: 'Even progress takes its time.' The cases of Evans and Trevithick are further confirmation of the historical-materialist viewpoint, according to which, in the capitalist system, inventions become part of progress only when they correspond to some real economic need; only when this happens can they be realised in social production.[83]

The railroad era began in the US in 1829. Four years after the opening of the Stockton–Darlington line in England, a 24-km line was opened between Baltimore and Ellicotts-Mills, the line on which Peter Cooper ran his Tom Thumb in 1830. Five years later, as the first railroad line was being built in Germany, the US had the largest network in the world, with 1,500 km of rail line; England at that time had 720 km. A decade later, in 1840, the US railroad, with 4,500 km of track, was bigger than the whole European network. In the following four decades, both North America and Europe experienced a parallel boom in railroad construction: 1850, 23,500 km in Europe – 14,500 km in America; 1860, 51,800 km in Europe – 49,300 in America; 1870, 105,000 km in Europe – 85,000 in America; 1880, 160,000 km in Europe – 150,700 km in North America. Then began in North America a 30-year boom in railroad construction which remains unique in transport history. Around 7,500 km of railroad were built annually: the North American rail network was 150,700 km in 1880, 270,000 km in 1890, 312,000 km at the turn of the century and 393,000 km in 1910.

This was the golden age of rail transport. In his history of rail travel, Schivelbusch quotes from a contemporary account of a train consisting entirely of Pullman Cars:

> Bathrooms with bath and shower, barber shops, manicure salons, lady's maids and man servants, telegraph offices, libraries, the latest magazines and newspapers as well as train timetables and hotel guides, smoking cars, a fantastic choice of wines and spirits – all such things were taken for granted on the luxury trains of that period. On the transcontinental line of Union Pacific they produced a daily paper that announced such events on board as music concerts and church services. The latter was made possible by the installation of two organs in the train.[84]

In May 1893, the New York Central Railroad Company announced that its trans-continental Rail Express had reached the record speed of 112.5 miles (181 km) per hour.

This massive expansion of the railroads in North America can be explained by six special factors. First, as long as the

North American railroads did not run parallel to canals or rivers, they had no competition. Roads did not exist and there was no lobby pushing hard for road construction. During the second half of the nineteenth century, rail transport proved itself so efficient that it began to replace water transport in certain parts of the country.

A second factor was the Civil War and the restructuring of capital investment in the transport sector that took place as a result of the war. The outbreak of war caught the northern states unprepared. A large transport capacity was needed on the rivers to carry troops and supplies; strategically placed railroad lines would also have to be built. But private investment in river and naval transport was now becoming a problem. According to Gustavus Meyers: 'After the outbreak of war, the waterways were taken over by privateers and the big shipowners now had a lot of superfluous ships on their hands.' They needed to find a use for their ships and at the same time a more secure place to invest their wealth. The solution was at hand. The state bought the ships for use in the war (at inflated prices) and the shipowners invested their money in the railroads. They also took advantage of the offer by the US state to give generous grants of land to companies that promised to build new rail lines. This was how the biggest railroad empire in the US was built, that of Cornelius Vanderbilt.[85]

Third, the US railroads were built at a tremendous cost to nature and human life. The railroads advanced into frontier land that was owned 'only' by the native Indians. Whereas in Europe the railroad companies had to spend large sums for the purchase of land, in North America they simply took whatever land was needed. The first continental link in North America was also built at a tremendous cost in human life. Very little progress was made in construction during the Civil War but, with the end of the war in 1865, an army of unemployed soldiers, adventurers and prisoners was put to work by the Union Pacific and Central Pacific on their Atlantic–Pacific line. Bad weather, snow storms and the resistance of the Indian population led to thousands of desertions during the next two years. It became almost impossible to find white workers for the job. The railroad companies then recruited over 10,000 Chinese workers, not just from San Francisco but also from

Shanghai, Peking and Hong Kong. It was these Chinese workers that laid the sleepers for the trans-continental railroad.
This railroad cost the lives of thousands of workers and an
even greater number of native Indians. The exact figures are
not known. US newspaper headlines suggested that 'Every
Sleeper Costs One Chinese Life'. But, in the end, it was only
the results that counted. The dead were forgotten when, on 10
May 1869, the Governor of California drove the golden spike
that linked Central and Union Pacific and joined New York,
via Chicago, with San Francisco.[86]

Fourth, the availability of labour and materials as well as
the cheaper access to land meant that the American railroads
were easier and cheaper to build. Whereas European railroads
tended to follow, where possible, a straight line, the American railroads followed a more natural river-like pattern in
order to avoid natural obstacles and difficult terrain. Where
the Americans went around a hill, the Europeans built a
tunnel. The material to build sleepers was plentiful everywhere in America and land did not cost anything. Rail construction in North America cost between one tenth and one
third of what it did in Europe. The narrower curve radials
presented a technological challenge. With the two fixed axles
of the European carriage, the American train would derail.
The Americans developed the bogie, the undercarriage piv-
oted below both ends of the locomotive or railroad car which
not only enabled it to master curves but also made it possible to have longer carriages.[87]

Fifth, the private American railroads received enormous
subsidies and concessions from the state, especially free grants
of land and favourable credits. For the construction of the first
trans-continental line, the US Congress granted the railroad
companies 52 sq km of land (generally along the rail line) and
between $16,000 and $48,000 cheap credit for each mile of
track. Within a few years the US railroad companies owned an
enormous amount of the best arable land. Since white settlements tended to follow the railroad, there was a very high
demand for land. The sale of this land was a major source of
capital for the railroad companies.

Prospective farmers had to pay the railroads exorbitant
prices for land. Very often they had not sufficient funds; a

mortgage or two would be signed; and if the farmer had a bad season or two, and could no longer pay the interest, foreclosure would result.[88]

A sixth and final factor was the role of the North American railroads in strengthening the socio-political consolidation of the continent. The railroads helped to hinder the break-up of the multi-national and class-divided society. In the midst of the Civil War, the US Congress decided to build the trans-continental railroad that would link loyal California with the North. The American Civil War was also the first major war in which the railroads played a crucial, almost decisive military role. The North had a much more developed railroad system than the South, a factor which contributed greatly to its victory.

That the railroads served private and not public interest was made absolutely clear in this number one railroad country in the world. William Henry Vanderbilt, the son of Cornelius and his successor as railroad king of America, became famous in history for four words uttered on 8 October 1882:

In response to the question of a reporter, whether the railroads should serve the public interest, the president of Central said that the railroad company had to serve only the interests of its shareholders, adding, 'The public be damned'.[89]

5

War, Colonies and Revolution: Militarisation of the Railways

One of the most important advantages of the whole system of railways will be that it will make the standing army superfluous or at least make it possible to reduce its size indefinitely. There will be no more wars of invasion.

Friedrich List, 1832

Without the railway, the Congo isn't worth two shillings; with the railway, however, it is worth uncountable millions.

Henry Morgan Stanley, 1884

Towards the end of the nineteenth century, an important factor that favoured nationalisation of rail was the growing realisation that it was essential in war. A private capitalist administration of the railways according to the profit principle could not easily be reconciled with the requirements of an effective long-term and centralised military strategy.

In Germany, troops were first transported by rail during the 1848 revolution. It was also in 1848 that the French workers dismantled the rail lines to prevent reinforcement of the counter-revolution.[90] The Russian Tsar made use of the newly constructed rail link to send troops to put down the Hungarian revolution of the same year. In 1855 the French, who occupied the Crimea, built a railway for exclusively military purposes. It linked the Black Sea port of Balaklava to the Franco-British forces that were besieging Sevastopol.

The Russians had to rely on overland marches to reinforce their own troops.

The first big test of the railway in war came in 1859 with the campaign of the French and Piedmontese against Austria. Between 20 April and 30 April of that year, the Paris–Lyon railway transported 8,500 soldiers and 500 horses per day over this 400 km stretch. Within three months the French railway had transported 60,000 men and 37,000 horses. This was six times faster than traditional marching time.

In the American Civil War the northern states established a special Bureau of United States Military Railroads. It established rail troops for the first time and put the private railway companies under de facto state control. In 1864 General Sherman made the Chattanooga to Atlanta line the nerve centre of his offensive against the southern states. Although he was 600 km away from his operational base, the railway enabled him to feed and supply his 100,000 men and 23,000 horses. It was in this war, for the first time, that the destruction of railway lines was carried out on a large scale and developed into an art.[91] This destruction was then raised to a much higher level in the two world wars. The *Schienenwolf* (railway wolf) was a specially designed carriage which, when pulled behind the locomotive, literally ploughed up the rail lines.

In 1857, the Prussian chief of staff, Hermann von Moltke, encouraged the government to build new railway lines, especially in an east–west direction towards the Rhine, to be used in the event of a war with France. Since there was very little economic use for such parallel lines, they were state owned. In 1864 the general staff was granted its own railway section so that military strategic planning could be done with much greater precision and with much more attention to the timetabling of troop transport. It was in the 1866 war against Austria that Prussia first made practical use of the railway in its deployment of troops. The Prussian general staff, with its own rail lines, was able to move its troops into Bohemia and Moravia much faster than Austria.

The 1866 war also demonstrated a factor which has become increasingly important since then, namely, the limited scope for *political* action that results from the use of modern war technology. When the Prussian deployment was

halted by the King, for political and tactical reasons, and the
Austrian position improved from day to day, Moltke insisted
on an immediate renewal of the operation: 'Once we have
mobilised, we shouldn't worry about accusations of aggression. Any hesitation only makes our own situation decisively
worse.'[92]

The Prussian experience was put to good use in the war
with France that came in 1870–1. Along its six east–west
railway lines, and on three more lines owned by its southern allies, Prussia deployed 462,000 soldiers within 18
days, all of them transported to their precise deployment
areas according to a previously worked-out plan. The regular French army, whose own transport dissolved into chaos,
was overrun.

The railway was an important factor in the Russian–Japanese War of 1904–5. With its attack on Russia, Japan wanted to
prevent the completion of the Trans-Siberian Railway, which
would have strengthened Russia's position in the Pacific area.
Russia was able to use the railway, which was almost
completed at the time, to transport reinforcements which
brought its strength in the war zone from 140,000 to 1 million
men. They arrived too late, however, to prevent the Russian
defeat.

Railway technology was also increasingly used in the military domination and economic exploitation of the colonies in
Africa. By 1913 the colonial powers had built 43,000 km of
railway on the continent.[93] Armoured trains were first used by
the British in the Boar War (1899–1902). In the German colonies, railway companies (mostly private) built a network of
4,179 km, 7.5 per cent of the rail network of the German
Reich. These rail lines were used exclusively for the purpose of
colonisation. This was particularly the case in south-west
Africa. Intensive settlement began at the end of the 1890s,
parallel to the construction of the rail link between Swakop-
mund and Windhoek. In 1904 a second line, the Otavi Line,
was built which went through the territory of the Hereroes.
The Otavi Mining and Railway Company demanded that the
Hereroes give up their land, without compensation, in a 40-km
corridor along the railway line. This land was to be settled by
an expected influx of German settlers. The Hereroes desperately mounted a resistance which was brutally put down by

General Von Trotha. In the three years between 1904 and 1907, German troops expelled the two main peoples living in this area, the Hereroes and Nama. By 1911, the number of Hereroes had shrunk from 80,000 to 15,310 and the Nama from 20,000 to 9,781.[94]

The economically exploitative character of the railway system was visible in the routes chosen. 'All the railways led to the sea', wrote Walter Rodney in his book on Africa. The United Nations Commission on Africa made a similar observation in its report in 1959: 'The predominant character of transport systems in Africa is their relative isolation within particular countries and areas. There are no links between countries and areas, even within the same region.'[95] Eduardo Galeano has also pointed to the differences between the railways in the capitalist metropolitan countries and those in Latin America. In Latin America,

> the railways don't form a network designed to link regions with one another; rather, they link production centres with the sea ports. On maps, the railway lines still present the image of a hand with extended fingers. Thus the railways, welcomed so often as the harbingers of progress, actually hindered the creation and development of an internal market.[96]

The militarisation of the railways reached new levels in the First World War. In all the European countries there was effective state control for the purpose of troop deployment and the transport of reinforcements and provisions. This was particularly true in Germany. The likelihood of a war on two fronts made it essential to be able to carry out a Blitzkrieg on one front, bring about a rapid conclusion and liberate troops for the longer war on the other front. Rapid mobility within the country was therefore crucial. Germany's deployment plan in the war, the Schlieffen Plan, depended crucially on the ability of the German railway to transport troops rapidly to the western front where the French, also in the possession of a modern railway network, would be quick to mobilise. A rapid victory here would liberate forces for deployment on the eastern front where, it was assumed, the Russians would mobilise much more slowly.

The Germans did indeed mobilise with amazing speed. Within 14 days, from 2 August to the fall of Lüttich on 16 August 1914, 11,000 German trains carried 3 million soldiers, 860,000 horses and a large mass of war material to the western front. But the French deployment was also rapid and precise. The Belgians, until then only a footnote in Germany's war plans, delivered an unexpectedly strong resistance, especially in the defence of the railway junction at Lüttich. The Russians mobilised faster than expected, largely because of previous French assistance in the construction of a rail network. Germany's war plan came to nothing. The war of attack became a long drawn-out war of position, precisely the outcome which the German military command had previously regarded as fatal.

The train was also to play its part in the Russian Revolution. The train transported Lenin and the leading Bolsheviks from Switzerland to Russia. This was the legendary 'sealed train' that is supposed to have changed the history of the modern world. The train that rolled across Europe in 1917 also contained two hostile territories – a diplomatic novelty. A chalk line separated German from Russian territory. Lenin and his comrades insisted on buying regular tickets for the journey; they travelled to the revolution on properly stamped third-class tickets.[97] The railway system and the ability of the Red Army under Trotsky's command to rapidly move its forces from one front to another also played a crucial role in the Russian Civil War.[98]

In the First World War and in the Russian Revolution the strategic importance of the railway became clear. In the practice of war, there was considerable friction between the needs of centralised military planning and the private organisational form of the transport system. Military administration of the railways during war time was not an adequate solution since the goals of private ownership did not lead to the construction of the strategic lines needed by the military. For general staffs war does not begin on the day war is declared; the strategic planning and practice begin much earlier. The outcome of this conflict was that the railways were increasingly militarised. The workers' organisations on the railways became increasingly subject to a kind of military discipline. One of the first 'sins' of the October Revolution was to abolish the independence of the Russian railway workers' organisation. They became 'transmission belts' for the Soviet authorities.

Originally seen as providing help in time of war, by adding greater mobility to the strategic operation, the railways soon became a determining factor in strategic planning. These military considerations were an important factor in promoting the idea of railway nationalisation in the twentieth century. It was only in the US that the railways remained in private hands for so long, but this had a lot to do with the fact that, since the Civil War, no major war has been fought on US territory.

The military significance of the railways has increased in the twentieth century. Military leaders now play a role in such decisions as railway electrification – electrified railway systems are more easily put out of operation by bombardment. Rail technology is also an important element of the modern nuclear weapons system: long-range nuclear missiles are transported on rail around the US in order to make them less vulnerable to attack.

Part II

The Resistible Rise of the Car – the Forced Decline of the Railways

First victory – then travel! Remember: the trains have to roll for victory!

German railway slogan in the Second World War

I love the car. It has given me the most beautiful hours of my life.

Adolf Hitler

Britain, then the most important of the imperialist powers, began the development of rail transport in the early part of the nineteenth century. From here, this new transport technology soon conquered continental Europe. The railways developed quite independently in the United States of America. Later, in the early twentieth century, it was the US, now the major imperialist power following the First World War, that brought a new transport technology to the rest of the world: the car and the truck (as well as its military variants, the jeep and the tank).

The promoters of the new technology were, however, confronted with a difficult task: in the early twentieth century, the train and the tram catered satisfactorily for all socially necessary transport in the industrialised countries. At that time, the car served as a luxury transport for only a small social minority. The intelligent and perceptive economist, Werner Sombart, felt very confident about the future of rail: 'This final epoch will end with a railway line in front of every house.'[1]

In the most important industrial countries the rail network more or less covered the whole territory, although less densely in the US and southern Europe than in Britain and central Europe. There was also a new technology at hand that would qualitatively improve rail travel and make it less expensive – the electric motor. For capitalist promoters of the motor vehicle, the goal was not to supplement rail travel (outside city centres or for distances of less than 50 km) but to replace it completely. The greater part of transport had to be taken off the rails and onto the roads. This meant that the entire rail system that had been developed in the previous 75 years would have to be brought to ruin.

It took another 50 years and another world war before the roads finally pushed rail into second place and it took another 25 years before rail transport was finally marginalised and no longer offered serious competition to the car. This was the historic victory of private capital over the mostly nationalised railways. In this battle, the nation state proved very beneficial for capital, in the massive public construction of roads, for instance, especially in the US after the crisis of 1929–33 and in fascist Germany and Italy. State-promoted and later nationalised motor industries also played a role (Volkswagen, Renault, British Leyland). Part II of this work attempts an analysis of the rise of the motor industry, its competitive battle against rail, the final triumph of motorised mass travel and the ideology of the car society. We will look concretely at the examples of the US, West Germany, East Germany and Western Europe as a whole.

6

The US: The First Car Boom, the Decline of the Railroads and the Car Society as a World Model

What's good for General Motors is good for America!

Charles Edward Wilson

The Beginning: Steam Cars and the Combustion Engine

The history of the automobile, defined as a self-moving vehicle, cannot be restricted to the 100-year-old type driven by a combustion engine. An electric car is still a car, as was the first steam-driven car constructed towards the end of the eighteenth century. In 1763, the French engineer, N.J. Cugnot, built a steam-powered vehicle for the transport of munitions. In 1770 he built an improved model but it was difficult to manoeuvre in the narrow streets of Paris – it went through a wall. After this first example of the car as public nuisance, the French government prohibited any further experiments.[2]

The first public demonstration of a roadworthy steam-powered car was in 1801. Richard Trevithick, whom we encountered in the previous chapter as the father of the steam locomotive, also built a 'diabolical car that ran like a horse, but ran only on steam'. He demonstrated his steam car in Camborne, England, and chose for his demonstration not a level but a poor and rather steep road.

Trevithick's full size engine was ready on Christmas Eve
1801 and the first load of passengers was moved by steam
on what was known in the neighbourhood as 'Captain
Dick's Puffer'. It was raining heavily, the road was rough
and the gradient steep but 'she went off like a little bird',
travelling three-quarters of a mile (1.2 km) up Beacon Hill
(to what became Camborne Railway Station) and home
again.[3]

Steam is not the ideal source of power for an automobile.
The stop-and-go operation required by the automobile places
too heavy a demand on the steam-powered engine, which
functions optimally in an even and regular operation. This
alone, however, does not explain why the steam-powered car
did not win the day – another factor was the private
monopolies on the railway. At the purely technical level,
there was a further development of the steam car; Trevithick,
for instance, built two other improved models. In the 1830s
there were steam-powered coaches and buses, and a regular
steam bus company began operation. The powers behind the
rail monopolies felt so threatened by this development that
they asked the British parliament to intervene. In 1836, and
later again in the 1860s, parliament introduced restriction on
the steam car which effectively finished it as a means of
transport.[4] Steam-powered coaches held out longer in France,
and were still in use at the end of the nineteenth century.
The good quality of French roads may have been an important factor here.

In 1860 in France, Jean Joseph Etienne Lenoir presented
publicly, for the first time, the technology that would eventually make the car a serious competitor to the train – the
combustion engine. It was a two-stroke engine powered by
lighting gas. The efficiency of this engine was three times
that of a steam engine of similar size. The engine was
intended for stationary use in smaller industrial enterprises.
For a quarter of a century the combustion engine was per-
fected and utilised in industry and in water transport. Only
at the end of this period was it used on a large scale in cars.

In 1861, a year after Lenoir's demonstration, Nikolaus
Otto, from Cologne, acquired the patent for a spirit-powered
combustion engine. In 1867 he built the first four-stroke

engine; finally, in the 1880s, he built an engine that was able to run on petrol. Gottlieb Daimler, working with Wilhelm Maybach, developed the first fast engine (880–900 revolutions per minute, 1.5 horse power); this was improved, at the turn of the century, by the addition of an electric starter, developed by Bosch. In 1893, Rudolf Diesel built the first engine to run on diesel oil. In 1886, Daimler mounted his engine on a four-wheeled coach and began his first trial runs. In the same year, Carl Benz demonstrated a three-wheeled motorcar. But these German car pioneers soon demonstrated their lack of patriotism: they sold the licence for the construction of their engines to France.

Whereas the Germans showed very little interest in the automobile, the French were enthusiastic. The much better network of roads in France was a positive factor. In 1894 the first car race was organised by two French car firms, Panhard-Lavassor and Peugeot, and the race was run between Paris and Rouen. The prizes went to the cars that were fitted with Daimler engines. But, unlike on the occasion of the first train trials some 50 years earlier, the speeds achieved here were very low, indeed lower than all other mechanised forms of transport – around 20 kilometres per hour.

A great number of horse-drawn carriages and bicycles accompanied the cars in the race, and the sports patron, Gordon Bennet, owner of the *New York Times*, had one of his journalists accompany the race on a bicycle.[5]

Car Production in the US: Henry Ford

It was in the United States that the car was first produced on a large scale, not in Europe where it had been invented and first used. And, unlike rail technology, it did not spread immediately to the other leading industrial nations. It was not until three or four decades after the advent of mass motoring in the US that a similar development occurred in Britain, France and Germany.

In 1899, Henry Ford left the Edison Company to 'devote himself to the car business'. The cars that were in use in America at that time were imported from Europe, mainly from Daimler and Peugeot. Ford's first attempt at production did not lead to any spectacular breakthrough. In 1905, he followed the European example and organised a car race in which he entered two cars, both built for high speed and not for regular use. In Ilya Ehrenburg's novel, *The Life of the Automobile*, Ford is quoted as saying: 'An automobile race is true democracy. The best man wins. If I achieve my goal, I will participate in ruling the country without having to bother with petty politics.' Whether authentic or invented, the fact is that Ford's model 999 won the race and, in Ford's words, 'made enough noise to half kill a man'. Now everyone knew 'that I could build fast cars'.[6] The first Ford plant was created.

In 1906, the number of cars sold in the US, 1,708, was sensational, but it was not enough to give the stimulus to mass production. However, these cars were designed and priced in such a way that their appeal was only to the upper layer of American society. They were luxury cars. In 1906–7, Ford dispensed entirely with the production of luxury cars and offered only three basic models. Prices sank from $2,000 to between $600 and $700. Soon five times as many cars were being produced. In 1909, he carried his basic concept to its logical conclusion and produced only one model, a 'car for the masses'.

Ford's idea, which was taken over quite literally by Adolf Hitler some 25 years later, was expressed as follows in his autobiography, *My Life and Work*:

> I will build a motorcar for the great multitude. It will be large enough for the family but small enough for the individual to run and care for. It will be constructed of the best materials, by the best men to be hired, after the simplest designs that modern engineering can devise. But it will be so low in price that no man making a good salary will be unable to own one – and enjoy with his family the blessing of hours of pleasure in God's great open spaces.[7]

Mass Production and the Ideology of Mass Motorisation

In 1910, having reached an annual production level of 45,000 cars, the Ford Motor Company had reached a point where assembly-line manufacture could be introduced. This then happened in 1913. Apart from modern slaughter houses, this was the first example of assembly-line production and the number of cars produced in the new plant increased dramatically.

Henry Ford was not merely a prosaic capitalist. His many sayings and speeches are permeated by a very definite philosophy, as in the following example from his autobiography:

> The average worker, I'm sorry to say, wants a job in which he doesn't have to put forth much physical exertion – above all he wants a job in which he does not have to think. Those who have what might be called the creative type of mind and who thoroughly abhor monotony are apt to imagine that all other minds are similarly restless and therefore to extend quite unwanted sympathy to the labouring man who day in and day out performs almost exactly the same operation.[8]

Maybe Henry Ford realised, in practice, that this was not the case. This was not, however, expressed in his philosophy, as it was in the analysis of Marx, who described the same phenomenon in quite a different manner:

> Factory work exhausts the nervous system to the uttermost; at the same time, it does away with the many-sided play of the muscles, and confiscates every atom of freedom, both in bodily and in intellectual activity. Even the lightening of the labour becomes an instrument of torture, since the machine does not free the worker from the work, but rather deprives the work itself of all content.[9]

Of course, Ford was aware of this 'terror of the machine' (the title of one of the chapters in his autobiography) but he saw it as progress and denied its harmful effects on the worker:

> I have not been able to discover that repetitive labour injures a man in any way. I have been told by parlour experts that repetitive labour is soul- as well as body-destroying, but this has not been the result of our investigations. ... Some of the operations are undoubtedly

monotonous – so monotonous that it seems scarcely possible that any man would care to continue long at the same job. Probably the most monotonous task in the whole factory is one in which a man picks up a gear with a steel hook, shakes it in a vat of oil, then turns it into a basket. The motion never varies. The gear comes to him always in exactly the same place, he gives each one the same number of shakes, and drops it into a basket which is always in exactly the same place. No muscular energy is required, no intelligence is required. ... Yet the man on that job has been doing it for eight solid years.[10]

With Ford's car plant, capitalism had reached that reversal of the relationship between the worker and the machine already analysed by Marx. In previous social formations, as in the early capitalist period, the machine was 'an extension of the human hand'; now the worker became an extension of the machine. The maximum exploitation of labour was now possible – the concentration of utilised labour power in minimal units of time. The goal was the maximum extraction of surplus value. At the same time, the application of machinery achieved its most rational form (rational in terms of profit, not human need). The outcome of Ford's entrepreneurial philosophy was the maximisation of average profit in the industry. As long as the Ford Company itself was technologically ahead of its competitors, as it was until the end of the 1930s, this meant super-profits for the corporation. Soon the company was able to announce an increase in productivity, as a result of assembly-line production, which achieved a fourfold increase in production without any increase in the labour force.

Henry Ford was also one of the first to recognise the importance of the 'consumer society' as a substitute for democracy:

'If they manage to adjust to exemplary machines, then their pay will go up, and the time will not be far when our very own workers will buy automobiles from us. ... I'm not saying our workers will sing Caruso or govern the state. No, we can leave such ravings to the European socialists. But the workers will buy automobiles.'[11]

An increasing amount of capital was now invested in the motor vehicle industry as a result of the promise of high profits, the widening market (linked to a large increase in income among wage earners), and the new production methods pioneered in the Ford plants. Other car producers began large-scale production, especially General Motors, Ford's major competitor; GM moved to number one position after the Second World War. The motor industry and the sectors that were closely linked to it (oil, chemicals, rubber) became the major growth sectors in the 1920s boom that followed the First World War, a boom that lasted until the world economic crisis of 1929. Between 1917 and 1919, the US motor industry produced more than two million cars annually, a figure that was more than doubled in the boom years of the 1920s. The number of cars registered at the beginning of the 1920s in the US was more than 10 million. At the end of the 1920s, the number exceeded 20 million and it never went below that figure even during the crisis years 1929–32. By the time of America's entry into the war in 1940, the number had increased by another 10 million. In 1950, the number of cars registered in the US reached 50 million. The car was now the dominant means of personal transport in North America. See Figure 6.1 overleaf.

On the wave of this mass motorisation, and the fundamental restructuring of the transport sector that this entailed, the US catapulted itself to the number one position among the industrialised nations, a position that rested on its immense economic power in world market competition. The great bulk of overall social investment in the US was in the civil productive sector; the state armaments sector remained relatively small. The economic power of the US made it possible for that country to peacefully acquire quasi-colonies in its efforts to promote its car industry. In 1924, the year Ford produced its ten millionth car, the American company, Firestone, a tyre manufacturer, signed a contract with Liberia, in West Africa, whereby it was granted a concession over an area of 40,000 hectares for the production of rubber. Henry Ford and Harvey S. Firestone were close friends. When the price of rubber subsequently fell on the world market, the big plantations in the British and Dutch colonies in South-East Asia, which up until then had a practical monopoly in this important sector, were

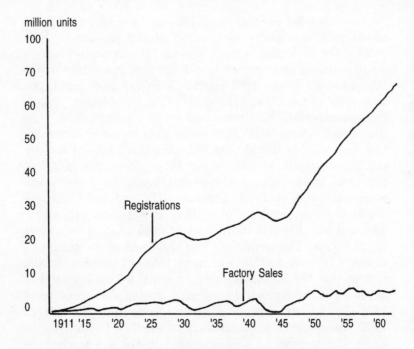

Figure 6.1
Passenger Cars: Factory Sales and Registrations, 1911–62
(Source: Baran and Sweezy, *Monopoly Capital*, p. 236)

thrown into a profound crisis. Numerous plantation workers lost their means of livelihood. In 1926, in the British and Dutch colonies, there were major insurrections which were brutally suppressed.

In Europe, it was not until after the Second World War that mass motorisation got under way. During the inter-war period, it was only in France, where Citroen and Peugeot had developed production earlier and where there was a good network of roads, and in Britain, where Ford had built a car plant as early as 1911, that there had been any significant developments. In general, the European continent had been more heavily burdened by the costs of military preparation, the economic crisis and the two world wars. The lower purchasing power of the general population also provided no basis for the development of mass motorisation.

But the wars themselves were the source of some auto-motive innovations. In 1902, the Archduke Franz Ferdinand, successor to the Austrian throne occupied by Franz Joseph I, arrived at the royal parade in a car – an affront to the staff officers who traditionally arrived at such an occasion on horse-back. The chauffeur of this royal car promoter was Ferdinand Porsche, a young technician from the Royal Coach Factory. In 1914, this same Ferdinand Porsche became technical director of Austro-Daimler in Vienna. On 28 June of that same year, his boss, the Archduke, drove in an open car, produced by the Viennese firm, Gräf and Stift (a kind of Austrian Rolls-Royce), through the streets of Sarajevo, where he was shot. In this long-prepared war, initiated by the shooting of the Archduke, the dominant transport technology was the train, as we have already described in Chapter 1. But military variants of the automobile were used in this war on a large scale, for instance in the battle of Verdun. The rail supply route was subject to German bombardment, so the French organised reinforce-ments by means of trucks – over a million soldiers and two million tons of supplies were transported to the front in rather primitive trucks. Similar developments took place on the Ger-man side. The director of Daimler, who profited greatly from the war, declared: 'War is a hungry beast, and its food is the automobile.' At the same time, the British brought their new invention to the Somme – the tank. It was for reasons of military secrecy that they were described as (water) tanks. It was not until the Second World War that tanks, trucks and jeeps were mass produced. The production of jeeps for military purposes made up for the shortfall in the production of ordinary cars during the war.[12]

The Decline of the American Railroads

A period of expansive growth ended with the beginning of the First World War. A depressive wave began then which was to last in America until the beginning, and in Europe until the end, of the Second World War. Between 1891 and 1913, industrial production grew in America at a yearly rate of 6 per cent; in the following period, between 1914 and 1937, the growth rate averaged only 2 per cent. Under these

Table 6.1 Average Yearly Investment in US Railroads

	1900–7	1908–15	Change %
New lines (miles)	5100	2800	−45.1
Increase in number of locomotives (units)	2300	1400	−40.5
Increase in number of rail cars (units)	87000	43800	−49.40

economic conditions, the new automotive technology, in order to increase its share of the profits, had to enter into a bitter competitive struggle with the railway. The railroad era actually began its decline in 1907, seven years before the onset of general economic decline in 1914. Table 6.1 compares the periods 1900–7 and 1908–15 with respect to the growth of the most important types of railway capital.[13]

The table shows a sharp drop in railroad investment of between 40 and 50 per cent. If we keep in mind the weight of the railroads in the overall economy, then this radical decline in growth in the railroads in the years *before* 1913 must have contributed in a major way to the general decline that began in that year. In their book, *Monopoly Capital*, Paul Baran and Paul M. Sweezy describe the end of the railway era as the end of

> the big shake-up which began even before the Civil War. ... it was in 1907 that the greatest external stimulus in capitalist history lost its tremendous force. ... The impetus provided by one epoch-making innovation had petered out. The next epoch-making innovation, the automobile, was just making its appearance on the economic scene and as yet exerted little or no influence on the economy as a whole.[14]

The rail network continued to grow, however, until 1925. From 311,000 km in 1900, it had grown to 392,808 km in 1910. During this decade in which the turning point was reached, the network continued to grow at an average rate of 8,180 km annually. By 1925, the network had grown to 420,580 km. But, as the period of mass motorisation got under way, the railways went into decline. By 1950 the network had shrunk to its size in 1905: 363,000 km. The first to be hit was the inter-urban electric railway. Begun in the 1890s, by 1916 it had grown to a network of 40,000 km (similar in size to the German railway at the time). In 1930, barely 15 years later, this network had practically disappeared – only a few lines were still in service and buses had replaced the electric trains. The biggest bus manufacturer was Yellow Coach, owned by GM, and the biggest bus company was Greyhound, also owned by GM.

The next to be affected were the long-distance railway lines. At the end of the 1970s, rail passenger travel in the US was 10 per cent of what it had been in 1925. In 1977, personal transport had the following structure: railways – 1 per cent; bus – 5 per cent; air – 11 per cent; car – 83 per cent. According to Brian Hollingsworth: 'Union Station at St. Louis had 276 arrivals and departures daily before World War One; 128 at the start of World War Two; and a mere eight today.' He makes the following assessment:

> The greatest factor in this decline is the wealth and industrial strength which the railroads helped to create, permitting, in its turn, near universal car ownership. The typical American small town grew up around the railroad depot, the railroad track itself often forming a convenient line of demarcation between the areas where lived the 'haves' and the 'have-nots' – hence the expression 'the wrong side of the track'. Alas, the centre-of-town station is no longer used – in contrast to the well-used European ones built as an afterthought well outside a typical town.[15]

It was during the period of railway decline that the steam locomotive went out of use. The market for steam locomotives had been a massive one: in the 120 years of railway history in the US, over 170,000 steam locomotives had been built

(78,000 of these had been built by the American Locomotive Company and 59,000 by Baldwins). The railways did not switch to electricity, as would have been expected from a perspective of long-term economic planning. The switch was almost exclusively to diesel, although the economic advantages of diesel over steam were insignificant. The reason for the switch to diesel rather than to electricity had to do with the emerging automobile industry and the importance of the diesel engine in American industry after the Second World War. The leading manufacturer of diesel locomotives for the US and world market was Electromotive Diesels, owned by General Motors, which was, by this time, the biggest company and also the biggest car manufacturer in the world.

The breakthrough in the transport of goods only came much later; until the end of the Second World War, 90 per cent of goods were still transported by rail. As late as 1957, 70 per cent of long-distance goods transport was by rail. It was not until the end of the 1970s that the turning point was reached; after this most goods were transported by road. This development is illustrated in Figure 6.2.[16] Mass motorisation and the publicly financed construction of the American highway network had made this possible.

The radical extent of the decline within a few decades becomes clear when we look at the revenue figures for the period 1920–36. In 1929, at the peak of the economic boom after the First World War, the revenue from goods transport on the railroads was only 10 per cent higher than it had been in 1920; in 1932, at the end of the 1929–32 crisis, revenue was just 60 per cent of the 1920 figure and in 1936 it was still only 75 per cent of that figure. In passenger transport the decline was even more catastrophic: revenue declined continuously after 1920, even during the period of economic boom. In 1932 it had fallen to 30 per cent of the level of 1920 and in 1936 it was still only one third of what it had been 16 years earlier.[17]

Part of this fall can, of course, be attributed to the Depression but, as the figures make clear, it was a feature of the boom years as well. This decline in rail transport becomes even more manifest when we realise that the rail network continued to expand until 1926 and, in the period between then and 1935, very few lines were actually closed

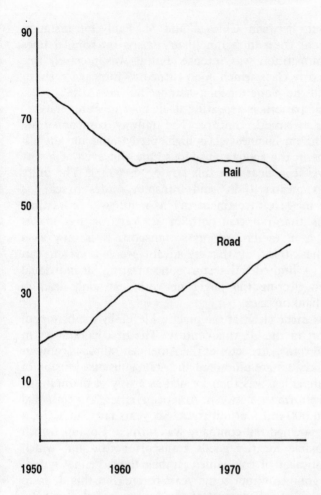

Figure 6.2
**Share of Road and Rail in Goods Transport in
the US 1947–77** (% of ton-miles)

down. Throughout this period there was a constantly increasing surplus capacity. The policy of the railroad companies during this period may actually have contributed to this decline. As a result of the Depression, with its mass unemployment and fall in real incomes, there was a decline in mass individual travel, so the railroads, during the 1930s, concentrated on goods transport and the luxury end of individual travel. Between Chicago and St. Paul, for instance, three different companies ran luxury trains on parallel lines and the competition was intense. But it was precisely this business luxury class which soon turned to the car for short-distance and the plane for long-distance business trips.

A similar pattern is repeating itself now in Europe at the end of the twentieth century. The railway companies are concentrating on business-class high-speed trains and on filling the gaps in the goods transport sector. But even at a very abstract level it is clear that this strategy is wrong. The unity of transport means (train) and transport routes (track), as well as the massive investment that is required in infrastructure, means that rail transport, by its very nature, makes sense only as a method of mass transport. It is only as a means of mass transport that its advantages as a system can be realised. A limited rail sector, concentrating on individual lines and neglecting the larger network, can only lead to losses and bankruptcies.

This was made clear, at the practical level, by the history of rail transport in the US this century. The first bankruptcy in the personal transport sector of the American railroads came in 1970. Amtrak, a state-promoted and state-subsidised fusion of existing companies, was then formed as a way of maintaining rail passenger travel between American cities. Amtrak had access to 26,000 miles of rail track. Six years later, in 1976, a second state-owned rail company was formed, Conrail, which was responsible for the goods transport sector and which merged a number of companies, among them Penn Central, which had gone bankrupt some years before. But this de facto nationalisation of a large part of the American rail sector did not really improve matters: the decline continued. The previous run-down had been too advanced and the scale of public investment in the new system was too small. The American state did not really develop a comprehensive transport strategy with a long-term perspective. The American rail network, at its peak, was one-third of the world network. Today around 200,000 miles of rail track, about 20 per cent of the world system, are in operation in the US, overwhelmingly in the goods transport sector.

American rail history is rich in symbols. The last nail was driven into the last sleeper (crosstie) of the first trans-continental line in 1869, an event comparable to the moon-landing a century later. This sleeper, preserved as a museum piece in San Francisco, was burned in the earthquake that shook that city in 1906, the same year that Ford began production of his cheap car. The motorist who travels on America's most famous highway, the Highway Number One that travels south to the tip of Florida, may well recall the Humphrey Bogart classic, *Key Largo*. Over a stretch of 180 miles, this highway has 42 bridges and crosses 32 islands, the biggest of which is Key Largo. Highway Number One links all the islands together and terminates in Key West, the southernmost point of the US. It was over 80 years ago that the islands were linked in this way to the mainland. But few people realise that it was not the highway that first achieved this. It was a railroad line which, in 1912, brought the 'American way of life' to these islands. The railroad operated for 23 years before it was extensively damaged by a hurricane which blew one train into the sea. The 42 bridges of the Miami to Key West line then formed the backbone of Highway Number One.[18]

World Triumph of the US Car Industry

Revolutionary changes in history, including economic history, cannot be explained monocausally. In what follows, I will point to eight different factors, not an exhaustive list and not all of them of equal importance, which help to account for the triumph of road over rail transport.

1. Behind the competition between road and rail there stood the intensive competition between different sectors of American capital, between the traditionally dominant group in the railways and heavy industry (Vanderbilt and Morgan) and the emerging, more modern sector (around Rockefeller), based mainly in oil (Standard Oil). The latter was to become the most powerful capital group in America and in the world.[19]

Until the 1870s, railroad capital was largely controlled by the Vanderbilt group. J.P. Morgan, until then mainly involved in the banking sector, became involved in the railroads in 1869. By the end of the 1880s, his was the dominant group in the rail sector and the most powerful capital group in North America. In the years that followed, this group also became a major force in the steel and mining industries: steel was used in rail and locomotive construction, while coal and iron were used in steel production, and coal was burned in the steam locomotives.

In the middle of the nineteenth century, the Rockefeller group became an important investor in the oil fields of Saudi Arabia (and later Mexico). Before the end of the century, it enjoyed an oil monopoly in North America, having made secret deals with the railroad companies (Morgan and Vanderbilt) for the cheap transport of petroleum. By 1910, both major capital groups, Rockefeller and Morgan, were similar in size; between them they controlled about $40 billion worth of assets, about a third of the total wealth in the US. Each group owned 'more than four times the revenue of the four European nations [Britain, Germany, France and Italy] and twenty times the revenue of the United States'.[20]

The interests of the Rockefeller group were in oil, petrochemicals, the car industry (Ford) and the banking sector. This group dominated the banking sector after the world economic crisis of 1929–32; the top Rockefeller banks are the Chase Manhattan and (after 1955) the First National City Bank of New York. After the Second World War, Rockefeller also entered atomic energy and the airspace industry. Its dominance in these modern sectors gave the Rockefeller group a competitive advantage over its only major rival, the Morgan group. It was the sectors dominated by Rockefeller that became the decisive sectors in the economies of all the imperialist powers after the Second World War.[21]

2. Economic crises and stagnation in the first quarter of this century hit the Morgan group, centred around rail and heavy industry, particularly hard. In general, the cyclical crises of the capitalist economy tend to hit the big traditional sectors harder. The overall mass of capital invested in these industries means not only high profits in periods of economic upswing but greater vulnerability in periods of crisis. Ford, for instance, was able to halt production for a whole year in 1926, having suffered major losses with its Tin Lizzie model; but, in 1927–8, it introduced its new Model A and was able

to survive the 1929–32 crisis quite well. For the big steel and railway companies, this was not an option. At the same time, the new technologies of the more 'modern' industries controlled by Rockefeller meant that this group was able to benefit from the super-profits which cushioned it against the economic crisis, while the traditional sectors enjoyed only average profits. In both crisis periods, 1907 and 1929–32, the Rockefeller group had an advantage over the Morgan group and eventually overtook the latter.

The Morgan group was hit very hard by bankruptcies and bank collapses, especially in the crisis of 1929–32. It was heavily involved in speculative share dealing. Ferdinand Lundberg gives the following description:

> The practice of the new holding-companies era was for a banking group, usually led by J.P. Morgan and Co., to induce the dominant families of competing enterprises to exchange their holdings for cash or for stocks and bonds in a consolidated enterprise. Securities of the new companies were then peddled like fish to a gullible public properly primed by glowing newspaper and magazine articles. The proceeds went to original owners of the constituent companies and, in the form of fat commissions and fees, to the bankers. The Morgan syndicate that floated the US Steel Corporation in 1901 exacted a fee of $62,500,000 according to the US Bureau of Corporations, whereas the tangible value of the entire property was only $682,000,000; the new securities, however, had a face value of $1,400,000,000.
>
> Most of the securities, as in the case of US Steel, represented at least half 'water', which made it possible for many corporations, US Steel included, to show even conservative earnings on the overcapitalisations; many of the new contrivances simply exploded in the bankruptcy courts during the ensuing three decades. Even where the combinations endured, the securities frequently sank in market value towards the zero mark. Small investors, again prompted by florid newspaper accounts, cleared out like frightened geese, with heavy losses, while the manipulators and original owners retrieved the depreciated holdings at far less than their true potential value.'[22]

The Rockefeller group itself also became involved with the railroad companies during this period, but their main interest here was to reduce rail travel and ruin the rail industry. As the new automotive technology made increasing headway against rail, the Morgan group began to shift its own interests to the car industry, leading to greater unity within US capital with respect to transport policy.

3. The big oil and car companies played a role in the decline of rail which can justifiably be described as conspiratorial. This was, in fact, the conclusion of the US government half a century later. As early as 1949, there was a report of a US Senate sub-committee which concluded that General Motors, the Morgan-owned car company, had been involved in the dismantling of hundreds of electric tram networks in order to have them replaced by General Motors buses. According to this report:

> By 1949, General Motors had been involved in the replacement of more than 100 electric transit systems with General Motors buses in 45 cities, including New York, Philadelphia, Baltimore, St. Louis, Oakland, Salt Lake City, and Los Angeles.[23]

Another 25 years were to pass before another US government study discovered that this dismantling by the big car companies existed on a much larger scale. This report, the Snell Report, published in 1974, gives a detailed account of this conspiracy in what is considered today to be the world's number one car city, Los Angeles:

> Nowhere was the ruin more apparent than in the Greater Los Angeles metropolitan area. Thirty-five years ago [in 1935] it was a beautiful region of lush palm trees, fragrant orange groves, and clean, ocean-enriched air. It was served by the world's largest interurban electric railway system ... with 3,000 quiet, pollution-free, electric trains. ... The Pacific Electric system branched out from Los Angeles for a radius of more than 75 miles reaching north to San Fernando, east to San Bernardino, and south to Santa Ana. ... Contrary to popular belief, the Pacific Electric, not the auto-

mobile, was responsible for the area's geographical development. First constructed in 1911, it established traditions of
suburban living long before the automobile had arrived. In
1938, General Motors and Standard Oil of California organised Pacific City Lines (PCL) as an affiliate of National City
Lines (NCL) to motorize west coast electric railways.

The National City Lines Inc. had been established in 1936
by General Motors, Standard Oil of California and the tyre
company, Firestone, all of them world leaders in their particular sectors. The goal of NCL, according to Snell, was to
'convert electric transit systems in sixteen states to GM bus
operations'. The report continues:

The following year PCL acquired, scrapped, and substituted
bus lines for the three northern Californian electric rail
systems in Fresno, San Jose, and Stockton. In 1940 GM,
Standard Oil, and Firestone 'assumed the active management of Pacific (City Lines)' in order to supervise its California operations more directly. That year PCL began to
acquire and scrap portions of the $100 million Pacific
electric system, including rail lines from Los Angeles to
Glendale, Burbank, Pasadena, and San Bernardino. Subsequently, in December 1944, another NCL affiliate
(American City Lines) was financed by GM and Standard
Oil to motorize downtown Los Angeles. At the time, Pacific
Electric shared downtown Los Angeles with a local electric
street-car company, the Los Angeles Railway. American
City Lines purchased the local system, scrapped its electric
transit cars, tore down its power transmission lines, ripped
up the tracks, and placed GM diesel buses, fuelled by Standard Oil, on Los Angeles' crowded streets. In sum, GM and
its auto-industrial allies severed Los Angeles' regional rail
links and then motorized its downtown heart.

In this report of 1974 we already find statements that
point to the destruction, even more evident today, which the
car has wreaked on the city and the broader environment:

Los Angeles is an ecological wasteland: the palm trees are
dying from petrochemical smog; the orange groves have

been paved over by 300 miles of freeway; the air is a septic tank into which four million cars, half of them built by General Motors, pump 13,000 tons of pollutants daily. With the destruction of the Pacific Electric rail system, Los Angeles may have lost its best hope for rapid rail transit and a smog free metropolitan area.[24]

The state also played a role in the promotion of the motor industry: as a job-creation measure during the Depression, Roosevelt initiated large-scale highway construction. Hitler and Mussolini carried out similar projects.

4. At the beginning of the twentieth century, advances in the technology of oil extraction made this energy source much cheaper. At the time of the outbreak of the Mexican revolution in 1910, oil reserves in Mexico were under US control. The uncertainties created by the revolution, and the threat to US economic interests, encouraged the US oil companies to rapidly extract large amounts of oil in a manner that was both wasteful and damaging to the reserves. As a result, the American market was flooded with cheap oil, precisely at the time when the competition between rail and road had reached a decisive stage. After the Second World War, a similar pattern was repeated when the US oil companies succeeded in acquiring monopoly control over the Saudi Arabian oil fields, the biggest oil reserves in the world. This monopoly lasted for three decades.

5. Both world wars also played an important role in the triumph of road over rail transport, initially in North America. At the time of the First World War, diesel-powered warships increased significantly the demand for oil. Standard Oil and Royal Dutch Shell were both beneficiaries of this development. The oil-related chemical industries were also given a large boost by the demand for explosives and chemical weapons.

During the Second World War, it was the general motorisation of the US army and the delivery of large numbers of motorised units to the allies that created a boom in the oil and motor industries. The decline in sales of civilian vehicles was more than offset by increased sales of military vehicles. The big car companies themselves (Ford, General Motors, Chrysler) had, in the meantime, also become directly involved in the armaments industry, manufacturing tanks and airplane engines. While the car and oil industries in America benefited from the war, the American railroads suffered from the decline in civilian transport conditioned by the war. Since the war fronts were situated in Europe and parts of Asia, the American railways played no strategic role in military actions.

It was in the Second World War that the car and oil industries demonstrated the truth of Marx's famous statement that capital has 'no fatherland'. In 1929, the leading German chemical company, IG Farben, and Standard Oil of America signed a cooperation agreement. According to this agreement, IG Farben was to maintain control of coal hydrogenation in Germany, in return for which it would not intervene in the international oil business. It kept to this agreement, even during the war. This was why the allies were so late in bombing IG Farben's hydrogenation plants: the first bombs to hit the Leuna plant fell on 12 May 1944 and the plants in Auschwitz and Monowitz were not hit until 20 August 1944. These plants were bombed just three weeks before the allied landing in Normandy and the purpose of the bombing raids was to deprive the Luftwaffe of the petrol they would need to launch an attack on the allied landing. Almost 95 per cent of the Luftwaffe's petrol was derived from coal hydrogenation. Up to that point in 1944, the Luftwaffe had not been deprived of its oil resources, which it needed to attack the Soviet Union.

US capital and the Nazi regime also had common interests in the motor industry. On 30 July 1938, the German vice-consul in Detroit bestowed on Henry Ford the Grand Cross of the Order of the Eagle, the highest order that Hitler could grant to a foreign national. During the war, the Ford plants in Berlin and Cologne, as well as the Adam Opel plant in Rüsselsheim, owned by General Motors, continued to produce armaments for the German war effort – 'without restrictions', as Henry Ford told his biographer, Robert Lacey. Snell also mentions this in his report:

From 1939 through 1945, the GM-owned Rüsselsheim facility alone assembled 50 per cent of all the propulsion systems produced for the Ju-88 medium range bomber.

According to the authoritative work of Wagner and Nowarra, the Ju-88 by 1940 'had become the Luftwaffe's most important bomber' and remained so for the rest of the war. The Rüsselsheim facility also assembled 10 per cent of the jet engines for the ME-262, the world's first operational jet fighter. ... Not until after World War II were the allies able to develop pure jet aircraft. By producing ME-262 jet engines for the Luftwaffe, therefore, GM's Rüsselsheim plant made a significant contribution to the Axis' technological superiority in the air.[25]

Because of its American ownership, the Ford works in Cologne were regarded by the local population as a safe area during bombing raids. When the alarms went off, thousands would rush to the factory, which they referred to as the 'bunker'. The Ford works in Cologne were not bombed during the war.

6. The extended time period between mass motorisation and the creation of a strong car industry in the US on the one hand, and the beginning of a parallel process in Europe, on the other hand, gave an added boost to the international triumph of the new automotive technology. It was during this period that the US developed from being a powerful imperialist state to being the dominant world power. At the end of the 1940s, when Europe and Japan were weakened by war damages and debt, the US was the only power in a position to dominate the world market. US companies and capital groups were the biggest in the world and they were the first to become active on a global scale. This US hegemony in the world market was further supported by the Marshall Plan, the leading role of the dollar and US capital exports.

US capital exports played a major role in the automobile and oil sectors. As early as 1911, Ford built his first car plant in Britain. Ford's first German plant was built in Cologne in 1925 and, in 1928, it began to assemble its Model A car at its plant in Plötzensee, near Berlin. The following year, in 1929, the Opel family in Germany sold 80 per cent of its shares to General Motors for a modest $25,967,000. The competition between Rockefeller and Morgan now continued on the European continent. In the

1930s, Ford and General Motors (Opel) controlled the greater part of the German car industry.

In spite of the massive changes that have taken place in the world since then – the decline in America's leading role, the creation of the European Community and the rise of Japan – US companies still controlled over a quarter of the European car market in the 1980s, making them the biggest national group on the continent of Europe.

The statistics for American direct foreign investment in 1972 (totalling $94 billion) show that investments in the oil industry accounted for as much as 28 per cent of the total. More than 50 per cent of all US direct foreign investment was concentrated in the oil and motor industries. Under conditions of US world hegemony, this massive capital outlay was a major force determining the direction of transport policy in Europe, especially at a time when the new transport technology and road transport was in its early stages of development on the European continent. No similar powerful international financial group supported an alternative rail policy. The railways were, by this time, mostly state owned.

7. This aspect of ownership/control brings us to a factor which is more important than all of the others mentioned so far. Rail transport, by its very nature, is most appropriately organised as a centralised (public) technology. In road transport there is a possible separation, based on modern technology, between the transport infrastructure (the motorway or road) and the means of transport (the car, truck, etc.). This transport technology can therefore be easily organised according to the principle: private appropriation of profit, socialisation of costs and losses. Private profits are appropriated by the vehicle manufacturers, the insurance companies and the motorway construction firms; costs are socialised by means of public financing of motorway construction, policing, hospitalisation of the injured and repairs to the environment.

8. Finally, among the factors that have helped to promote the car, one has to mention psychological factors and patriarchy. The car society has shown itself to be an ideal appendage to both the bourgeois and the bureaucratic post-capitalist social formations. In both of these social formations, people are

denied the most basic freedoms, for instance, the freedom to determine the products of human labour – what is produced, how, and for what purpose. What they have are substitute freedoms, small freedoms which allow them to escape from the unfreedoms of day-to-day life. The car is one such substitute. The pattern of patriarchal domination is also re-created in the car society: the private car reinforces patriarchy in a number of ways, for instance, in the unequal access of men and women to private transport on a daily basis. This is also a factor which will be dealt with in greater detail in Part III.

7

Germany: The Decline of the Railways and the Rise of the Car Industry

> The Germans, having constructed a stable democracy, have now moved their death wish and other peculiar spiritual needs to the roads.
>
> *The Times*, 1964

The US undoubtedly led the way in the worldwide promotion of road transport. The US was not the only player, however, and increasingly from the 1960s other countries developed their own dynamic towards mass motorisation. Germany is one such example, the country that twice this century used war as a means to win control of the European economy and which today is the strongest economy in Europe and possesses the second strongest export industry in the world. An important part of the foundation of Germany's economic strength is its powerful motor industry.

German Railways 1900–1933:
State Plundering and Reparations

The development of the German railways in the first decades of this century parallels that of the US railways in many respects: declining investment in a largely state-owned network, profits siphoned off to promote other projects. The profitability of rail transport in this period demonstrated the potential of this technology. In Prussia, for example, the state administration of the railways, for a

Table 7.1 Growth of German Railways 1900–33

	1900	1913	1925	1929	1933
Track length in km	51678	63378	57684	58183	58185
Number of locomotives	19462	30444	29205	26310	22865
Person kilometres (mn)	20187	41393	50089	48132	30726
Ton kilometres (mn)	36992	67750	60199	77071	48223

long time, was able to finance other government departments with its surplus. In 1913, the last year before the
war, the railways in Prussia, Baden, Bavaria, Saxony and
Württemberg brought in a profit of 1,025 billion marks. In
other words, profits from the railways amounted to 30 per
cent of the total expenditure of the Empire.[26]

From the beginning of the century, however, and up to
the Second World War, the expansion of the German rail
network was very modest. There was a significant increase in
the transport of persons and goods but the stock of locomotives increased at a much lower rate, as demonstrated in
Table 7.1.[27]

Between 1900 and 1913, the transport of persons more
than doubled and goods transport increased by 83 per cent, but
the locomotive stock increased by only 56 per cent. The rail
network in this period grew by 11,700 km, around 23 per cent,
an average yearly growth of 900 km. In the period 1870–80,
the annual average growth had been 1,500 km. During the
initial period after the First World War, however, between 1920
and 1933, the rail network hardly grew at all. And this was in
spite of the fact that, in this period, the railways were organ-

ised as a single company and were in a position to develop an extensive national network. Before the Depression of 1929 the stock of locomotives actually decreased by about 20 per cent. During the Depression years there was a further decline of 13 per cent, with the result that, in 1933, the locomotive stock had declined to the level of 1905, 30 per cent below what it had been in 1921, the year in which the national rail network, the Reichsbahn, was founded. The transport of goods increased rapidly in the 1920s, by 30 per cent between 1925 and 1929, and this happened on a stagnating network that had lost about 20 per cent of its locomotive stock, evidence of the greater efficiency of the newer locomotives.

Even at the time of its founding, in 1921, the Reichsbahn was burdened by heavy debts. For the first time in its history, the railway made heavy losses in 1918–19, largely as a result of the war and amounting to 4.1 billion marks. This had to be paid from its own assets.[28] The Dawes Plan for Germany, in 1924, established a new framework for reparations payments. The Reichsbahn was reorganised and its finances placed under allied control. The Reichsbahn was made responsible for war reparation payments amounting to 11 billion gold marks, which would have to be paid either from its profits or through the sale of assets. The annual rate of payment was set at 600 million marks. In addition to this, there was to be an annual transport tax of over 200 million marks, payable to the Reich government or the allies, and an annual contribution to a pension fund of 160 million marks. In the period between 1925 and 1930, this amounted to a total payment of 5.5 billion marks. In other words, in each of those years in which the economic recovery would have allowed the railway to consolidate and expand, it was forced to pay out 1 billion marks. In spite of this massive drain on its resources, the railway continued to be profitable, except in 1930 and 1931.

The success of the railways during the years of economic recovery in the 1920s, in spite of the external demands on its resources, demonstrates the potential for development that this transport technology had to offer. The development of transport in Germany in this period was not the product of 'free competition' between different transport systems. The private exploitation of the rail network was followed, after

nationalisation, by the external imposition of heavy reparation and other payments from which, in the final analysis, it
was the car and oil industries that benefited.

Rail Transport and the Nazi State

The Reichsbahn, like other economic sectors, profited from the
economic recovery of 1934–7 and a number of advances, such
as the fast Interurban network and the electrification of over
2,000 km of rail line, already set in motion during the Weimar
Republic, were carried to fruition during the 1930s and claimed
as Nazi triumphs. In 1936–7, the Reichsbahn Company was
dissolved and replaced by the new Deutsche Reichsbahn; the
government had already refused to continue making reparation
payments.

These publicly proclaimed successes, however, were deceptive: the Nazi state had, right from the beginning, opted for the
new automotive technology and had directed the biggest investments to this sector. The advances made by the Deutsche
Reichsbahn in this period were limited to a few areas; there
was no move to develop an extensive national network. The
relationship between the Nazi state and the publicly owned rail
network was meant to serve military and not societal needs.
The railway was militarised in preparation for the coming war.
This neglect of the civilian function and the reorientation
towards war are evident from the statistics for this period (see
Table 7.2).[29]

Although the transport of passengers and goods increased by
more than two-thirds between 1933 and 1937, the locomotive
stock grew by only 3 per cent. This changed dramatically just
before the war and during the war years, but this was for
obvious military purposes. In 1936, for instance, the Reichsbahn had 660,000 employees; this grew to 1.6 million by 1943.
The Reich transport minister, Dorpmüller, claimed in that
year: 'Every eighteenth person in the Reich either works for the
railway or is part of a railway worker's family.'[30] Most of the
male workers were active in the occupied territories, while
women were increasingly employed in the inner-German network. At the peak of the war, more than 200,000 women were
employed by the Deutsche Reichsbahn.

Table 7.2 Growth of German Reichsbahn 1929–43

	1929	1933	1937	1943
Track (km)	58183	58185	59126	152000
Locomotives	26310	22865	23594	35000
Person-km (mn)	48132	30726	51064	–
Ton-km (mn)	77071	48223	80564	–

German Railways and the Holocaust

The attempt, in 1940 and 1941, to liquidate the Jews in Europe by means of the traditional methods of mass murder proved both time-consuming and likely to lead to public outrage. The Nazi leadership, therefore, in 1942, decided that the 'final solution to the Jewish question' would have to resort to more efficient industrial means. In the next few years, millions of Jews, moved to specially constructed extermination camps, were murdered by means of poison gas or some other method. This placed heavy demands not only on the German chemical industry, for instance, the delivery of adequate supplies of Zyklon B by the IG Farben subsidiary, Degesch, but also on the Reichsbahn. Although its transport capacity was not sufficient to satisfy all military requirements, it succeeded in making sufficient capacity available to the SS to transport these millions of Jews to their death.

The Reichsbahn management and the ministry of transport organised the special transports so that the trains could regularly and punctually carry their loads to Belzek, Treblinka, Auschwitz and Majdanek. Recent and very detailed research[31] has painted a disturbing picture of the German thoroughness with which thousands on the railway (office workers, drivers, guards, timetable planners, etc.) became part of the extermination machinery. It is a picture in which the Reichsbahn haggled with the SS over the rates of payment (passenger or goods rates), in which time-tables were worked out and return trips were put to good economic use by transporting the clothing of the murdered Jews back to Germany for distribution to bombed-out families.

No special departments were needed for these transports; they were simply integrated into the normal business and timetabling of the Reichsbahn. The SS, as a rule, was unable to provide adequate guards for these transports, so ordinary police were used. The Reichsbahn charged four pfennig per kilometre for adults, two pfennig for children; babies were carried free. These corresponded to regular third-class fares. The wagons used, however, were cattle wagons. The bills for transport were passed initially to sur-viving Jewish organisations, later to the head of security or to the Gestapo.

Transport was timetabled to fit optimally with other war goals. Götz Aly and Susanne Heim report:

Between 25 January and 4 February 1943, the same train carried 1,000 people from Zamosc in Poland to Berlin for forced labour. In Berlin the train picked up 1,000 Jews and their families and transported them to Auschwitz. The train then returned empty to Zamosc where 1,000 Poles considered useless and dangerous were loaded and transported back to Auschwitz.[32]

'I did not know they wanted to exterminate the Jews. It was not easy to take in the whole complex situation. ... I mean, for me, as an ordinary citizen.'[33] The 'ordinary citi-zen' who said this to a German court was Albert Ganzen-müller, state secretary in the Reich transport ministry and, as such, responsible for the coordination of the Reichsbahn and the SS in the 'final solution'. The West German court that tried Ganzenmüller in 1973 agreed with this argument and declared him innocent. Other Reichsbahn officials that had been active in the organisation of the holocaust were to occupy, after the end of the war, leading positions in the Federal German Railway, the Bundesbahn.

Fascism and the German Car Industry:
Foundation for the Post-War Mass Motorisation

The German car industry, largely American-owned, was very under-developed before the Nazis came to power. Around 40,000 vehicles were produced in 1925, this number rising to over 100,000 in 1928. But with less than half a million registered vehicles altogether, one cannot speak of mass motorisation. The depression brought the German car industry to the edge of ruin: in 1928 the industry employed 90,000 workers, in 1933 this had sunk to 40,000. Productivity was also much lower in Germany than in the US. The price of a car in Germany was therefore much higher, three to five times higher than the annual average wage of a worker, so mass sale of cars was out of the question. Production was concentrated on trucks, buses and motor cycles rather than cars. In the period 1929 to 1935, cars and vans made up only one-third of vehicles on the road. The proportion of cars and vans in that part of the industry controlled by German capital was even lower. Opel, owned by General Motors, accounted for 30 per cent of the German vehicle market, but its share of the smaller vehicles appropriate for private transport (those between 1000 and 1500 cc) was 80 per cent.[34] Even in the 1930s, the German car industry had little interest in mass motorisation. There was no market for cars among the working class and the car plants were organised on the old workshop principle. Assembly-line production was an exception and the strong market position of General Motors acted as a disincentive to the German firms (Daimler-Benz, Adler, Audi, Horch and BMW). The market for industrial transport vehicles as well as the anticipated contracts from the fascist state continued to concentrate the interests of the German vehicle industry on the non-private sector.

Within days of coming to power, at a speech to the International Automobile and Motor Cycle Exhibition in Berlin, Hitler presented an extensive programme for Volksmotorisierung (people's motorisation). There was to be a massive reduction in transport tax; new car purchases were to be tax free. The two most important elements of the Nazi state's planned Volksmotorisierung were autobahn construction and the Volkswagen 'the people's car'.

As early as 23 June 1933, the necessary legislation was passed establishing the Reichsautobahn Company (*Reichsautobahngesellschaft*). The new autobahn company stole not just the form of its name from the railway company, the Reichsbahn, but also its money: the new Reichsautobahn was a subsidiary of the Reichsbahn. The railway had to provide the starting capital for its competitor. In addition to direct support in the form of 60 million marks, the Reichsbahn also had to provide the administrative apparatus and had to deliver construction materials at a cheaper rate.

Although a previous 'autobahn' had been opened as early as 1932 between Cologne and Bonn, it was not until the end of 1936 that the new 1,000-km autobahn was opened to traffic. Another 1,000 km was added in the following year, the highest ever yearly rate of construction. In railway construction in the nineteenth century, this had been the annual rate of construction for every year between 1860 and 1870 – with a similar amount of labour expenditure per kilometre, with a much lower level of construction technology and without the fascist labour regulations.

It was the Austrian engineer, Ferdinand Porsche, who was given the task of designing the new small car, the Volkswagen, announced by Hitler at the automobile exhibition in 1934. The initial capital to build the autobahn was robbed from the railway and now the money for the new car was robbed from the people. In 1938, with a great fanfare of propaganda, a new saving scheme was announced, the 'Power through Pleasure Saving Scheme (*Kraft-durch-Freude-Sparsystem*), whereby people could put down money regularly for the later purchase of a Volkswagen. As many as 337,000 people took part in this scheme, which lasted until 1945. Each 'KdF car owner' paid a minimum sum of five marks per week, had to subscribe to a monthly magazine, and received driving instruction as well as ideological indoctrination from the 'National Socialist Vehicle Corps' (*Nationalsozialistischer Kraftfahrzeugkorps* – NSKK). A participant who had saved 75 per cent of the purchase price (990 marks) was given an order number from the regional office. The participant also had no right to withdraw from the scheme.[35] Before the scheme came to an end in 1945, 280 million marks had been contributed in this way to the Volkswagen venture. Not a single 'KdF car owner' ever received a Volkswagen. Before 1945, only 630 civilian versions of the 'Beetle' were produced; they all went to leading Nazi officials.

The language of *Volksmotorisierung* is well adapted to fascist ideology. Just like the 'people's radio' (*Volksempfänger*), the 'people's car' (*Volkswagen*) is aimed at the individual or the nuclear family. To the mass of ordinary people, economically exploited and denied any political participation, it promises a surrogate satisfaction. According to Hitler, driving satisfies 'people's natural desire for freedom'; the car 'is not only useful to those social layers whose life possibilities are restricted, but it is for them, on Sundays and holidays, a source of pleasure and happiness'. He himself liked 'in particular to drive around the country in a car because no other means of transport makes it possible for the traveller to have such a close relationship with the people and the countryside as does the car'.[36]

Foreign observers at the time agreed with these sentiments. *L'Auto*, in Paris, on the occasion of the presentation of the first Volkswagen prototype, wrote: 'The Volkswagen encourages all Germans to become car drivers. This is the car that we need. What we also need is a car-friendly government.' In London, *The Times* was equally enthusiastic: 'The people's car of Herr Porsche beats everything. England will have to learn from the Germans.' The *New York Times* was aware of the links between Detroit and Wolfsburg: 'They've copied our "car for everyone", but have refined it. We should study the result.'[37]

But, just as in the case of the Reichsautobahn, the Volkswagen, for the Nazi authorities, was not primarily a civilian but a military project. What was being created were the preconditions for a militarisation of society, for a new imperialist war of aggression. Modern war needs a high level of motorisation, rapid transit routes, etc. France and Britain, in the 1930s, had a higher level of motorisation than Germany. The language of 'people's motorisation' was only a propagandistic front for war preparations. The specifications which the Nazi authorities gave to Ferdinand Porsche were clearly determined by military interests. The car had to be 'operable everywhere';

it was to have 'the highest possible road clearance' and 'cross-country mobility'; wear and tear was to be minimised by keeping the maximum rpm at a fairly low level; the costs were to be kept down by assembly-line production and low energy use. The Automobile Association initially suggested a three-wheel vehicle, a cross between a car and a motor cycle, because this would be cheaper and more accessible for workers on low incomes. This suggestion was rejected by the authorities. Their specification was that the Volkswagen was to have 'room for three adults and a child' which, translated, means 'three men and a machine gun'.[38]

The result was the jeep or 'bucket car' (*Kubelwagen*) of the German *Wehrmacht*, mass produced at the Volkswagen plant in Fallersleben (Wolfsburg). The design was based entirely on Porsche's design for a 'civilian' car. Before the end of the war, this plant produced 52,000 *Kubelwagen*, over 14,000 amphibious jeeps, 500 special VW vehicles for use by Rommel in Africa and a small number of VW cross-country vehicles. The plant constructed a chassis on which a variety of civilian or military vehicles could be mounted.

The Volkswagen plant was built to serve the military needs of the Nazi state. The other two main German car manufacturers, Daimler Benz and BMW (Bavarian Motor Works), both controlled by the Deutsche Bank, soon integrated their industrial production into the Nazi military project. According to an American report of 1946–7, both car manufacturers, 'long before the outbreak of war, had shifted from civilian car production to the production of airplane engines', tanks and armoured trucks. During the war, these two car companies 'produced two thirds of all German airplane engines'.[39] Military production, between 1935 and 1945, allowed Daimler Benz to increase its turnover six times, while BMW, in the same period, was able to achieve a tenfold increase.

After the war, the German car manufacturers returned to civilian production. Volkswagen began its post-war success story with the production of a civilian version of the Kubelwagen, the Beetle. General Motors (Opel) and Ford, which had, during the war, produced for the Nazi war machinery, also renewed civilian production. The Deutsch-Amerikanische Petroleum Gesellschaft (DAPAG) became Esso and IG Farben was broken up into BASF, Bayer and

Hoechst. IG Farben, presumed dead after 45 years in official liquidation, reappeared in 1990, after unification, to claim massive tracts of land in the ex-GDR as its property.

West Germany Since the Second World War

The new East German state, the German Democratic Republic (GDR), saw itself, in its transport policies as well as in its general politics, as an alternative to what had gone before and what continued to exist in West Germany. The West German state, however, the Federal Republic of Germany (BRD), saw itself juridically as the successor state of the German Reich. In its transport policy its practice was a continuation of pre-1945 developments. Volkswagen is just one example of this continuity.

Post-war West Germany inherited a road network of some 350,000 km, in generally good condition. War damages were repaired by 1949. The Deutsche Bundesbahn, the West German successor to the Reichsbahn, inherited a rail network of around 30,500 km, with a high level of war damages. The division of Germany also represented a qualitative weakening of the rail network. This was partly a result of the geography of the German Reich and partly a result of the previously described military strategy which ensured that most major lines ran east–west. The north–south lines were already very weak before the division of the country. The foundation of separate states in east and west in 1949 meant that the rail networks in both east and west were severely truncated. Before the war, there had been 18 east–west lines and only four north–south lines. Only a massive investment in expanding the network in a north–south direction would have overcome this handicap. But the number of north–south lines remained the same until 1990.[40] For road traffic, the division of Germany on a north-south axis did not present any special problem. The larger network of roads and motorways was better able to adapt to the new situation than the more rigid and less extensive rail network. The autobahn network was still relatively under-developed. The greater part of autobahn construction did not take place until the 1960s and 1970s, and then they were adapted to the geographical features of the West German state.

The transport policy of all post-war West German governments, whether dominated by the Conservatives (CDU,
CSU) or Social Democrats (SPD), was based on the following
priorities:

• the road network was to be expanded and improved.

• the rail network was not to be restructured in keeping with
  the new geographical reality – after 1960 it was gradually
  dismantled.

• the canal and river system was to be massively expanded to
  absorb the goods previously shipped by rail.

The development of this transport policy between 1950
and 1980 is demonstrated in Table 7.3.[41] As the table makes
clear, it was not until the 1960s that the major shift from
rail to road began. Road construction in the 1950s was
relatively modest but in each decade between 1960 and 1980
the road network was expanded by around 50,000 km. The
autobahn network grew by 1,500 km in the 1960s and by
more than 3,000 km in the 1970s (under the SPD). During
the same period, the rail network declined by around 4,400
km, 12.5 per cent.

These figures, however, only reflect the quantitative
dimension. The factors that were decisive in the victory of road
over rail were qualitative. The road network constructed in the
1960s and 1970s was qualitatively far ahead of what the Nazi
state had constructed. The wider roads and the better road
surfaces meant higher speeds and much shorter transport time
for both individual travel and goods transport. No such qualitative improvement took place on the railways: the trains still
rolled on the tracks from the previous century.[42] The average
speed on the German railways actually sank below the level of
the 1920s and 1930s. Many smaller regional and commuter
lines were closed: in 1971 there was a work-day average of
18,000 short-distance and local trains running, but in 1982
this had been reduced to 14,504, a reduction of around 20 per
cent in only ten years.[43]

This unequal competition between road and rail led to a complete transformation of transport services. Public transport,
predominantly rail, not only lost its dominant position but

Table 7.3 Growth of Transport in West German 1950–80 (km)

	1950	1960	1970	1980	1990
Total road network	346555	368651	432410	479492	498000
Autobahn	2128	2551	4110	7292	8822
Total rail network	36608	36019	33100	31600	29800
Passenger rail network	30000	28300	25000	23500	20800
Canals and Waterways	2800	–	4393	4322	4350

became rather marginal. This development is illustrated in Figure 7.1 overleaf.[44] Individual private transport (mainly by car) increased by 1,700 per cent between 1950 and 1980; travel by public transport increased in the same period by only 6 per cent. As a proportion of all transport, public transport accounted for 67 per cent in 1950, but only 21 per cent in 1980. Rail travel declined sharply from a share of 38 per cent in 1950 to 6.5 per cent in 1980. Air travel increased dramatically in this period. It provided around 2 per cent of all transport services in 1980, almost one-third of that offered by rail.

The railway's share of goods transport sank from 62 per cent in 1950 to 31 per cent in 1980, while road transport increased its share from 11 to 38 per cent. It is an interesting fact that road transport of goods increased dramatically in the 1970s (from 23 to 38 per cent) in spite of the oil crisis. The railway's share of goods transport in that same decade decreased from 40 to 31 per cent, in spite of the public campaign that encouraged companies to shift their goods by rail.

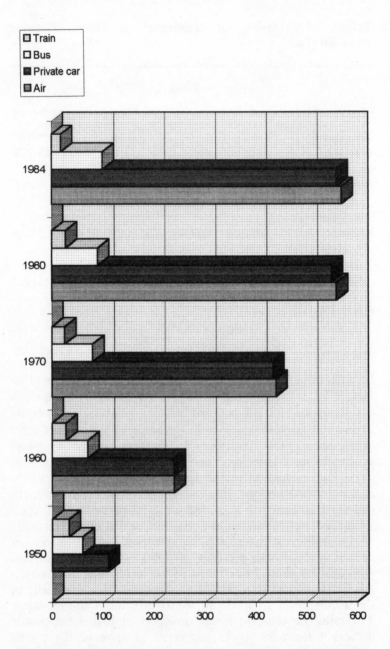

Figure 7.1 Passenger Transport in West Germany 1950–84
(in million person-km)

Table 7.4   Cars and Goods Vehicles in West Germany 1950–90 (mn)

	1938*	1950	1955	1960	1970	1980	1990
Cars	0.73	0.54	1.75	4.5	13.90	23.20	30.70
Goods vehicles	0.30	0.40	0.61	0.70	1.00	1.30	1.40

* estimated for territory of post-war West Germany

Mass Motorisation in West Germany

The number of vehicles, especially cars, in the early post-war period in West Germany was quite low; mass motorisation had hardly started at the beginning of the 1960s. The growth in car (and goods vehicle) ownership is demonstrated in Table 7.4.[45] There were actually fewer cars in West Germany in 1950 than there had been in 1938 (in the same area). In 1960, with 4.5 million registered cars, its is clear that car ownership was still the privilege of a small minority. The trend really began in the early 1960s; in the first half of the decade, the number of cars almost doubled.

The view that mass motorisation began in the 1960s is confirmed when we look at the social status of car owners in that period. As Table 7.5 overleaf demonstrates, until the end of the 1950s it was mainly entrepreneurs and the self-employed who registered new cars.[46] As late as 1960, white-collar and manual workers accounted for only 42.6 per cent of new car registrations. Although wage earners made up more than 80 per cent of the population, they still accounted for less than half of car buyers. Table 7.5 illustrates the gradual shift in the social composition of car owners, a shift downwards through the social hierarchy. At the beginning of the 1950s, car ownership was an almost exclusive privilege of the elite, the entrepreneurs and self-employed. In the latter half of the 1950s and by 1960, higher officials and top-

Table 7.5 Car Registration by Social Layer (per cent)

	1950	1955	1960	1965	1970	1973
Entrepreneurs & self-employed	93.5	71.9	47.3	35.9	28.1	27.1
Top civil sevants	1.4	4.8	7.0	8.0	8.9	8.8
White-collar	4.2	14.2	21.8	25.5	30.5	31.9
Blue-colour	0.1	7.1	20.8	27.2	27.3	25.8
Unemployed	0.8	2.0	3.1	3.4	5.2	6.4

salaried white-collared staff now made up almost a third of car owners. After 1970, the majority of car owners were workers (blue and white collar).

We could summarise the developments in German transport since the end of the Second World War as follows:

• Between 1945 and 1980, the railways and public transport declined from a dominant to a marginal position in the delivery of transport services for persons and goods. In the same period, road transport rose to become absolutely dominant.

• The process of mass motorisation took place over a relatively short period of time. Between 1960 and 1975, the number of cars and vans in Germany increased by more than 13 million. By 1975, with a total of 18 million cars and vans, every fourth German was a vehicle owner.

• The most important cause of this development was a transport policy that promoted mass motorisation by means of massive investment in road construction, dismantled the rail network and generally neglected the public rail system.

- The purchase of 50 million cars and the construction of 130,000 km of new roads and autobahns between 1950 and 1983 presents us with another example of the privatisation of profit and the socialisation of costs. The workers during this period, in addition to paying for their cars, also paid an increasing share of the general tax burden (6 per cent in 1950, 23.1 per cent in 1974).[47] In the case of the earlier, privately owned railways, it was the private owner who was responsible for providing both means (train) and way (track) for travel. The revenue from the business, in principle, had to pay for both. With the privately purchased car, however, travelling on publicly financed roads and autobahns, it is the individual citizen that pays for both, as car purchaser and as tax payer. What car owners pay, however, through their taxes, is only part of the cost. A big part of road building and maintenance, not to speak of ecological costs, are covered by general taxes paid by many millions of people who do not own cars.

  From the mid-1970s, the expenditure of an average wage-earning household now included the payments for their car. This extra expenditure did not signify a better quality of life or a higher standard of living. On the contrary, by now the car had become a *necessity*: the means of transport that previously had been provided by the state or private companies, and which was essential for the satisfaction of everyday travel needs, was no longer adequate. The individual citizen was *forced* to purchase a car.

- Mass motorisation was a powerful programme for stimulation of the economy. It led to a complete restructuring of the whole economy, at the centre of which is now the car industry and its related sectors. This new late-capitalist development model has enormous destructive potential, which I will return to in Chapter 10.

8

East Germany:
The Non-Capitalist Road –
What was Different?

The highway blocked
is this my end
to follow a Mercedes Benz?

The Kinks

We use cars more sensibly than the Americans. We will continue to build more taxi garages where people can rent a car. Who needs a car of their own?

Nikita Khrushchev

Khrushchev's prediction in the 1950s was not fulfilled, either in the Soviet Union or East Germany. In its development tendencies, transport in the German Democratic Republic (GDR) was not all that different from what we have seen in West Germany. In general, GDR development followed the West German model but lagged behind. The GDR development was also characteristic for most of the other countries in the Eastern bloc in this period, especially Czechoslovakia, Poland, Hungary and Yugoslavia.

From the 1960s, the GDR was on the road to becoming a car-owning society in which both public and non-motorised transport (bicycles, walking) was in decline. The time-lag with West Germany was around two decades. At the time of the collapse of the GDR state in 1989–90, car density and the overall share of private transport was roughly what it had been in the US in 1950, in West Germany in 1970 or in Britain in 1975. In other words, it had reached the stage where it could be described as a highly motorised consumer society.

It was not until after 1960 that there was significant growth in car ownership: the number of cars rose fourfold between 1960 and 1970, from 300,000 to 1.2 million. The number doubled again in the following decade until, at the time of unification in 1990, it had reached 4 million (in a population of roughly 17 million). The GDR was, at this point, a car society, with a degree of car ownership comparable to Japan in 1985.

This east–west comparison, in the case of transport development in the two Germanys, is not a specifically German phenomenon. The path followed by the GDR is characteristic for all countries that are part of the industrialisation process, regardless of their social system. As cities expand, and as more people become involved in industrial production or the service sector, public sector transport and non-motorised forms of transport gradually give way to the private vehicle. Measured in person-kilometres public transport was dominant in Britain until the end of the 1950s, and in Italy until 1961. In 1970, Britain had 200 cars per 1,000 inhabitants; in 1980, it was more than 300. The GDR crossed the Rubicon to private sector dominance in 1975. This is illustrated in Figure 8.1 overleaf. In this figure, the x axis represents the number of cars per thousand inhabitants, while the y axis represents the ratio between public and private transport. The dotted line represents, as it were, the Rubicon: here public and private transport are equal in terms of number of person-kilometres travelled. The GDR was just above the dotted line in 1975.

The reasons for the triumph of private motor vehicle transport in the developed capitalist countries has been dealt with in Part I. But why was a similar path followed in the non-capitalist countries, the countries of what was known as 'really existing socialism'? This requires a more detailed examination than can be undertaken here, but some general observations can be made. What we are dealing with here is something very fundamental to these societies; transport was not an exception, but was part of a general phenomenon. The countries of Eastern Europe repeated just about all the mistakes of the industrialisation process in the West,

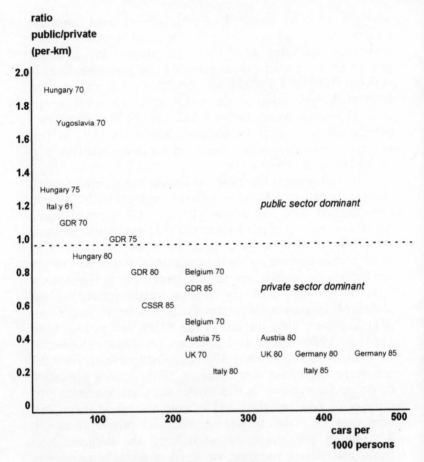

Figure 8.1 **Public and Private Transport in Europe between 1970 and 1985**

sometimes in an even more extreme form. These non-capitalist societies, all of them behind the West in their levels of industrialisation, copied, by and large, the production technology of capitalism. They did not pursue an independent path in increasing their productive forces; they did not have a qualitatively different concept of production. In the early stage, having abolished the private capitalist system, this was a result of the importance of resolving very basic needs: housing, nutrition, reconstruction, energy production and creation of an adequate infrastructure. At a later stage, when these basic needs had been fulfilled and repression had somewhat lessened under de-Stalinisation, the ruling bureaucracy saw the Western consumer model as an important means of stabilising its power.

The ruling elite in the GDR were also aware that, in the absence of elementary democratic rights, the danger of collective revolt could be diminished by providing greater scope for freedoms and pleasures in the individual sphere. In this respect, the car and the possibilities for individual leisure played a similar role in both East and West. The private car is an ideal substitute satisfaction. In the sphere of transport it offers individual compensation for what people have lost collectively in the sphere of production, namely, control. Freedom of movement through the environmental landscape compensates for immobility and unfreedom in the political landscape.

This interpretation of GDR transport policy is supported by a comparison of goods and personal transport. In goods transport in the GDR, the railways remained dominant. The proportion of goods transported by road increased until the mid-1970s, at which time there was a decisive shift away from road transport, in both word and deed. Table 8.1, over-leaf, illustrates this development.[48]

The decision of the GDR policy makers to reduce road traffic and shift goods transport to the railways as much as possible was influenced by the oil crisis of 1973 as well as by the increase in Soviet oil prices. It was both economically and ecologically a good decision. But they pursued precisely the opposite path in the sphere of personal transport, a decision which was to prove economically and ecologically destructive for the whole of that society.

The development of the private transport sector in the east was accelerated after unification. By 1994, the proportions of public and private transport were more or less the same in both parts of united Germany, which meant, of course, that rail transport of goods in the east had been cut back drastically. In the goods sector, rail transport services were at a similar level in both Germanys in 1987, around 70 million ton-kilometres (ton-km) in each country. In 1994, the level of rail transport of goods was below 70 ton-km for the whole of united German railways. Rail transport of goods was reduced by half within seven years.

Table 8.1 Goods Transport in East Germany (GDR) 1950–88
Amount (mn ton-km) and share (per cent)

Means of transport	1950	1960	1970	1980	1987
Rail	15064	32860	41513	56395	76738
Share	81	82	67	71	77
Road	1945	5002	18269	21021	15554
Share	10	12	29	26	20
Inland waterways	1579	2252	2358	2152	2361
Share	8	6	4	3	3
Total transport* (=100 per cent)	18588	40114	62140	79568	76738

* not including air transport or coastal shipping

The growth of transport services in the GDR and the modal split between road and rail corresponds, in essentials, to the model of the Western car society. With individual motorisation, the amount of travel increased dramatically, doubling in the GDR between 1960 and 1985. The main increase, of course, was in private travel by car, which increased almost two and a half times between 1970 and 1990. Cycling and walking declined.[49]

The specific form of this increase is closely linked to the increase in what will be described in the next chapter as 'artificial travel'. Urban spread increased the distances to work, school and shops, which could only be reached now by some form of motorised transport. The quality of the environment in the cities deteriorated to such an extent that people chose to travel even over short distances that they would previously have walked. Public parks and gardens and other recreational areas were being destroyed, a result of the specific model of industrialisation. This, in turn, meant that people had to travel

greater distances for recreation; the dacha in the country
became more necessary as life in the city became less bearable.
This expansion in individual travel took place on the basis of
an antiquated and inadequate transport infrastructure. The
GDR transport policy of increased rail transport for goods and
an expanding private car sector for personal transport required
very high levels of investment in both sectors. But GDR society
lacked the social resources to finance such investment.

At the end of the 1980s, a study carried out by the
Transport Institute in Dresden stated that:

> Almost 70 per cent of all roads are in condition III and
> IV (extreme wear and tear, road bases destroyed, roads in
> need of renewal or complete replacement). ... Road repair
> would require annual resources of 4 billion marks; the
> existing repair fund (1987) is 2.5 billion marks.[50]

Local passenger services presented a similar picture in this
period. From the end of the 1970s, there was continuous
deterioration in the quality of service: old coaches, inadequate
personnel, trains seldom on time. Dissatisfaction increased the
turn to private transport. At the end of the 1980s, local passenger services had only 75 to 80 per cent of the personnel needed
to maintain an adequate service.

The GDR railway, the *Deutsche Reichsbahn*, was in a
particularly bad state. A study in 1989 concluded that state
investment in rail was 'no longer adequate for the maintenance and expansion of the basic infrastructure', leading to
a 'permanent reproduction deficit'.[51] In other words, continuous underinvestment meant that the railway was wearing
itself out. This negative development is a very sad one, especially when we bear in mind that the GDR was, after Switzerland, Europe's second 'railway country'. The average GDR
citizen travelled by train 37 times a year, twice the West
German average and more than three times the British average (see Table on p. 119).

The history of GDR transport policy, up to the time of that
country's collapse in 1989, could be summarised as follows:

• From the 1960s, the GDR transport system moved in the
  direction of the classic car-society model such as exists in
  the West.

- Most goods were transported by rail, especially from the mid-1970s, but in the field of personal transport, the authorities operated on the assumption that each citizen wanted to have his own car. This need was, to a large extent, created by the structural changes in GDR society (urban spread, industrialisation) and by the deterioration in public transport.

- The main driving force behind this development was not, as in the West, a powerful motor industry and car lobby. On the contrary, from the point of view of its economic structure, the GDR was more dependent on rail than on road transport. The attempt to maintain rail transport while, at the same time, promoting the private car sector, meant that the GDR had to maintain very high levels of investment in both sectors. In the end, this placed too high a demand on the GDR economy. But this was a question of policy; more so than in the West, this was a conscious option for private car ownership. This copying of the Western consumer model, and of the Western car society in particular, represented a conscious attempt to stabilise the one-party dictatorship under conditions of de-Stalinisation.

- The leadership and policy of the SED (Sozialistische Einheitspartei Deutschland – Socialist Unity Party of Germany) thus prepared GDR society from within for its later integration into the Western model. In 1989, this society was ripe for such integration. Only a small minority in East Germany defended a 'third way' that would not repeat the mistakes and failures of either East or West Germany. The Citizen's Movement (Bürgerbewegung) of the GDR in 1989–90 fought a hopeless war on two fronts: on one side, against the glittering consumer model of the West and the political and economic offensive of West Germany; on the other side, against the GDR population itself which, repelled by the realities of SED policies, had lost its faith in alternative values and wanted to 'catch up' with what the West had to offer. On the roads also, this meant that the GDR citizens, in their two-stroke Trabants, had to 'catch up' with their West German counterparts driving Volkswagen, BMW or Mercedes.

9

Western Europe:
The Car Society at the End
of the Twentieth Century

Every morning after breakfast the family gathered in the garage to bestow their daily ration of admiration and respect on the two Chevrolets while, on the television, an untidy and unemployed actor, Budweiser, swore fidelity.

Raymond Federman

Mass Motorisation

Since the 1970s, at the latest, road transport has been the dominant form of transport for persons and goods in all the highly industrialised capitalist countries. In the seven major industrial powers, the Group of Seven (G7), the motor industry (including related sectors such as oil and tyres) is now the centre and major driving force of the economy.

The process of mass motorisation, which we have already encountered in the US and Germany, has been generalised throughout the OECD states since the 1970s. Canada and the US were in the lead, having started earlier, and, although the European countries have been rapidly catching up, car ownership has, at the same time, continued to increase in North America. In 1965, motor vehicle density in Europe was highest in Sweden, France and Britain; in 1983, it was Germany, Switzerland, Italy and Britain that had the highest number. This development is demonstrated in Table 9.1.[52]

In the 1990s, in the major countries of Western Europe, car density will reach what has always been considered saturation

Table 9.1 Car Density in Industrial Countries 1965–83
(cars per thousand inhabitants)

Year	US	Canada	Sweden	France	Britain
1965	379	262	224	178	165
1970	437	306	279	240	208
1975	495	380	329	290	245
1980	530	430	346	345	268
1983	538	440	352	377	288

Year	Switzerland	Italy	East Germany (GDR)	West Germany
1965	157	98	–	158
1970	223	179	61	230
1975	280	263	100	289
1980	340	306	143	369
1983	382	345	175	390

point: more than 500 cars per thousand inhabitants. Car density in Germany went beyond this point in 1994, in spite of the absorption of the 'under-motorised' GDR: in that year, there were more than 40 million automobiles for 80 million inhabitants. This growth in car ownership takes place at a time of growing poverty and when an increasing minority is deliberately deciding not to have a car, while some households have two or three. The distribution of cars is therefore an increasingly unequal one. A survey carried out by the Berlin city government in 1993 revealed that 48 per cent of all households in the city did not have a car. There were, interestingly enough, no significant differences, in this respect, between East and West Berlin.

The triumphal march of mass motorisation in Europe followed a recognisable pattern:

- The state, in its official transport policy, promoted and subsidised road construction.

- Throughout this period, motorisation as a 'way of life' was promoted on a very large scale by a propaganda campaign that was very similar everywhere. The initial vehicle of mass motorisation in all of these countries was based on Ford's Tin Lizzie or the German Volkswagen model – the small, inexpensive 'people's car'. In France it was the 2CV (deux chevaux), the Renault R4 and the Simca 1000. In Italy it was the Fiat 500 and 600. In Britain it was the 'Mini'. Over five million British Minis rolled off the assembly lines before 1993. It celebrated its 35th birthday in 1994 and the 'people's car' ideology that informed this motorisation drive is clear in the following report from the Guardian in 1994: 'The Mini defies logic and convention. Nobody would buy a mildly updated version of the Vauxhall Victor or Hillman Minx. But Minis are still built or, as some say, "born", on one of their original production lines at the Rover Longbridge plant. ... A child of the late fifties, the Mini seemed to have been purpose-built for the swinging sixties.'[53]

- Rail transport was neglected and downgraded. This transport technology, which at the time was more than 125 years old, was in need of investment for renewal and improvement, especially for electrification. But these investments were not made. It was clear what the result had to be – a massive shift from rail to road.

Road and Rail in Western Europe 1970–89

We have already seen how the railways declined in North America after the Second World War. A similar decline took place in the world's second major economic power, Japan. *The Economist* reported in 1985: 'In Japan, between 1950 and 1980, the share of the railways in goods transport fell from 39 to 7 per cent. The decline in rail passenger travel was almost as dramatic.'[54] Developments were similar in Europe, as illustrated in Table 9.2 overleaf, based on figures published by the

Table 9.2 Transport of Persons and Goods in Western Europe 1970–89

	1970	1980	1989	1989 as % of 1970
Goods (mn ton-km)				
Rail	274	269	263	−4
Road	439	687	928	114
Inland waterways	113	118	118	4.4
Persons (mn person-km)				
Rail	222	255	280	26
Public transport (bus)	254	343	366	44
Private transport	1568	2277	2969	89
Road accidents				
Injuries (000)	2024	1950	1935	−4.4
Deaths (000)	81	68	62	−23.4

European Conference of Ministers of Transport (ECMT), which includes 19 European countries.[55]

As these figures demonstrate, road transport of goods in ECMT countries more than doubled between 1970 and 1989, growing by 114 per cent. Individual road travel grew by 90 per cent in the same period, reaching 100 per cent the following year. Transport of goods by rail fell by 4 per cent. Individual rail travel grew by 26 per cent, a significant growth, but bus travel grew much faster, by 44 per cent.

Road injuries remained high throughout the period, around 2 million per year. The number of road deaths declined between 1970 and 1980, but at 60,000 per year in 1980 it was still very high. Between 1970 and 1989, according to these official figures, 1.4 million people were killed in road accidents in Western Europe. Between 1960 and 1994, around 5 million people lost their lives on the roads, similar to the number that died in the First World War.

Table 9.3 Share of Rail/Road in European Countries
(in bn person-km/ton-km)

	1970	1980	1989	1989 as % of 1970	1970 as % of total	1989 as % of total
West Germany						
Goods/rail	71	64	61	−14	36	22
Goods/road	78	124	161	106	40	58
Persons/rail	39	41	42	8	9	6
Persons/car	351	470	563	60	80	86
Italy						
Goods/rail	18	18	21	17	23	11
Goods/road	59	120	167	183	76	89
Persons/rail	33	40	44	37	12	7
Persons/car	212	324	481	127	77	79
France						
Goods/rail	68	66	53	−22	46	30
Goods/road	66	104	117	77	45	66
Persons/rail	41	55	65	57	11	10
Persons/car	305	453	574	88	82	85
Britain						
Goods/rail	25	18	19	−24	22	12
Goods/road	85	90	130	53	74	86
Persons/rail	30	30	34	13	8	5
Person/car	289	395	556	92	78	88
Switzerland						
Goods/rail	6.6	7.4	8.2	24	61	47
Goods/road	4.2	6.0	9.0	114	38	53
Persons/rail	8.2	9.2	11.0	34	13	11
Persons/car	50.7	72.6	87.2	72	83	86

Continued on next page

Table 9.3 Share of Rail/Road in European Countries *cont.*
(in bn person-km/ton-km)

	1970	1980	1989	1989 as % of 1970	1970 as % of total	1989 as % of total
Austria						
Goods/rail	9.9	11.0	12.0	21	71	58
Goods/road	2.9	7.9	6.7	131	20	33
Persons/rail	6.3	7.3	8.4	33	–	11
Persons/car	28.0	43.5	53.8	92	–	71
Netherlands						
Goods/rail	3.7	3.4	3.1	–16	8	5
Goods/road	12.4	17.7	22.1	78	27	36
Persons/rail	8.0	8.9	10.2	28	11	6
Persons/car	72.1	111.1	137.0	90	79	86
Denmark						
Goods/rail	1.9	1.6	1.7	–11	19	15
Goods/road	7.8	7.8	9.2	18	80	85
Persons/rail	3.4	4.3	4.7	38	8	7
Persons/car					81	79
Spain						
Goods/rail	10	11	12	16	17	8
Goods/road	52	90	142	175	83	92
Persons/rail	15	15	16	7	15	8
Persons/car	64	131	157	144	64	74
All ECMT countries						
Goods/rail	274	269	263	–4	33	20
Goods/road	439	687	928	111	53	71
Persons/rail	222	255	281	27	11	8
Persons/car	1568	2277	2969	89	75	80

Table 9.3 gives comparative figures for road and rail travel in the 19 ECMT countries for the period 1970 to 1989.[56] These figures reveal interesting differences among the countries concerned but confirm the overall direction of development.

In the case of the leading European countries, Germany, Britain, France and Italy, the decisive trends were as follows:

- Rail transport of goods declined particularly strongly in three countries – 14 per cent in Germany, 22 per cent in France, 24 per cent in Britain. The average decline for all European Transport Ministry (ECMT) countries was 4 per cent. Only in Italy was there an increase. The decline in Britain was particularly strong because it was in this period that the Beeching Plan, with its massive reduction of rail services, began to have its effect.

- The average increase in road transport of goods for all ECMT countries was 111 per cent. Britain fell well below this, with a growth rate of 53 per cent, which may be a result of the fact that Britain's motorways are the oldest in Europe and, like the London Underground, are in need of billions of pounds of new investment to enable them to meet the requirements of the 1990s. The rate of increase in Italy was well above the average, at 183 per cent, a three-fold increase. This was probably a result of the massive construction of motorways after the Second World War, combined with an industrialisation drive.

- The railway's share of goods transport in 1970 in these four countries was not high, between 22 per cent in Britain and 44 per cent in Italy. The decline in this share over the next two decades was dramatic. In Britain, Germany and France there was an absolute decline, in Britain by as much as 24 per cent (from 25m ton-km to 19m ton-km). As a proportion of overall goods transport, rail declined by a third in France and Germany and by half in Britain and Italy.

- In all four countries, the railways shared in the overall growth in individual travel. Average growth of individual rail travel for all ECMT countries was 27 per cent. Britain and Germany were below this average but Italy was, at 37 per cent, well above it. In France, rail passenger travel increased at more than twice the average rate (57 per cent). This growth in individual rail travel, however, did not take place mainly in the high-speed sectors. During the period in question, Italy did not have any high-speed trains, while the decisive growth in individual rail travel in France took place in the period 1970–80, before the introduction of the TGV in the mid-1980s.

It is also of interest that the overall share of rail in individual travel fell not only as an ECMT average; it fell also in those countries where there had been an above-average growth in the rail sector. This was because the car sector grew at a much faster pace. In Britain, for instance, rail travel grew by 13 per cent but the railway's share in individual transport overall fell from 8 to 5 per cent. In France, although individual rail travel grew by 57 per cent, overall individual travel grew by 88 per cent in the same period, with the result that rail's share in individual transport fell from 11 to 10 per cent.

The second group in Table 9.4 (Switzerland, Austria, Holland and Denmark) are all relatively small countries, without an indigenous car industry and therefore with a weak car lobby. These countries have been traditionally praised for their enlightened public transport policies and for bucking the trend towards car mania. A closer look at the figures in Table 9.4, however, leads to a more modest assessment: there have been some singular positive developments in this group of countries, but overall the trend is similar to elsewhere in Europe. The growth in rail transport of goods in Switzerland and Austria is positive, but in Denmark road transport of goods has increased at a very high rate.

In all four countries individual rail travel has increased by an average of 26 per cent, well above the ECMT average. Although Switzerland and Austria have a car density similar to Germany or Britain, the train continues to be used by many people. In the mid-1980s, Swiss citizens made, on average, 43 train journeys a year, travelling an average 1445 km. The British yearly average is 11 train journeys and 542 km. A suggested explanation for this is the high quality of rail travel in Switzerland. (see Table 9.4).

Table 9.4 Rail Travel in European Countries 1985–6

Country	Rail journeys per person per year	Person-km per person per year
Switzerland	43	1445
East Germany (GDR)	37	1370
Poland	34	1532
Czechoslovakia	27	1275
Austria	23	964
West Germany	17	804
Romania	17	1360
France	13	1097
Britain	11	542
Sweden	9	788

Spain is typical for a group of countries that would also include Portugal, Greece and Turkey. The industrialisation and motorisation process in these countries was not as developed in 1970 as it was in Central Europe and Britain, but they were en route to the car society in seven-league boots. Road haulage in Spain, in this period, was 50 per cent above the ECMT average and individual travel increased at twice the ECMT rate. At the end of the 1980s, Spain had just about caught up with the rest of Europe. In Portugal and Greece, individual travel increased fourfold between 1970 and 1989.

The balance sheet for Europe is a clear one: the trend towards the total car society continues unabated, in both personal and goods transport. There are no real exceptions. Spain, Portugal, Turkey and Greece are examples of less-developed countries that, in a few years, have repeated all the mistakes made over decades in the developed countries, in spite of everything that has been learned in economics as well as ecology. They give us a foretaste of what we can expect in the developing transport sectors of Eastern Europe and the ex-Soviet Union.

The Automobile Industry

World automobile production and the big international automobile manufacturers are concentrated in the six highly industrialised capitalist countries: the US, Japan, Germany, France,
Britain and Italy. At the end of the 1970s, a dozen automobile
companies controlled 70 per cent of global automobile production and 90 per cent of production in the capitalist West.[57]
These transnational corporations have a corresponding structural weight in the economy and export of these six countries.
Motor vehicle manufacture, excluding related sectors, accounts
for between 5 and 7 per cent of industrial production. The
export quotas of the French, Italian, British, German, and
Japanese car companies are between 40 and 60 per cent; they
account for around 10 per cent of the total export of these
countries.[58] At the end of the 1970s, the automobile industry
in these six countries employed 3.5 million people. If we
include the supply industries, the number of workers rises to
between 9 and 11 million in this sector alone. This does not
include the workers in the non-industrial transport sector. In
West Germany, in 1980, the total number of workers in the
motor manufacturing and transport sector was 2,865,000,
almost 3 million. This was around 11 per cent of the whole
workforce at the time.[59]

In assessing the weight of this sector in the economy as a
whole, its dynamic is as important as its absolute size. In the
US between the 1920s and the 1970s, the growth rate of the
motor industry was well above the growth rate for the economy
as a whole. In other words, the car industry acted as a motor
for the whole economy. In Japan, it is the growth of its motor
industry which has been behind that country's expansion and
growing strength on the world market. In Germany, the motor
industry was the most important element in the long
economic boom after the Second World War. Between 1953
and the beginning of the 1970s, the West German motor
industry not only had a growth rate well above that for the
economy as a whole, it was also the biggest sector. Figure 9.1
illustrates this development. While industry as a whole grew by
around 130 per cent, the construction and coal industries fell
below this level. The motor industry led the way. Between

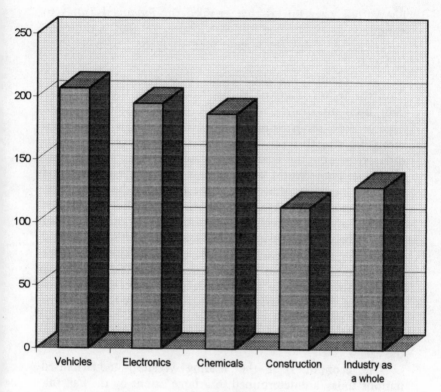

Figure 9.1
Growth of West German Industrial Branches in Relation to
Overall Industrial Growth 1953–71

1953 and 1971, it grew by 207 per cent, 90 percentage points above the rate of growth for industry as a whole. In the 1950s, the motor industry accounted for around 5 per cent of total industrial production; by the beginning of the 1980s, this figure had reached over 10 per cent.

Among the seven countries with indigenous car production, it is only Britain that has undergone dramatic decline. By the end of the 1970s, Britain had lost its place on the world car market, a factor which contributed strongly to that country's general decline on the world market. It was massive investment from foreign corporations (Nissan, Honda, Toyota) and the takeover of British companies (Ford took over Jaguar,

BMW took over Rover) that enabled the *Financial Times* to announce in 1994: 'The full year total car output is thus certain to exceed 1.4m, the highest total since the 1.53m achieved in 1974.'[60]

This positive impulse for the whole economy that came from the motor industry in the period before the 1970s also had, from an immanent capitalist economic viewpoint, its negative side: the growing dependence of industrial growth and industrial structure on car manufacture and export. The car industry became the heart of late capitalist society. Before and after the First World War, it was the steel, mining and machine industries that were at the centre of the West European economy; today these are third-rate industries. The chemical and electrotechnical industries that seemed to lead the field between the wars yielded first place, after the Second World War, to the car industry. The other industrial branches have become today, to a large extent, suppliers to the car industry or are closely linked to it (steel, electronics, petrochemicals). The construction industry has been heavily influenced by the new transport system: suburban housing estates, green-space industrial parks and shopping malls all depend on the car.

The economies of the leading Western industrialised nations today are determined to a large extent by the car, oil, and oil-processing industries, as demonstrated by Tables 9.5[61] and 9.6[62].

The figures in these tables make three things clear:

1. In all three imperialist centres, a surprisingly identical 'growth model' has been developed which we have no hesitation in describing as a 'destruction model'. The alpha and omega of this growth model is the car society. The corporations of the car society (the motor, oil, tyre and oil-processing industries) make up around 50–60 per cent of the 20 leading industrial corporations. They, with the banks and insurance companies linked to them, are the key players in this capitalist order of things.

2. The tables concretise this structure of the car society for each individual country in industrialised Western Europe. The corporate structure of West Germany, the most power-

Table 9.5 The 20 Biggest Companies in US, Japan and Western Europe

No.	US ($mn)		Japan ($mn)		Western Europe (DMmn)	
1	Exxon*	115	Toyota*	72	Shell*	170
2	GM*	105	Matsushita	56	BP*	95
3	Ford*	88	Hitachi	55	Daimler Benz*	95
4	IBM	65	Nissan M*	42	Siemens	76
5	Mobil*	63	Toshiba	33	VW*	76
6	General E	60	Honda*	31	Fiat*	75
7	Phlp Morris	56	Sony	29	Unilever	68
8	Chevron*	41	NEC	26	ENI/Agip*	67
9	Du Pont	39	Mitsubishi E	24	Veba*	60
10	Texaco*	37	Nippon Steel	23	Elf Aquitaine*	59
11	Chrysler*	30	Nippon Oil*	21	Nestlé	58
12	Boeing	29	Mitsubishi M*	20	Philips	51
13	Amoco*	28	Mazda*	20	Renault*	49
14	Proctor & G.	27	Mitsubishi HE	18	Hoechst	47
15	United Tech.	21	Bridgestone*	14	Peugeot/Citrn.*	47
16	ITT	20	NKK	14	Alc.Alsthom	47
17	Atl. Rich.*	19	Sumitomo Mt	13	BASF	47
18	Dow Chem.	19	Showa Shell*	13	ABB	45
19	Eastman K.	19	Cosmos Oil*	13	Total*	42
20	Xerox	18	Isuzu*	12	Bayer	42
Total turnover:		899		549		1316
Total turnover owned by car society companies		526		258		835
Share (%)		58.5		47		63.4

Abbreviations:
M = Motors   HE = Heavy Industries   E = Electric
Mt = Metal

Table 9.6 The 12 Biggest Companies in Germany, Britain, France and Italy (by turnover in DMmn)

No.	Germany		Britain		France		Italy	
1	Daimler*	95	Shell*	59	Elf*	170	Fiat*	76
2	Siemens	76	BP*	49	Renault*	95	Eni/Agip*	67
3	VW*	75	BAT	47	Peugeot*	40	Enel	26
4	Veba*	60	ICI	47	Alcatel	36	Montedison	21
5	Hoechst	47	Aerospace	42	Total Oil*	31	Feruzzi	24
6	BASF	47	GE	26	Usinor	26	Pirelli*	13
7	Bayer	42	Ford*	25	Rhone Poulenc	18	Olivetti	12
8	Thyssen	36	British Steel	22	Peciney	13	Alitalia	8
9	Bosch*	33	Guinness	21	Thomson	12	Tamoil*	7
10	BMW*	29	IBM UK	20	Michelin*	12	Efim*	6
11	Opel/GM*	27	Esso*	22	St Gobain	11	Esso Italy*	6
12	Ford*	22	Rolls-Royce*	17	Schneider	10	Erg Petrol*	6
Total turnover:		589		397		474		272
Total turnover owned by car or car-related companies:		341		217		304		181
Share of turnover owned by car or car-related companies (%):		57.9		54.7		64.1		66.5

* indicates car or car-related company

ful economy in Europe, is one in which around 60 per cent of the 12 biggest corporations are 'car society' corporations. France and Britain are in a similar position.

3. The figures in these tables actually underestimate the real influence of the 'car society' corporations because they contain only those companies that represent the car society in a narrow sense. We could also add the airline industry, which is completely dependent on oil. The chemical and petrochemical corporations are in a similar position. There are also a whole range of companies that depend, to an increasing extent, on the car society. A list of such companies would include, for instance, Siemens in Germany, General Electric in the US, British Steel in Britain, and so on. If we were to also include the banks and insurance companies that are integrated into the production mechanisms of the car society, then we would find that the economic structure of the most powerful states on this planet are more dominated by this destructive model than even the tables suggest. It would probably still be an underestimation to say that two-thirds of the economic resources of the capitalist economy are concentrated in this destructive model.

The chairman of General Motors (GM), the biggest corporation in the world, said once that 'what is good for General Motors is good for America'. In a certain superficial sense, this was true for the period in which the capitalist economies were enjoying a new period of growth: in the US after the world economic crisis and depression, in Western Europe after the Second World War. In the meantime, however, we have witnessed two important changes. Firstly, since the mid-1970s we have been in a period of declining growth rates and increasingly severe crises that are pointing in the direction of a new world economic crisis and a new depression. Secondly, this is now combined with an ecological crisis which is, to a large extent, a direct product of this car society. This growth model, with the car at its centre, is a destructive model. The partial rationality of the individual car becomes, with quantitative growth (500m world-wide), the irrationality of the car society.

10

The History and Poverty of
Urban Public Transport

The population of Greater London grew from just over
4,200,000 in 1875 to about 6,000,000 in 1895. From information collected for the Royal Commission on London
Traffic at the beginning of the present century ... it would
seem that the number of journeys made by train, tram, and
omnibus perhaps increased from 270,000,000 per year to
about 1,000,000,000 per year during the same period. So,
while London's population grew by rather less than 50 per
cent in these 20 years – in itself a remarkable rate of growth
– the number of journeys in the London area appears to
have risen by nearly 300 per cent, and the number of journeys per head of London's resident population from about
65 to over 165.

T.C. Parker and Michael Robins,
History of London Transport

Early capitalism of the eighteenth and nineteenth century revolutionised agriculture, caused a flight from the land and created
cities. It is generally assumed that this coincided with the
creation of urban public transport, especially in the bigger cities. But this was not the case. The major urban centres of early
capitalism, those with over one million inhabitants, existed for
more than half a century without large-scale public transport.
In the major cities of Britain and the US, up until the middle
of the nineteenth century, most people experienced modern
mobility only in the form of an occasional excursion on the
train. This was the case in Germany until the end of the

nineteenth century. It was only after this period that the creation of public transport led to the revolution in daily mobility in the big cities. Its golden age was the first three decades of this century. The history of public transport, which reached its peak in the 1920s, helps us to understand the poverty of public transport today in our car-dominated cities. In the present chapter, I will examine the development of public transport in London and Berlin.

1. *The big cities of early capitalism were without mass public transport for decades. People went to work and did their shopping on foot. In these cities, distances were short. Urban transport conditions, as well as the conditions of housing and work, were poor.*

There was little travel in the daily lives of people in pre-industrial and early industrial society; people went on foot or made use of primitive means with the help of animals. The peasants, the craftworkers, and the workers of the early industrial period did not have far to go to work. Shopping played only a minor role since people were largely self-sufficient. The creation of big cities did not bring an immediate change. Initially, the pre-urban social model was simply transferred to the city. Workers lived in the vicinity of the factory – in rather poor housing. People also shopped in the local neighbourhood or even purchased some of their necessities in the workplace itself.

London in 1860 had 2.8 million inhabitants, only half a million less than united Berlin in 1995. The only means of mass public transport were the horse-drawn omnibuses that carried well-to-do passengers. In 1860, around 40 million omnibus journeys were made, 14 journeys per inhabitant in that year. Travel to and from work was therefore insignificant.

Berlin in 1870 had 1 million inhabitants and 370 horse-drawn omnibuses; there were 10 million journeys, 10 per inhabitant in that year, even fewer than London. Before the advent of the omnibus, the rivers and canals (in London the Thames and the city canals, in Berlin the Spree, the Havel, and the city canals) were the primary means of transport for occasional trips to the outskirts of town on weekends or holidays.[63]

2. Public transport in the cities was a major breakthrough but it was affected, from the beginning, by land speculation, extreme centralisation and structurally enforced travel. The structure of modern cities has been partly determined by the negative developments of this period. The undeniable progress which public transport represented was partly offset by these negative features.

Mass transport in the new urban centres was largely commuter transport for the middle and working classes. It was the result of residential dispersion, the rise of sprawling suburbs located outside the urban centres. The move to the suburbs was prompted by the unhealthy conditions in the traditional working-class neighbourhoods. The conservative Prussian politician, Heinrich von Treischke, gives the following picture of Berlin in 1874:

> Our capital city, at the present moment, resembles a young person in that charming age when arms and limbs are growing too long for their clothes and tropical vegetation begins to cover the facial skin. A mass of human beings live at close quarters in exorbitantly priced dwellings; there is a complete lack of a developed transport system which alone could enable these circumscribed lives to have some contact with nature.

But these gentlemen and most of the promoters of urban transport had little interest in the health and living conditions of the working class when they set about developing the public transport system.[64]

In the middle of the nineteenth century, the City of London had 124,000 inhabitants; by 1891 the number had fallen to 50,000; today there are fewer than 5,000 people living in the City of London. As the population moved away from the City, the transport system grew rapidly to accommodate the hundreds of thousands of people that had to come to the City daily to work. Whenever the underground or tram lines were extended a few miles into the countryside, new suburban developments sprang up. The value of land rose at an incredible rate. People described it as 'Metroland' and the first underground company in London was the Metropolitan.

The transport companies profited in many ways from this development; the building materials for the new suburban developments were carried on the new lines; the new suburban estates also increased the number of passengers. The population of Uxbridge, for instance, grew from 4,000 in 1901 to 30,000 in 1931; Harrow grew from below 50,000 in 1921 to 220,000 in 1951. According to Bernhard Strowitzki, in his study of the London underground:

> For the city as a whole, the surface area being developed increased at a faster rate than the population. For an increasing number of inner-city residents, even those with mid-level incomes, the daily trip to work on the underground or electric suburban train was taken for granted. The state soon became involved in the construction of rail lines ... with guaranteed interest for private owners who invested.[65]

In Berlin, this development took place under the watchful eyes of the Prussian planners, but the result was the same. In 1858 the Prussian official and architect, James Hobrecht, presented a plan for the city which was to largely determine Berlin's development for decades to come. Street planning was centralised around the old city centre. In 1870, the statistician, Ernst Bruch, made a critique of the plan which could have come from a town planner or critic of the late twentieth century: 'The basic mistake of the plan is its exaggerated centralisation. None of the projected suburban settlements will be able to develop an independent life.' To the Hobrecht image of Berlin with its single centre, Bruch suggested an alternative in which the new suburban centres 'would maintain their own independent existence, constitute their own centres of gravity and, with their own satellites, fit unconstrainedly into the looser and more flexibly constructed whole'.[66]

The Hobrecht plan extended far beyond the city, driving up the price of the surrounding farmland. Private entrepreneurs, with the help of state subsidies, brought rail lines and horse-drawn trams into the countryside around Berlin. Train stations were built on greenfield sites, for instance, the station in Lichterfelde built by the speculator, Carstenn, in 1868. Rent in the centre of Berlin rose threefold in the

period 1860 to 1880. This encouraged the move to the suburbs. The dependence of the suburbs on the centre led to a
large amount of daily traffic. The Prussian minister for trade
and public works wrote in 1871:

> The city of Berlin, as a coherent built-up area, has already
> grown on such a scale that it can no longer be traversed
> on foot. It seems essential, therefore, to make it possible
> for people who work in the centre of the city to have
> their dwelling at some distance from the centre. It is for
> this reason that we have recently considered the construc-
> tion of a network of horse-drawn trams.[67]

3. *Public transport expanded rapidly in the final quarter of
the nineteenth century, devoted largely to commuter traffic.
Until the 1930s, it grew at a faster rate than the population.*

London's population doubled between 1875 and 1920 but the
number of journeys on public transport increased 20 times
during the same period. The discrepancy remained enormous
even beyond this period. For instance, in the period 1890 to
1930, while the population increased from 4.2 to 7.7 million
(80 per cent), the number of journeys on public transport
increased fourfold.

There was a similar development in Berlin; between 1875
and 1920, the population increased threefold but the amount
of traffic on public transport increased 40 times. In the later
period, 1890 to 1929, when the population doubled, the volume of public transport increased nine times. By far the greater
part of this was commuter traffic. Some forms of transport
specialised in commuter traffic. London's horse-drawn trams
experienced the fastest growth after 1875 and, by 1920, were
the most important means of urban public transport. Workers
made up a very large proportion of this traffic. In Berlin it was
also the trams that were the main carriers of commuter traffic
and which grew the fastest during this period.[68]

There was indeed one form of transport which was an alternative to public transport at this time, certainly over short and
medium distances, but it was prohibited: on 15 April 1864, the
Prussian government restricted 'the riding of bicycles, which
has become fashionable' on most Berlin streets. The private

owners of the urban transport systems had pressurised the government into banning the bike.[69]

4. *The modern means of public transport gave a mobility to the people of the big cities that was superior to that which they enjoy in today's auto-metropolis. The golden period of public transport was the 1920s. There were a number of forms of transport in this period: steam-driven suburban trains, electric trams, underground and elevated railways, and buses. At the peak of this development, it was the electric tram that played the key role.*

The principal measure of mobility in cities with public transport is the number of journeys per inhabitant per year. At the peak of development in this period, the yearly number of journeys per inhabitant was 503 in London and 448 in Berlin. New York had an even higher number, 545 journeys per inhabitant in 1925. Taking into account that the elderly and children used public transport very little and that the working week was six days, then we arrive at a figure of two journeys per day for the average adult plus about a dozen trips each year on weekends and holidays.

Table 10.1, overleaf, compares public transport in London and Berlin during the period 1875 to 1960.[70] There are three aspects of these figures that I would like to emphasise:

(a) For a certain period, the trams had the largest share of the market in London (1920: 36 per cent); in Berlin, the trams at one time could even attract as much as 50 per cent of the market.

(b) With the decline of the trams, it was not the underground but the buses that experienced the greatest growth. This meant a rapid growth of *street traffic* (buses and private cars) after 1930.

(c) During the peak period of public transport, London and Berlin had a relatively small number of cars. Although the car had already been in existence for half a century, it failed to make a breakthrough in this period. The high level of mobility of people in cities like London and Berlin, which

Table 10.1
Public Transport in London (1875–1960)
and Berlin (1875–1962)

London	1875	1890	1920	1930	1960
Population (mn)	3.5	5.5	7.4	8.1	8.2
Journeys by public transport	183	850	3057	4070	3860
By tram	48	200	1100	1100	312*
By Underground	15	300	690	600	674
By main line rail	70	150	370	420	600
By bus	50	200	900	1960	2275
Journeys per person	52	154	413	503	471
No. of vehicles (000)			26	180	1200

Berlin	1875	1890	1920	1929	1962**
Population (mn)	1.1	2.0	3.9	4.3	3.3
Journeys by public transport	32	235	1425	1928	1430
By tram	18	143	788	925	390
By underground (U-Bahn)			101	275	260
By main line rail (S-Bahn)		64	528	445	220
By bus	14	28	9	279	560
Journeys per person	28	120	367	448	433
No. of vehicles(000)			20	40	300

* in trolley buses   ** For both parts of Berlin

Table 10.2 Tram and Underground Compared

	Tram	Underground	Underground as % of tram
Energy used (mn kwh)	103.40	88.20	85
Passengers (mn)	501	209	42
Energy per journey	0.21	0.42	200
Capital invested per km (mn RM)	0.50	6.30	1250

were also cultural capitals and models of urban planning, was achieved without the private car.

5. *In all major cities with a developed underground system, it is the underground that takes by far the largest portion of the capital invested in public transport. This is in spite of the fact that its share of passengers is relatively small. There are a number of reasons for the preferential treatment of underground systems in big cities but they have little to do with a rational transport policy.*

It was in London in the early 1920s that the London Underground achieved its highest share of passengers – 23 per cent. The Berlin underground reached its highest level, 18 per cent, in the early 1930s.[71] By 1960, the share of the London tube was down to 17 per cent, comparable to the Berlin figure of 18 per cent at the same time. By 1994, this had declined further, to 15 per cent in London and to 11 per cent in united Berlin.[72]

This relatively small share of passenger transit contrasts with the large share of the capital invested in this specific form

of public transport. In the 1920s, the construction of one kilometre of underground was 10 times more expensive than a
similar stretch of tram line. Today it is 15 to 20 times more
expensive. The Berlin transport authorities in the 1920s and
1930s published figures for the construction and operation of
the underground and tram lines which allow us to make a
comparison. These figures are given in Table 10.2.[73]

For each kilometre of track, the underground was 12
times more expensive than the tram. The underground also
used twice as much energy, and this was before the existence
of a large number of high-energy escalators.[74] At the end of
the 1920s, it was the view of the town planner, Werner
Hegemann, that 'all the underground systems in the world
need state subsidies to avoid bankruptcy'.[75] Of course, most
public transport systems at the time were privately owned
and profitable.

The argument that the underground systems are faster
also does not stand up to close examination. The greater
distances between underground stations, compared to trams,
as well as the distance from the street to the underground
platform, more than make up for the time saved by greater
speed. The claim of the city planners that the underground/
subway trains offer a rapid means of transport in the inner
cities that could not be achieved by any other means does
not stand up to examination. The Batelle Institute in Frankfurt carried out a study of one of the main underground lines
in the city, the A1 line. It compared the underground line
with the tram that had previously run on this route and its
conclusion was that, although the underground train was a
faster train, the longer distances that travellers had to walk
to reach the underground platform meant that there was no
real saving of time. The conclusion of the Batelle Institute
study is described by Michael Busse:

Travel time by tram is longer than by subway. But this
advantage is cancelled out by the shorter time it takes to
reach a tram stop. Without the subway train, car traffic
would be slower [because the removal of the tram lines
provided an extra two lanes]. So who benefited from the
subway? The answer is clear: only the car driver.[76]

Why then do underground systems have such a prominent place in the public transport system of most big cities? Some of the main reasons are the following:

• The construction of underground systems avoided the problem of land purchases in the inner cities where land was expensive. At the same time, the construction of an underground station made the surrounding land even more valuable. The underground was a boost to speculation in inner-city property.

• The building of the early underground was itself part of a major speculation, even though the results were not always as expected. This was particularly true of the London Underground, the first stretch of which was begun in 1856, with a large amount of support from the City of London, and put into operation in 1863 (the Paddington–Farringdon Street section of the North Metropolitan Railway). The high costs involved were a disincentive to British investors. Later projects were also to end in cancellation as a result of bankruptcy, for instance the Baker Street and Waterloo Railway (later the Bakerloo). The speculator behind this project, Whitaker Wright, committed suicide to avoid a seven-year sentence for falsifying the balance sheet. US speculative capital was heavily involved in the London Underground (Charles Tyson Yerkes, Albert Henry Stanley, later Baron Ashfield of Southwell). According to T. C. Parker, in his study of the history of London transport: 'The travelling public of London owes a considerable debt to the ill-advised American (and other) speculators. ... If the backers [of the underground] had not indulged in such an unfortunate speculation in the early years of the century, how long would London have had to wait for such a vital additional railway provision?'[77]

• Some of the underground lines of this early period were part of much larger projects in which the low profitability of the underground section was compensated for by advantages elsewhere. A number of railway companies built underground lines to link their major lines that ended in terminal stations. For instance, the inner ring of London's Metropolitan Line was completed because it was to be part of a larger railway line from Manchester, through the Thames tunnel and the Metropolitan underground line, to the south coast of England, then through a tunnel under the Channel to the Continent and on to Paris. According to H. J. Dyos and D. H. Aldercroft, in their history of British transport: 'Under its deluded chairman, Edward Watkins, the Manchester, Sheffield & Lincolnshire Railway, which had undertaken some of the most costly works in the country and knew penury all too well, worked up to a more ambitious and debilitating swipe at three well-nigh impregnable companies with London termini as part of a quixotic plan to form a single undertaking serving the North, Midlands, London, and the Channel ports. It failed. The ordinary stock of the Great Central Railway, as it had become during the constructional phase, never yielded a dividend.'[78]

The construction of the Channel Tunnel had already begun, with a test bore of two kilometres.

• Underground lines were almost always monopolies. Having granted a concession for a stretch of underground, the urban authorities seldom allowed competition on the same line.

• State subsidies were an important element in underground construction (in London, from the 1920s). This was soon followed by the consolidation of the different companies involved in public transport: the London Passenger Transport Board was established in 1933. The London Underground was taken into public ownership in 1945. The Berlin underground and elevated railways were subsided right from the beginning. The first line to be opened (in 1902) was the line that linked Stralauer Tor to the Zoo Railway Station and Potsdamer Platz.

• The construction of an underground line, compared to other forms of transport, is a very big undertaking. The contracts are very large and, for this reason alone, are attractive to the world of business, especially since large-scale public subsidies allow 'the socialisation of losses and the privatisation of profit'.

- The construction of underground lines also leaves the surface area free for other forms of transport. This was a great advantage for the operators and manufacturers of buses. From the 1920s, it also made possible an increase in car traffic in the city centres.[79]

6. *The end of the tram system in London and West Berlin was the result of political and not economic considerations. In this, it is similar to developments in the US where, as a government report has officially confirmed, the car industry conspired to buy up the public transport systems in the big cities in order to replace the trams with buses.*

Trams have an atmospheric advantage in that they are driven above ground where the experience of travel is qualitatively better than it is in underground tunnels. Because of their easier accessibility they are friendlier to the elderly and the infirm. The lines also tend to follow the established routes and communication lines of the existing urban structure. Transport studies have confirmed that the tram is the most popular form of public transport. It is no accident that present-day Zurich, in which the tram is the backbone of the public transport system, holds the record in Western Europe for the use of public transport. It is the only city with more than 500 journeys per year per inhabitant, a figure reminiscent of the golden age of urban public transport.[80]

The underground and tram competed for passengers in 1920s Berlin. W. Hegemann made the following assessment in 1930:

Transport statistics tell us clearly what the great majority of Berliners think about the advantages of travelling through the cellars. Every summer, the underground loses one fifth of its passengers to the tram. Only when the weather is cold or wet, when sitting in the slow and poorly heated trams is too much to bear, is there an increase in underground travel.[81]

In the faster and well-heated modern tram, these structural disadvantages are no longer present.

In addition to the general factors outlined above that led to the promotion of underground and bus systems in most big cities, there were a number of specific factors in certain cities. For instance, through the whole period of its existence the tram was not allowed to operate in central London, which was a major structural disadvantage for the London tramline system. The trams could not travel through the city and journeys had to be interrupted.[82]

The London trams had to serve the travel needs of the working population. This meant that cheap fares were subsidised and, as early as 1899, the city took over the operation of the horse-drawn trams, the core of the later electrified tram network. The competition between tram and underground was therefore, at the same time, a competition between communal and private transport and, as long as profits are to be had from transport, a society dominated by private capital will tend to promote the private at the cost of the public sector.

The consolidation of the companies involved in public transport in London in the London Passenger Transport Board (LPTB) was a consolidation of what were mainly privately operated transport systems. The first head of the LPTB was Lord Ashfield, who had invested the greater part of his money in the Underground. The first important decision of the LPTB was to close 95 kilometres of tram line. The process of line closures began shortly afterwards. The last tram ran in 1952.

In Berlin, shortly after the municipalisation of the tramline system in 1919, there were two events which came close to being deliberate sabotage of this form of transport. At the height of the inflationary crisis of 1923, the Berlin tramlines, the biggest part of the city's transport system, were shut down completely for one whole day (10 September). All the employees were sent home, a new tram company was formed and, when transport resumed on the following day, it was with only one-third of the former employees and a smaller number of trams. It took the tram system six years to recover from its losses in the transport market. The other sections of the public transport system (underground, commuter trains, buses) were not subjected to such a shock. Later, in 1928 and 1929, there was a major investment in modernisation; 300 new motor carriages were bought. In the next three years, these had to be completely re-equipped –

because of major technical faults. These carriages had been delivered by the Nationale Automobil Gesellschaft (NAG), a car producer and daughter company of AEG, a company whose main interests were in the underground.[83]

In 1953, the West Berlin Senate (local government) decided to completely close the tram system although it was, at the time, the most popular form of transport in the city. The decision was taken at a closed session of a committee which did not have the formal authority to even take such a decision. It was only revealed to the public much later and in piecemeal fashion.[84] In East Berlin, the tram continued to run successfully. When the city was reunited in 1990, the opportunity existed to extend the East Berlin tramlines into the western part of the city. Five years later, only a symbolic stretch of some 100 yards has been extended.

The shut-down of the trams was made palatable for the public by promising it would be replaced by the trolley bus. A lot of paper was printed at the time to convince the travelling public that the trolley bus combined the advantages of the tram (low energy use, no emissions) with those of the autobus (greater mobility in the streets). In reality, the trolley buses ran for a few years before they were completely replaced by the diesel-driven bus.

For urban transport in Europe, we still do not have a comprehensive study comparable to the Snell Report commissioned by the US government in 1974. This Report showed, as I have already mentioned, that the reduction and closure of the American urban rail systems was the result of an organised conspiracy by the US car companies.[85]

7. *The poverty of public transport in the big cities of today is the result of the history outlined above, of the continued destruction of these cities, and of the destruction of the collective urban life-world by profit, speculation in property and the promotion of individualism.*

Since the end of the 1920s, we have been experiencing a continuous decline in public transport and a steady increase in private car traffic in cities. Between 1929–30 and 1960–2, the number of registered private cars in London and Berlin increased eight times. Since then, there has been a further

fourfold increase. In both cities there is now one car for
every 2.5 persons (elderly and children included). With the
advent of the two-car and three-car family, the distribution of
car ownership is still very unequal. In East Berlin in 1993,
49 per cent of households did not have a car; in West Berlin
the number was only slightly lower, 47 per cent. This means
that practically every second household has to walk, use a
bicycle, or depend on public transport.[86] But public transport
services in cities like Berlin and London have been in continuous decline. In these two cities, in the mid-1990s, the
yearly number of journeys undertaken per inhabitant on public transport is between 50 and 60 per cent of what it used
to be in the 1920s.[87] Public transport is no longer profitable;
in most cities, public transport systems cover only from 30
to 50 per cent of their costs. The cost of maintaining an
underground system is enormous. The buses that carry most
public passengers in Berlin and London are generally stuck in
traffic.

There is an immanent logic in all of this and its consequences are unavoidable as long as present transport policies
– and urban planning policies – are adhered to. In the golden
age of public transport, it was the systems of mass transport
that accounted for the overwhelmingly greater part of motorised transport. They were oligopolies in the transport market.
Public transport was, at the same time, present everywhere
and around the clock. It is still present everywhere today and
there is an increasing demand that it should be available
around the clock (night lines, night taxis, women's taxis,
etc.). But public transport today only accounts for a minor
part of the motorised transport market. The demands placed
on it (everywhere and around the clock) can not be satisfied
on the basis of its small share of the market.

The official response to this contradiction is to raise fares,
reduce services, break up the public transport systems and
privatise the different parts. The subsequent deterioration in
the quality of the service will lead to a further loss of passengers. At the end of this road is a city completely dominated by
the car. Apart from perhaps a few central lines, public transport will not be profitable. In public transport, we are returning
to the situation that existed before the turn of the century,
made worse by the damages that the car society has caused in

the meantime. In real existing capitalism, developments are tending to favour motorised individual transport and to increase the deficit in public transport. This development could be described as 'the privatisation and centralisation of leisure time and leisure travel'. At the same time, there are increasing demands for public transport at peak times.

The winning of Saturday as a work-free day was a social and political success. From the point of view of public transport, however, this was a problem because transport needs during leisure time are usually catered for by the private car. On 28 per cent of days there is now no commuter traffic – the key area of public transport. There was a parallel decline in the use of public transport for evening visits to the cinema or theatre and for similar visits at weekends. In 1948, greyhound racing in London attracted 11.2 million spectators; in the mid-1960s it attracted less than half that number. Television gradually took the place of the cinema, and when people go out they tend to use the private car.

The disparity between peak and slack hour traffic is increasing. Already in 1936, the LPTB reported that: 'The result of the increasing use of private means of transport is to accentuate the disparity which exists between the peak and slack hours traffic and to influence adversely the cost of the Board's operations.'[88]

The result is an even higher deficit for public transport.

8. *A comparison of transport in Western Europe with that in the United States demonstrates that these destructive tendencies can get much worse.*

Energy use per inhabitant in US cities is three times higher than in Western Europe, although the population density in the US is half of that in Europe. The population density of New York, Chicago or Boston is between 13 and 20 persons per hectare; in London, Amsterdam or Berlin the comparable figure is between 50 and 65. The lower the population density of the city, the greater is the need for a private car, next to the airplane the most wasteful form of transport in terms of energy use. Energy use per head in Detroit is 65 Mj, five times higher than London with 13 Mj. The figures are similar for other cities.

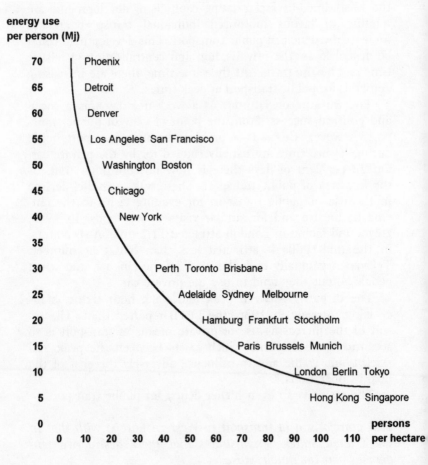

energy use per person (Mj)

70 Phoenix

65 Detroit

60 Denver

55 Los Angeles San Francisco

50 Washington Boston

45 Chicago

40 New York

35

30 Perth Toronto Brisbane

25 Adelaide Sydney Melbourne

20 Hamburg Frankfurt Stockholm

15 Paris Brussels Munich

10 London Berlin Tokyo

5 Hong Kong Singapore

0

0 10 20 30 40 50 60 70 80 90 100 110 **persons per hectare**

Figure 10.1 Population Density and Energy Use

Figure 10.1, illustrates this dramatic situation.[89] It is the result of a steady dissolution of traditional dense urban structures and the dispersal of people over wider areas. During the previous period, there was only one tendency towards the dissolution of traditional urban structures – the depopulation of city centres and the move to the suburbs. In the modern autopia, however, there are a number of often conflicting disintegrative tendencies, all of them potentially very destructive and all of them made possible by the increasing dominance of individual motorised mobility.

The German parliament's Commission of Enquiry into Protection of the Earth's Atmosphere described this development in its 1994 report:

As a result of the possibilities of individual transport, new settlements can be established today on green sites in the surrounding countryside, no longer limited by the historical axes of development. Up to the present, the road connections have been provided by the state. In spite of this dispersive and supra-regional relocation, the big core cities retain their central importance. In fact, as providers of new services, their importance could increase. This, in turn, will attract even more traffic into the centres which will accentuate the deterioration of living conditions in these cities and lead to an even greater exodus of the urban population.[90]

Part III

The Car Society:
Myth, Mania and Machismo

I love cars. I love my father's cars and my mother's cars.
I loved my first car. I adored and worshipped my MGB –
I even polished the copper plates on the engine. I love
cars of all shapes and sizes. Cars are a good thing.

Robert Key, Transport Minister,
in *Auto Express* magazine, July 1993

Mrs Thatcher three years ago lauded 'the great car
economy'.

Geoffrey Lean,
in the *Observer*, 15 August 1993

The first claim of the car society is that the car is for everyone: everyone either has a car or wants to have one. In fact,
only two-thirds of all adults have a driving licence. If we
include those below the age of 18, then only half the population is potentially car-mobile. And this statistic is true for
the most highly motorised countries of Western Europe.
Likewise, the possession of a driving licence does not auto-
matically mean possession of a car. In Germany, only 50 per
cent of adults have access to a car on a daily basis. This
means that only a minority of the whole population has
independent access to a car in their daily life.[1]
Estimates for the future also indicate that, even in countries
with the highest car density, only a minority of the population,
around 50 per cent of adults, will have daily access to a car.
Those without a car will be a large minority. It would be

impossible to either finance or organise a transport system and a road network in which a large majority of the population made daily use of a car. As André Gorz once said, such a transport system would be similar, in principle, to every French family having a villa with a private beach on the Cote d'Azur.[2] Or, we could add, similar to every ski enthusiast driving straight to the best ski slopes in his own car. But such were, in fact, the promises and ideals of the 1960s. An article on the Swiss ski resort of St Moritz in the British magazine *Country Life* in 1964 ended with the statement: 'It must be confessed that the Engadine lifts are less comfortably linked. To get the best out of the St Moritz skiing it is an advantage, and a great saving of time, to have a car.'[3]

The results are well known. The offer of a private villa on the beach became the rabbit-hutch apartments and the concrete hotel blocks of the Cote d'Azur, Costa Brava, Mallorca, Crete, Cyprus and Tenerife. The coastal regions that the first motorway fanatics forgot – such as Cinque Terre in Italy – now advertise themselves as 'car free'. The Swiss ski resorts now have to strictly limit car access or, as in the case of Zermatt, pride themselves on being totally car free. The car's promise of 'freedom for everyone' has given us the familiar and universal traffic congestion, the rush-hour and weekend traffic jam.

With such a massive gap between promise and reality, a grand ideology is needed to help close that gap. This is the ideology of the car society, an ideology which expresses itself in such statements as: the car makes us mobile, the car is an advanced high-tech product, the car creates more free time, the car is a rational transport system, the car is essential. There are, in addition, the psychic, social-psychological and patriarchal aspects that are inherent to this form of transport: if the citizens in our society have no significant influence on the politics or social conditions that determine their existence and their consciousness, they have at least the substitute satisfaction of the private car. If our society creates alienation, then the resultant aggression can be deflected in a manner that does not challenge the dominant structures. If the great majority of society lives in conditions in which they are dominated, then the car offers at least the male section of society the chance to optimise its patriarchal power within the existing framework or relations.

11

Necessary and Artificial Transport

A week of action was launched yesterday to highlight the plight of the small grocers. *Independent Grocer* magazine, which is leading the campaign, has written to Mr John Gummer, the Environment Secretary, calling for a moratorium on superstore developments, and to Mr Heseltine, the Trade and Industry Secretary, warning that 'endless bureaucracy' is crippling small grocery businesses. It says that tens of thousands of small grocers have closed in the past two decades, although the sick, the elderly, the disabled and those without transport rely on them.

Financial Times, 17 March 1993

According to the German Ministry for Urban Construction, 96 per cent of all motorised travel is local, i.e. within a distance of less than 50 km. One-third of all car journeys are within a radius of less than 3 km, an ideal distance for walking or cycling.[4]

It may well be that the construction of long-distance motorways and the run-down of long-distance rail connections have contributed to the fact that millions of people bought a car. But by far the greatest proportion of motorised travel is local and it is in this area of local travel that there has been the greatest increase – in and around towns and shopping centres. A part of this may be due, as the sociologist and psychoanalyst, Alexander Mitscherlich, has argued, to the fact that the car is not just a means of transport but also a 'status symbol, a shelter for lovers, and a drug for those with a strong addiction to movement'.[5] The explosive increase in motorised travel is a product of structural developments in our society that have little to do with 'greater mobility'. It is the result of what I would describe as 'artificial' or 'enforced' transport.

The Segregated City

Artificial transport was created wherever the car society established itself. The development followed a general pattern. Industrialisation led to flight from the land and the growth of urban centres. In these urban centres, people generally lived near their place of work. The development of local public transport made it possible to have the workplace a little further from home. The advent of the car, with the simultaneous demolition of the local public transport network, led to a radical relocation of urban populations. This happened in the US in the first half of this century with the radical separation of home and workplace, decline in local public transport and the destruction of local recreation areas. Distances travelled every day became longer, making the car a necessity. In Western Europe, this development was not significant until after the Second World War. The major change began in the 1950s when buildings and streets in city centres began to be taken over by business and commercial outlets. This process accelerated in the 1960s, when city centres were completely dominated by department stores, offices, banks, building societies and insurance companies. The earlier population was forced into the suburbs where they lived in high-rise blocks or, as was more frequently the case, on large estates of semi-detached houses.[6] The spatial separation of home and work now took place on a massive scale. The shift of populations from the centres of the big cities had already begun before the advent of the car but, with the car's arrival, this development accelerated and affected not only big but also medium and small towns. The new suburban developments were also beyond the reach of the existing urban tramways and, in many cases, had little or no access to any form of public transport.

The massive increase in suburban car-owners made a complete mess of urban planning and created what, in the 1960s, was already being described as urban transport chaos.

The official responsible for urban planning in the German
city of Hannover wrote at the beginning of the 1970s:

> In 1948 we had a ratio of 68.6 residents to one car. Our
> plan for the reconstruction of Hannover assumed a future
> ratio of ten to one, as was also assumed in countries like
> Sweden and Switzerland at the time. But now we have
> already reached a ratio of four to one.[7]

However, as the planners were overtaken by developments, and
the ratio deteriorated, there was no fundamental change in
urban construction or transport policy. And it was not city
planners who raised the alarm in the 1970s, but a few sociolo-
gists and psychologists.[8] The new streets were built to accommodate the extra cars. From the mid-1960s there was a street-
building boom: first the four-lane outer ring, then the various
inner 'rings' that soon began to choke the big cities. Whoever
sows streets harvests traffic, and the asphalt city was soon
taken over by the car.

This was followed by a new development which began in
the United States: a ring of shopping malls grew up on the
outskirts of the city. With their massive car parks, their
appeal was to the motorised customer. The shopping malls
were followed by furniture centres, DIY centres, and other
similar outlets. Shopping moved from the locality to the
'green spaces' beyond the town. The miles to be travelled
increased enormously.

Finally, the offices and factories themselves were built in
the new green spaces or relocated there. In *Country Life* this
was seen as

> a major advance towards the American ideal in office and
> laboratory planning. In brief, these ideals consist of
> imposing buildings in attractive settings and interiors
> designed for maximum comfort. ... They are achieved by
> acquiring a beautiful site and by using air-conditioning
> and artificial lighting instead of, and not in addition to,
> natural light and air.[9]

This 'segregated' or 'demixed' urban society required even
more travel. The new streets and motorways, the suburban

sprawl, the shopping malls, the new industries and service centres destroyed the traditional areas of recreation in and around the cities. Travelling 'to the countryside' was now a much bigger undertaking and required a car – more traffic, new roads, more destruction.

The segregated city broke up the original spatial unity of residence, work, shopping and recreation, creating new travel needs. Developments in public transport promoted this pattern. The urban trams, the backbone of public transport in most of the cities of Europe and America before the Second World War, were demolished. In the cities of West Germany between 1970 and 1990, more than 2,000 km of tram lines were removed, more than half of the entire network. There were 526 km of tram lines in London before the Second World War, accounting for about one-third of public transport and bigger than the underground system.[10] The underground or subway system is no substitute for the tram, nor is the system of urban trains (the German *S-Bahn*). With their star form, radiating out to the suburbs from the centre, these latter systems are more appropriate to the 'segregated' city and actually promote this type of development. With the longer distances between stations and the more difficult access (which includes underground tunnels and escalators), the underground/subway and the urban trains are more appropriate for travelling these longer distances. But there is seldom a comfortable and efficient public transport system that links the train or subway station with local streets. The system of urban segregation therefore puts enormous pressure on households to purchase a car and, in many cases, a second car.

Urban streets, now with four or more lanes, often with a barrier in the middle, are increasingly difficult to cross. Pedestrian crossings are spaced far apart. Streets, once lines of communication, are becoming dividing lines: movement is generally only possible up and down one side and traditional communicative connections are being destroyed.

Large numbers of cars and major roadways are synonomous with loneliness, with having few friends and acquaintances. This was confirmed in a study carried out in San Francisco. The study looked at residential areas with different levels of traffic. In areas of high vehicle density (16,000 vehicles per day, 1,900 vehicles during rush hours) the inhabitants claimed to have an average of 0.9 friends and 3.1 acquaintances each. The statements that met with the highest levels of agreement included: 'This isn't a friendly street, nobody helps you'; 'People only use the streets as a way of getting somewhere'; 'People are afraid to go on the streets because of the large amount of traffic'. In areas with lower levels of raffic (2,000 vehicles per day, 200 vehicles in rush hours) the inhabitants had an average of 3 friends and 6.3 acquaintances each. The statements that met with the most approval included: 'I feel at home in this locality. The people here are warm and I don't feel alone'; 'Everyone knows everyone else'; 'A friendly street – people gossip, wash their cars. People drop in for a visit'.[11]

Already in the early 1970s there were complaints about the destructive effects of this kind of traffic and about the absence of serious planning. The German daily, the *Frankfurter Allgemeine Zeitung* wrote at the time:

> The tragedy of our cities in the car era is that the loss of character has been greater even than that caused by the fire bombing during the war. There is no historically significant big city in Germany today that hasn't been changed beyond recognition by this termite-like army of cars.[12]

As Alexander Mitscherlich once said: 'operation (transport planning) successful, patient (city life) dead'.[13]

From Utopia to Autopia

What were the principal causes of this irrational development that created artificial travel and damaged the quality of life? One of its causes was certainly the fact that most planners and architects from the mid-1930s accepted the basic concept of the segregated city. The triumph of the car in North America and the effect of this on North American urban development and highway construction were a major influence.

It began with the Athens Charter of 1933, an international congress of architects that declared the segregation of different functions (living, working, physical and mental recreation, circulation) as the key element of modern urban construction. The Athens Charter stipulated, in Article 77, that: 'The keys to town planning are in the four functions: Living, Working, Recreation, Circulation'. Article 47 added that 'the industrial sectors should be independent of the living quarters and separated from each other by verdant zones'. The Charter also said about these living spaces, in Article 23, that they should occupy 'the best sites within the urban area, with respect to topography, climatic conditions, orientation for sun, and available green spaces'. According to a commentary that accompanied the Charter: 'The raw materials of urban construction are sun, space, green space, steel, and concrete – and in that order.'[14]

According to Le Corbusier, the most important architect of this school: 'the conception of "Living, Working, Cultivation of the Body and Mind, Circulation" is antagonistic to the existing framework of road, pavement, street alignment, enclosed courts, and embellishments'. He rejected the rows of houses along traditional streets, houses in which 'the windows of half the facades open directly on this tumult (of our present cities); windows of the other half give on to courts, more or less abominable'. In what he described as the 'town-planning revolution':

> The house must leave the street (and the notion of street alignment must be abandoned). The interior court must be repudiated. A sufficient number of dwellings must be assembled in one building to liberate, by their concentration on a point, a considerable area of open ground. The dwelling units would have to be of an adequate size, i.e. for 1,000, 1,500 or 2,700 inhabitants.[15]

Radical solutions were the order of the day. All of Le Corbusier's model cities had this in common: 'a motorway that crosses right through the whole city'. He is impressed by 'the sensational highway crossovers in New York and the parkways in Connecticut'. He is enthused by urban transport arteries that run underground and by massive highways mounted on concrete stilts:

> Stilts, 'the key to the problem of circulation posed by great cities' (to quote Professor Maurin of the Faculty of Science in Paris, 1933), have been regarded, since 1937,

as the essential element of the new official edifices of Rio de Janeiro, bringing with them wherever they are used a beginning of the liberation of the ground. One fine day, the city fathers will comprehend, and stilts will be recognised as the indispensable foundation of town planning. The rule will appear in all its simple clarity: high blocks of dwellings, palaces, schools, houses, etc. will be orientated according to the sun and the best view; the ground, level or undulating, will be furrowed by communications entirely independent of the buildings.[16]

The German urban architect, Walter Schwagenscheidt, who, like the majority of his West European colleagues, shared the ideas of Le Corbusier, wrote in the mid-1950s:

Houses can no longer get away from the car. Where there are houses, there will be traffic. ... Every apartment will be able to have a window that looks out to the motorway. It will be exciting to watch the cars as they rush past and overtake each other, one travelling faster than the other.[17]

In the view of these city planners, public transport would have to be situated away from the space given to the car. According to Fritz Jaspers, writing at the beginning of the 1960s:

American experts are of the view that public transport in the future will have to be situated at a second level, mainly underground. ... The earlier view that a subway could only be feasible for a city with more than one million inhabitants is probably no longer valid. ... There is no doubt that the costs would be enormous and, up to now, the financing and realisation of such a project has seemed impossible. But we can no longer evade this rather unpleasant necessity. ...[18]

Looked at from the perspective of the 1990s, these earlier concepts of the city planners and architects may seem naive. Any criticism of these conceptions, however, would have to be relativised in at least four ways. First, these conceptions of urban construction were formulated at a time when there was little critical opposition, least of all with respect to urban construction and transport. For everyone, including the big majority of the traditional organisations of the labour movement, the road that led to the car society was the road that led to a prosperous society.

Second, the motivation of these urban planners and architects was an eminently social one: living conditions in the inner cities for the mass of the wage-earning population were quite inhuman during the first three decades of this century. Compared with the cramped living quarters, with no bath and an external toilet, in narrow, dirty and impoverished streets, the high-rise blocks and suburban estates appeared as a desirable alternative. Le Corbusier was very aware of the alienation of people in their modern urban environments:

> The modern age is spread before them, sparkling and radiant – on the far side of the barrier. In their own homes where they live in a precarious ease, since their remuneration bears no relation to the quality of their work, they find their uncleanly old snail-shell, and they cannot even think of having a family. If they do so, there will begin the slow martyrdom that we all know. These people too claim their rights to a machine for living in, which shall be in all simplicity a *human* thing.
>
> Both the worker and the intellectual are precluded from following their deepest instincts in regard to the family; each and every day they make use of the brilliant and effective tools that the age has provided, but they are not enabled thereby to use them for themselves. Nothing could be more discouraging or more irritating. Nothing is prepared. We may well say: Architecture or Revolution.[19]

Third, it would be wrong to assume that today's unfriendly and inhuman urban structures are identical with the naive models of these city planners and architects. Where these models were naive is in their assumption that these 'green cities', with plenty of nature, big parks and children's playgrounds, were compatible with the car society.

Fourth, it was the combination of these conceptions with an economic order and urban structure exclusively oriented towards profit and rent that led to the urban destruction and quadrupling of traffic that we are familiar with, that led, not to the utopia of these early planners, but to what Mitscherlich has named the 'autopia'.

The objective tendencies of the car society, tendencies that unfolded, as it were, behind the backs of these architects and planners, were partly the product of the specific property relations of these societies: it was private property and speculation in both land and real estate that determined developments in modern urban centres. The importance of city centres for business meant that land prices and rent rose at a phenomenal rate in these areas. It was the lower land prices outside the city centres that later attracted the shopping malls and cut-price supermarkets to these locations. A similar pattern was to emerge in the family-house construction boom. In most of the industrialised Western countries, this form of housing was publicly supported (with tax concessions) and was promoted as the ideal form of housing for the middle classes. The effect on traffic was inflationary as the city expanded relentlessly into the greenbelt.

City and local government administrations also supported and promoted this relocation and dislocation of urban populations. With slogans such as 'greater efficiency' and 'greater savings', most public administrative functions were centralised, regions and smaller towns were dissolved and fused into larger conurbations, smaller local recreational facilities were replaced by large expensive centralised projects (recreation complexes). These developments did much to erode the feelings of local community and added, once more, to the total amount of traffic.

These structural changes that have been described so far, and which have led to dramatic increases in the amount of travel necessary for the average citizen, are not changes that have now come to an end. These changes are part of an ongoing process and, in different periods, can move in diametrically opposite directions.

The early phase of the car society, with its segregation of residence, work and recreation, created new centres and promoted a relocation of urban populations. But these new structures were themselves soon overtaken. The city of St. Louis, Olympic city in 1904 and then the fourth biggest city in the US, lost half of its population between 1950 and

1980. Between 1970 and 1980, after the car society had fully established itself in the US, cities such as Buffalo, Cleveland, Detroit and St. Louis lost 20 per cent of their populations; other cities, such as Baltimore, Atlanta, Boston, Chicago, Cincinnati, Kansas City, Minneapolis, Philadelphia, Pittsburgh, Washington and New York lost more than 10 per cent of their populations in the same decade.

In the recent period, new structures of residence, work, and recreation are being established in what appears to be an anarchic process. A study by Andreas Falke identifies a number of reasons for these structural changes in US society at the end of the twentieth century. One of the main reasons is the decline in the traditional industries and the decay of the old city centres. Federal subsidy programmes promote the construction of new industrial sites instead of the maintenance of older ones. Land prices also favour relocation of industrial sites away from the cities. The better-paid professional classes now prefer to live outside the decaying cities, leading in turn to a decline in income for the urban administrations and further inner-city decay. The impoverishment of the old urban centres and the decline in public transport lead to a declining mobility for city dwellers and accelerate the process of social impoverishment. The relocation of new industries to the less densely inhabited green spaces leads then to a dramatic increase in traffic in these new areas, where all the old mistakes are repeated.

The costs of this enforced mobility are partly socialised (publicly financed motorway construction and the future costs of repair to environmental damage) and partly paid for by the individual consumers. The transport costs of the individual are increased dramatically and this is a generalised phenomenon that results from the new spatial order. The city dweller,

> in order to be able to live in the city, has to reunite the different aspects of life that the profit criterion has separated. He is forced to overcome ever greater distances. All travel that goes beyond what could be considered as individually and socially necessary and reasonable, we describe as *enforced mobility*.

The German authors, Linder, Maurer and Resch, from whose

book, *Erzwungene Mobilität* (*Enforced Mobility*), published in the mid-1970s, the above quotation is taken, see this development as an extension of commodity production into spheres wherein previously the relevant goods had been freely available to all:

> Industrial commodity production now sells to the consumer what it had previously taken from him elsewhere. Changes in the way urban dwellers spend their free time, the loss of recreational spaces in the cities, the break-up of traditional communicative spaces, the decline in local pubs/cafes, squares, and parks leads to an increase in the sale of 'private environment' and new consumer goods: larger houses or apartments to make up for the loss of a natural environment; fitness training equipment to make up for the loss of physical movement.[20]

The city of Munich provides a positive example of the importance of the kind of functional unity we have described. In the very heart of the city is a large park, the English Garden. According to the Munich city authorities, the existence of this park means 30,000 fewer car trips to the countryside every weekend; in the course of a year this amounts to a reduction in travel of 200 million person-kilometres.[21] The preservation of the functional unity of residence and free-time recreation brings three advantages to the city: the park is a 'green lung', improving the quality of air and counteracting the harmful effects of the car; it helps to reduce the amount of traffic in the city and surrounding countryside; it improves the quality of life for residents of the city.

This is not the tendency, however, in most big cities. In Berlin, which recently became the capital city of a united Germany, the big park in the city centre, the Tiergarten, is now threatened by new buildings above ground and the construction of a massive network of tunnels underground. In other cities, most of the big urban parks have disappeared. An article in the English magazine, *Country Life*, 'The Vanished Great Gardens of London', begins with the following statement: 'The great gardens of the past, with their splendid orchards, vineyards, shady walks and beds of sweet-scented herbs and flowers, have gone forever, lost in a maze of crowded streets and modern buildings.'[22]

The two sectors that benefit from this segregation of urban life are the owners of real estate and the car industry. The price of property in the old and new city centres has risen dramatically while the value of land in previously rural areas has increased many times as a result of new-town construction, industrial relocation and the increase in extra-urban shopping centres. The development of the segregated city also made the purchase of a car essential for many millions of citizens who previously would have got by without one.

What is Mobility?

Mobility, as an improvement in the quality of life, should not be reduced to number of miles travelled. Mobility has to be measured rather in terms of goals achieved. The decisive questions are: how many reasonable movements from one place to another have people made, either as a result of individual desire or the requirements of society, and how much time do people devote to these? I will deal with the question of time below. I will look first at the question of travel or spatial movement itself.

The different growth rates for distance travelled (person-kilometres) and the number of journeys made is instructive. In the period between 1950 and 1980, the annual amount of travel, of person-kilometres, rose in West Germany from 84.7 billion to 600 billion, a 700 per cent increase. In the same period, the number of journeys made increased from a yearly rate of 8.3 million to 37 million, an increase of 450 per cent. In other words, the number of journeys made increased at a much smaller rate than the distance travelled (person-km). The number of journeys made, the product of human purpose or necessity, expresses a qualitative determination of mobility. The distance travelled, the number of person-kilometres, expresses a purely quantitative determination. While distance travelled is important for the estimation of social cost, the number of trips is more important in an attempt to assess mobility as a human need.

But a more than fourfold increase in mobility, thus under-stood, simply did not happen. A large part of the registered increase in distance and journeys resulted from the fact that journeys previously taken by foot or by bicycle were now being taken by car or bus. Since journeys by foot or bicycle are simply not expressed in the statistics, which only express motorised travel, the scale of the increase in mobility is deceptive. In some cities, in the 1980s and 1990s, there was a marked increase in the use of bicycles, with a decrease in car use (although the number of cars increased). In terms of the usual statistics, this would have amounted to a decline in mobility. But no transport minister has ever made such an absurd claim, although they continue to base their arguments on a definition of mobility linked exclusively to motorisation. In general, how-ever, the trend, following the advent of mass motorisation and the destruction of people-friendly urban structures, has been towards a greater use of motor transport, even in travel over short distances previously covered on foot or by bicycle. One study has shown that one in every three journeys covers a maximum of three kilometres.[23] When we take into account that a good 700 metres (roughly 23 per cent of the distance covered) is devoted to finding a parking place and getting from the parking place to the intended destination, then we have to conclude that the car is actually quite an inefficient way of covering such distances. A three-kilometre journey is, however, ideal for a bicycle, which could cover the distance in seven to ten minutes. In a pedestrian-friendly environment, the same distance could be covered on foot in 30 to 45 minutes. A great part of the alleged increase in distance travelled is simply accounted for by the motorisation of routes previously covered on foot or by bicycle.

The actual increase can be accounted for in terms of artifi-cial transport, in other words, the enforced mobility brought about by the kinds of structural changes that have been described earlier. These are journeys that result, not from some clearly defined human need, but from a specific irrational organisation of social life. For instance, in the period 1960 to 1976 in West Germany, journeys to and from work increased from 5.6 billion to 9.5 billion, an increase of around 70 per cent.[24] During this whole period, however, the number of workers remained constant at around 26 million; holiday periods were extended and Saturday work ended for most people. In absolute terms, fewer people actually went to work. The increase in work-related traffic can only be explained by the fact that many people who previously had been able to get to their factory or office on foot or by bicycle now had to use some motorised form of transport. It was only when they had made this change that they were counted as 'traffic'.

A similar picture emerges when we look at shopping or getting to school and university. Although the growth in population in this period was only around 9 per cent, the increase in shopping trips was over 30 per cent, and this during a period when the trend towards once-a-week (weekend) shopping should actually have led to a decrease. Shopping had become motorised. Travel by school and university students increased by more than 300 per cent, although the number of students increased by only 60 per cent. The increase in student traffic was a result of the amalgamation of smaller schools, the expansion of school busing, the greater danger in riding to school by bicycle, the construction of university campuses and student residences outside of the urban centres, an increase of car ownership among students and increasing pressure on parents to drive their children to and from school and university. Getting to school has also been motorised.

If we incorporate all of these changes into the estimates, we would have to conclude that there was actually very little increase in mobility. The workers go to and from work five days a week (previously six), while the students continue to go to and from school and university. The average householder goes shopping three or four times a week. At the weekend, the average citizen makes one or two trips to the countryside or to visit friends and relatives and, during the week, may go out again, for instance to the cinema. This was how it was in 1929, in 1950, and it is not essentially different in 1995. It is only in the sphere of holiday travel that there has been any significant change. Although there has been a big increase in holiday travel, this still only constitutes about 1 per cent of the number of journeys made. The big change in holiday travel has been in the number of miles travelled; between 1960 and today this has doubled. This is a result of the greater distances that are now travelled to holiday resorts. Whether the recreational value, for the average British holiday-maker, is significantly higher in Greece, Spain or Tenerife than it is in Scotland, the Lake District, Ireland, or Cornwall, cannot be so simply answered. Holiday travel is a commodity produced and sold in a highly competitive and deregulated market. In the summer of 1994, the British daily, the *Guardian*, reported that 'it would cost twice as much for a family to stay in Penzance, Cornwall, for a fortnight, compared with a similar period in Spain – including air fares'.[25]

The increase in mobility, therefore, is really a myth. Traditional non-motorised journeys to work, school and shopping have become motorised and, in the segregated cities, the distances travelled have increased dramatically. The cost, in terms of quality of life, has been high.

12

The Car as Advanced Technology

Meet Warrant Officer Ron Audrain. Ron is an engine nut. He lives, breathes and talks cars. Even in his sleep. Just the sort of chap you'd ask along with you when making an attempt to drive round the world in record time. A not inconsiderable feat just achieved by two teams from the Royal Army Ordinance Corps. Their cars? Both of them Rover 827 Si Saloons. They drove 26,000 miles, crossed six continents and were back in just thirty-nine days. And Ron, bless him, along with his box of spares, followed them all the way. The trouble is, he needn't have bothered. The spares box remained unopened for the whole journey. Which left Ron feeling like a spare part himself.

Advertisement for Rover in
the *Guardian*, 23 July 1990

The American author and consumer campaigner, Ralph Nader, has, since the mid-1960s, uncovered a large number of major structural faults in particular car models, forcing the big car companies to recall many models. In 1966, for instance, as a result of Nader's campaign, General Motors was forced to recall over 1 million cars because of a manufacturing error in the braking system. In 1970, in West Germany, a quarter of a million Ford Escorts and Capris had to be recalled. In 1985, Volkswagen had to recall 1 million cars manufactured between March 1983 and May 1984, about one-third of all VW production during this period. In early 1995, Opel/General Motors, along with a number of other car manufacturers, had to recall many hundreds of thousands of cars because of the danger of an explosion when filling with petrol. Without the kind of campaigning carried out by Nader and others, many more thousands of people would have died in road accidents attributed, as in almost all cases, to 'human error'. What Nader's investigations have demonstrated is that the technology of cars makes this form of transport extremely dangerous. It is a technology which has not made any significant advance in the past 100 years.

A very comprehensive critique of car technology has been published in Germany by Jörg Linser, a highly qualified machine construction engineer who worked for some years in the car industry before becoming professor for propulsion technology and transport at a German university. His study is titled *Unser Auto – eine geplante Fehlkonstruktion (Our Car – A Planned Faulty Design)*.[26]

Contrary to all propaganda from the car manufacturers, energy consumption of cars is today more or less the same as in the 1950s and energy consumption for each person-kilometre is even higher than it was half a century ago. According to official figures from the German transport ministry, average car consumption of energy reached its peak in the mid-1980s with 10.9 litres per 100 kilometres. This had gone down slightly to 10.1 litres per 100 kilometres by 1993. These official government figures were 30 to 50 per cent higher that the figures published by the car manufacturers. This slight decline in energy use per car also has to be set against the declining rate of occupancy per car. In the 1950s and 1960s average car occupancy was 2 persons; this has since shrunk to 1.2 persons. The trend to heavier cars is likewise irrational. This was the view of the *Financial Times* in 1995: 'At a time when we should be worried sick by pollution and the rapid drain of oil resources, engines are again of the same wasteful size as in the industry's dark ages, suggesting that their manufacturers are mad.'[27]

This can be only partly explained by the fact that an increasing number of car-owners are opting for greater horse power. With improved road quality, energy use should actually have declined by about 15 or 20 per cent. The ongoing high energy use is even more surprising when we realise that in other areas of energy use there have been considerable savings, especially since the oil crisis of 1973.

The life expectancy of a car has also gone down continu-

ously since the 1950s. Whereas cars built in the early 1950s
had a life expectancy of 14 years, that had sunk to 10 years by
the early 1970s and remains at that level today. Average
annual distance travelled per car went down in the same period
from 15,000 km to 12,000 km. Linser has demonstrated that
practically all car parts today are manufactured with a life
expectancy of 100,000 km, many of them, such as clutch and
brakes, even less. What has become clear is that these are
conscious decisions. All of these components are capable of
being manufactured to last three to five times longer, which is
indeed the case in lorries, buses, and other industrial
machines. The price increase that would result from using
longer-life components in cars is insignificant compared to the
longer-term savings in the economy as a whole that would
result from doubling or tripling the average life of the car.
Making car bodies rust-free, for instance, would add a maximum of 400 dollars to the cost of a car.

According to Linser, the car manufacturers have 'in a very
suspect fashion, sought to establish consensus among themselves about the manufacture of car engines that have greater
revolutions per minute (rpm)' but smaller cylinder size.[28] The
Volkswagen Beetle reached its peak with 4,000 rpm, but by
1975 the 50hp Golf had reached 6,000 rpm. It is a simple
consequence of the laws of physics that the wear and tear of an
engine increases with increasing movement of the piston in
the cylinder.

What becomes clear from any objective study of the car as
technological product is the fact that the basic construction
principles involved have not significantly advanced for over a
century. There has been no major innovation in car technology
this century. During the same period, the railways developed
two completely new forms of traction and, with the advanced
high-speed trains of the 1990s, have made a significant qualitative advance. There has also been a technological revolution in
aerospace technology. In its basic constructional elements,
however, the car of the 1990s is not qualitatively different from
the car of 1900. Linser's assessment: 'There is no other industrial branch of comparable importance in which there has been
no real innovation. In spite of this, the car industry is presented in the professional literature as in the vanguard of the
most modern technology.'[29]

The combustion engine – similar to the steam engine in many respects – was developed in the first instance for stationary use. Built into the moving automobile, it had to have incorporated in it a number of technical 'crutches'. 'Long since overtaken by technological progress, these crutches, which, in their structure and mode of functioning are typical of the late 19th century, are still part of the modern car.' An example of this antiquated technology is the clutch. Linser suggests that a hydrostatic transmission, of the type used for many years in agricultural machinery, locomotives and industrial vehicles, would have provided a better technology. The combination of a combustion engine and a hydrostatic transmission would make it possible to run the motor at different car speeds while maintaining a constant number of revolutions. According to Linser: 'Every combustion engine gives its best performance at a certain number of revolutions. ... A hydrostatic transmission would make it possible to maintain the motor constantly at this optimal number of revolutions.' This would mean lower energy use, lower toxic emission and less noise pollution.[30]

All of these possible innovations are well known in the research and development departments of the big car companies. They are, in fact, used by these same companies in the industrial vehicles which they deliver to the manufacturing industry. They are not used, however, in the mass-produced car. When we look at the descriptions of 'new features' in cars that are presented at the car shows in Paris and elsewhere, we find that these are external, stylistic and rather superficial innovations. In a report from the Paris Car Show we find, for example, that the

new Renault creation for the year 2000, named 'Megane', is electronically equipped and resembles both an airplane and an automatic game machine. The doors have no handles and no visible locks: they are opened noiselessly by infra-red remote control. The rear-view mirror is replaced by a camera and screen. Installed computers allow the driver to reserve a hotel room while en route or request travel information. The boot/trunk pulls out like a drawer for easier loading.

Similar descriptions are given for Peugeot's new sports car, the 'Oxia', which has air conditioning and automatic tyre pressure control.[31]

The *Financial Times* described the Mercedes Benz S-Class as a dinosaur:

> Take the Mercedes 600 as the ne-plus-ultra-wagen of the company chairman (and of the banana politicians too). Its twelve cylinders and the best part of four hundred horses can whisk him to a mile a minute in six seconds, but does he really want G-forces to distort his tender liver and compress it with other soft organs in the rear upper regions of his rib cage? Is there even an occasion between his house in the leafy purlieus of nether Kensington and his office near Cornhill when his two-and-a-half tons of metal Behemoth can be urged to even half its maximum speed of 160 m/h? ... Such is the vanity of men that the big car has become the Ship of Fools, the silly self-flattery of men who see in it the implications of wealth, power and status – transitory things when attached to objects of brief fashion and immediately declining value.[32]

Speed Limit: The German Controversy

The Federal Republic of Germany is the only highly motorised country in which there is no speed limit on motorways (see Table 12.1).

In the discussion of German demands for the Europe-wide introduction of the catalytic converter, the other European governments have been very critical of this aspect of German policy. The German car industry's demand that the no-speed-limit rule has to be maintained in order to demonstrate the high quality of German cars has been met with the counter-claim that this would constitute an unfair advantage for Germany according to the international agreements regulating competition.

The claim that speed limits are, in any case, neither observed nor enforced is only partly true. This happens in those areas where the police and officials do not bother to enforce the limits and where public opinion regards speeding as

Table 12.1. National Speed Limits (km per hour)

Country	(a)	Speed limit (b)	(c)	Alcohol limit*
Germany	50	100	–	0.8
Belgium	60	90	120	0.5
Denmark	60	80	110	0.8
France	60	90	130	0.7
Greece	50	80	120	0.5
Britain	48	96	110	0.8
Italy	50	80	130	0.8
Netherlands	50	80	120	0.5
Norway	50	80	90	0.5
Austria	50	100	130	0.8
Sweden	50	70	110	0.2
Switzerland	50	100	120	0.8
Russia	60	90	90	0.0
Spain	60	90	120	0.8
Czech Republic	60	90	110	0.0
Turkey	50	90	90	0.0
Hungary	60	80	120	0.0
Japan	50	70–80	70–100	
US	40–50	98	98	

(a) residential (b) non-residential (c) motorway/freeway
* in December 1994

a minor offence or racing on the highways as a male virtue. This is often the case in Italy, France and Spain. But in the US a mile over the limit can cost $50 and most commentators agree that the speed limit is generally observed in Britain. In Japan every car has an inbuilt alarm which goes off whenever the car exceeds the 100 km/h limit. In addition, there exists in Japan another effective speed limitation: more than one-third of all roads are not asphalted. Economic programmes for the 1990s are trying to remedy this.[33]

It was Ronald Reagan who perhaps raised some doubts about the embarrassing lead which the Federal Republic of Germany enjoys in this field. On his official trip to Germany in 1985, between his visit to the concentration camp in Bergen-Belsen and his visit to the SS cemetery in Bitburg, he was asked by a reporter: 'Mr. President, if you could really do whatever you wanted to, what would you do here in Bonn?' Reagan's face lit up with enthusiasm and he replied: 'I'd drive on the autobahn. To drive very fast for a while, that would be fun. Before I became president and before I became governor of California, I came to Munich with Richard Nixon. We drove on the autobahn. It was fantastic.'[34]

The major argument for the introduction and strict enforcement of speed limits is its effect on the number of accidents and deaths on the roads. It is high speed which is the main cause of road accidents. In all countries the number of accidents and road fatalities declined sharply when speed limits were introduced. In the US, the introduction of the 55 m/h limit reduced road fatalities by 20 per cent.[35] According to the US Department of Transport in Washington, there were four times as many road accident fatalities in Germany as in the US in the mid-1980s, relative to the amount of traffic.[36] In Denmark, the number of road fatalities declined by almost 50 per cent following the introduction of the speed limit.[37]

One of the first measures of the Nazi state was the abolition of speed limits for all vehicles. Following this, the number of road accidents reached new records. In 1937 and 1938 there were 8,000 road deaths each year. Speed limits were imposed after 1945 but were lifted again in 1952, whereupon the number of road deaths jumped from 7,750 to 11,299, an increase of 45 per cent. In 1957 local speed limits of 50 km/h were introduced, which reduced the number of yearly fatalities by 1,000.[38]

A similar development took place in the aftermath of German unification. When the previous speed limit on East German motorways was lifted in 1990, the number of road fatalities doubled. The increase in fatalities on East German roads in 1990 was ten times the number of people that had been killed by GDR border guards in the three previous decades.

According to German police statistics, the principal cause of injuries and deaths on the road is 'inappropriate speed'. Some reports suggest that as many as 50 per cent of all accidents are caused by speeding. The link is clear: neither a perfect braking system nor human ability can alter the fact that the braking distance for a car travelling 50 km/h is around 30 metres, for 100 km/h it is 80 metres, and for 160 km/h it is 200 metres. If a car travelling 160 km/h has to brake in a space of 150 metres, it will still hit its object at 68 km/h, enough to seriously injure or kill car occupants.[39]

The repeated claim that the more expensive cars, which also claim to have the best safety standards, are a better protection against road accidents is not borne out by the statistics. The figures used by the insurance companies indicate that, in the case of accidents where the driver is at fault, the expensive cars with the greatest speed potential are also the cars that cause the most accidents (for instance, the Jaguar XJS, all Porsche models, the BMW and Audi from the medium and upper range, and the Golf GTI). In the middle we find the classical middle-class cars where the accident rate is average. The lowest number of accidents occur with the smaller and weaker models (the VW Polo, the Mini, the Renault R4, and the Fiat Panda).[40]

In the German debate, however, it is not the number of road accidents and fatalities that are seen as most important – an indication of how unserious this discussion really is. At the centre of the debate is the relation between lower speed and the reduction of toxic emissions.

The federal environment ministry, in the mid-1980s, admitted that the death of the forests in Germany was a result of air pollution. An article in the weekly, *Der Spiegel*, based on figures from the environment ministry, claimed that a reduction of the speed limit on the autobahn to 100 km/h was essential if air quality was to be improved. At speeds above 100 km/h 'the emission of toxins increases rapidly; nitrogen oxide, for instance, goes up from 4.5 to 6.2 grammes per kilometre, carbon monoxide rises from 5.9 to 13.8 grammes'.[41]

A number of scientific studies were published at the time, all of them, with the exception of one study financed by Daimler Benz, agreeing that a speed reduction to 100 km/h on the motorways and to 80 km/h on other roads would bring major savings and cut down significantly on toxic emissions. There was general agreement among all the experts on the potential reductions in nitrogen oxide, the main culprit in the creation of acid rain. Estimates for the reduction in nitrogen oxide caused by a 100–80 km/h speed limit varied from 70,000 to 300,000 tons. The latter figure would represent a reduction of 10 per cent of total nitrogen oxide, 20 per cent of the nitrogen oxide produced by traffic. And such a reduction could be achieved immediately, unlike the medium or long term reductions promised by the catalytic converter.[42]

The Catalytic Converter Demagogy

The debate about speed limits for German motorways, therefore, came to nothing. What developed, instead, was a Europe-wide debate about low-emission cars and a mandatory catalytic converter. The outcome was a new set of EU emission standards that are weaker than those already in operation in the US and Japan. The German car industry celebrated a triple victory: there was to be no speed limit, they could evade a mandatory catalytic converter for new cars, and they could promote their cars in future as low-emission and environment friendly, with major new tax concessions.

The success of the catalytic converter in the US and Japan since the end of the 1970s is not disputed. Between 1972 and 1982 in Japan, air pollutants declined by a third, in spite of the fact that the number of cars increased three-fold during the same period. The source of this decline was the mandatory catalytic converter, combined with strictly enforced speed limits. Just as in Germany and in the rest of Western Europe, the Japanese car lobby, led by Toyota, claimed that the proposed regulations were both technically and financially unachievable. Toyota continued to build its cars without the catalytic converter and it was eventually public pressure and competition from Mazda that forced Toyota to conform. The Toyota chief, Toyoda, was forced to apologise to the Japanese parliament.[43]

Western Europe experienced a similar 'theatre of the absurd' in the mid-1980s. The announcement that the catalytic converter might become mandatory was met with stiff resistance from the car industry, especially from the manufacturers of small- and medium-range cars. Gradually, under German leadership, the European Commission watered down the proposals until they had virtually disappeared. Cars that have reached a low minimum standard for emissions are now sold as 'low emission' cars. The emission standards are much lower than they were in the US in the mid-1970s. The German argument that the other EU partners could not be forced to adopt a higher standard is really a very poor argument, especially for Germany, which has pursued its own national opt-out on the question of speed limits. Austria, Switzerland, Denmark and the other Scandinavian countries also have much tougher emission standards than the EU.

The catalytic converter itself is not really a satisfactory solution to the problem. Basically, it is an apparatus attached externally to the engine which captures or blocks some of the environmentally dangerous substances. These dangerous substances are not themselves reduced at source. Theoretically, the catalytic converter should be able to block 90 per cent of some specific toxic emissions. But there is serious doubt that this will actually be achieved in practice. Catalytic converter-equipped cars, for instance, have to use lead-free petrol. A single filling with leaded petrol, which is cheaper in the US, would render the catalytic converter practically useless, irreparably so.

The catalytic converter also only begins to be effective after the engine has warmed up, in other words, after about three kilometres of driving. On distances of less than one kilometre the catalytic converter has no effect whatever. However, about half of all car journeys in cities are below five kilometres; one in every ten journeys is less than one kilometre. In other words, for most journeys the catalytic converter has no effect.

The life expectancy of a catalytic converter is 50,000 kilometres; with increasing use, it becomes less and less effective. With all these limitations, in the context of a low level of environmental consciousness, experts in the US estimate that about 40 per cent of all catalytic converters in that country do not operate properly.[44] Only with an extensive checking system and rigorous enforcement would the catalytic converter be able to achieve the reductions that are claimed for it.

There is an additional problem in countries where there is no speed limit or where the limit is not properly enforced. The catalytic converter functions optimally in conditions of stable speed, temperature and air-petrol mix. The stop-and-go of most city traffic already limits its effectiveness, but it is the radical differences of speed (from 20 km/h in the city to 200 km/h on the autobahn) and temperature (between −20C and +30C) that create the biggest problem for the catalytic converter.

The catalytic converter itself also represents a potential hazard. The German authors, Till Bastian and Harald Theml, have written of one particular danger:

> Per kilometre, every catalytic converter gives off 1 to 2 grammes of the heavy metals platinum and palladium into the environment. A small proportion of this may end up being breathed in by someone. Platinum is linked with asthma. Experiments have also linked platinum with the growth of tumours. There is as yet no evidence linking these phenomena to the platinum emissions of catalytic converters.[45]

Scientific studies have also claimed that the catalytic converters contribute to global warming. This was the conclusion of a study produced in an apothecary journal:

> Bad news for the environmentally conscious car driver: the much praised catalytic converter increases global warming. This is the unanimous conclusion of studies carried out by a number of laboratories in different institutes. According to these studies, a combustion engine with catalytic converter produces five times as much nitrous gases as a similar engine without catalytic converter or a diesel engine. These nitrous gases are considered responsible, along with carbon monoxide and methane, for trapping the infra-red light from the sun inside the atmosphere and creating the greenhouse effect. Researchers are now searching frantically for some solution and for some way to change the catalytic converter so that it doesn't give off these nitrous gases.[46]

Finally, the catalytic converter stimulated the widespread use of lead-free petrol. Lead-free petrol, however, contains much more benzol than does ordinary leaded petrol. It has been well known for over 30 years that benzol is a carcinogen, but it is only in recent years that many people have become aware of it. Sadly, there was even a British company called National Benzol, which as late as 1958 was still advertising itself: 'Go Super National Benzol, the high-octane, light aromatic mixture.'[47]

The best that can be said about the catalytic converter is that it helped prevent an even greater increase in toxic emissions and helped to pacify public opinion so that the further expansion of the car society could continue unhindered. Emissions have continued to rise in Europe since the introduction of regulations for 'low emission'. The reductions that have been achieved are more than nullified by the increase in motorised traffic.

13

The Speed Myth

Let's look at the world from the perspective of a gas pedal [accelerator]: constantly being kicked, persistently humiliated by rough footwear. But even a gas pedal wants to be handled with sensitivity. Perhaps it secretly dreams of the gentle touch of soft rubber. A special gas pedal shoe has now been invented in America, the J.P. Tod's. The manufacturer, Della Valle, distributes prototypes of the aristocratic shoe to prominent people. The story goes that the Fiat boss, Giovanni Agnelli, was the first to go public with the J.P. Tod's. ... Today, more than 600,000 drivers worldwide want to have their J.P. Tod's and are willing to pay DM 300 for the privilege, often in advance.

Süddeutsche Zeitung Magazin, no. 22, 1995

Senna is not dead. He's with God on the podium.

Banner in Sao Paolo during
the funeral of Ayrton Senna, May 1994

The speed myth is part of car travel. The great majority of car drivers firmly believe that the car is the fastest way of getting anywhere. The car manufacturers promote this belief by making their cars faster and more powerful every year. Practically all car models are capable of speeds far in excess of the speed limits laid down in Europe and America, or of the speed limits recommended in Germany (130 km/h).[48] A few models are capable of speeds which, only a few decades ago, were only achieved in racing. It is no longer unusual to find non-racing cars that can do 200 km/h or more.

More Horsepower

The speed and power stakes were raised in the 1990s. The headline in the *Frankfurter Rundschau*'s report of the International Car Show in Frankfurt in 1989 was: 'Is a 300-Horsepower Car a Technology for Humans?' In the report that followed, the Audi manager, Jürgen Stockmar, made the usual claim that the production of super-fast and aggressive cars was a response of the car industry to the demands of the market: 'Visitors to the show are interested in the highlights. A Cabriolet or a car for DM 220,000 is always surrounded by viewers but hardly anyone pays attention to the new low-energy environment-friendly Turbo-Diesel.'[49]

But it was precisely Volkswagen, the Audi parent company, that had done so much in the 1980s to popularise high speed as part of 'people's motorisation'. Before any other manufacturer came upon the idea, Volkswagen produced its Golf GTI in 1976, a racing car in Golf clothing. The German weekly, *Der Spiegel*, in 1990, described the typical mentality of a Golf GTI driver: 'Up front is an old grandpa in his Daimler and he thinks, it's only a Golf behind me, and then I step on the pedal – it's a fantastic feeling.' According to the Volkswagen representative, Herbert Schuster, it is 'an understatement car, in keeping with our GTI philosophy'.[50]

The VW campaign was a very successful one; between 1976 and 1994, 1.4 million Golf GTIs were sold. There are over 100 GTI clubs, sponsored by Volkswagen, with tens of thousands of members. Every summer they organise a GTI Festival on Wörtersee (a lake in Carinthia, Austria), where they have erected a monument to the GTI.

In the mid-1980s, the Golf GTI achieved a speed of 200 km/h. Between 1976 and 1990, Volkswagen produced four new and more powerful models of the Golf GTI. According to *Der Spiegel* in 1990:

Outside of Germany, the Golf GTI has become a status symbol. It began in France, where car thieves apparently will only take a black one, but Italy and France were soon to follow. At the moment, there is a GTI craze in Spain.[51]

Soon all other car companies had to follow suit and, in
1989, the Opel Kadett (Vauxhall Cavalier) replaced the GTI
as the top-speed car for the first time. The Volkswagen
empire soon struck back; the new Golf GTI G60 reached
216 km/h, exactly 1 km/h more than the Opel Kadett.

Foreign car companies prefer to display their high-speed
cars on German motorways. In 1989, Toyota carried out
what it called 'Operation L': the company flew US journalists
to Germany and let them drive the new Lexus model at
speeds of up to 260 km/h on the autobahn between Munich
and Cologne. In the US, 'autobahn-proved' is considered a
special quality seal. This continuous increase in top speed,
and the speed myth of which it is part, are in rather stark
contrast to what is the actual average speed. When the German weekly, _Stern_, claims, as it did in 1989, that it is now
possible to drive between Cologne and Wiesbaden in one
hour, at an average speed of 150 km/h, then one has to ask:
when, on what days, and at what time of day?[52] The
increased speed capabilities have no effect whatever, in practice, on the real average speeds of everyday travel. In German
cities, this average speed is between 20 and 30 km/h; on the
A roads, it is between 60 and 75 km/h; on the motorways it
is around 100 km/h. These speed averages are valid regardless of what model is being driven.

> The goal of all motorised travel is to get a large number
> of people from A to B in the shortest possible time. A
> single car, driving very fast, would get its passengers to
> their goal very quickly. But a number of cars on the same
> road, driving in the same direction, have to maintain, for
> reasons of safety, a minimum distance from each other,
> whereby the risk to safety increases with speed. The
> result is a long line of cars and the level of achievement,
> measured in terms of the number of people per minute
> that reach their destination, is quite modest. ... Where the
> number of cars is quite large, the minimum safety dis-
> tance between each car results in a very low average
> speed. The optimum speed can be estimated exactly and,
> for a normal two-lane highway, it is 80 km/h.[53]

This average estimate is for continuously moving traffic; if we include starting, stopping and traffic jams, then the average is much lower.

Average Speed

'Time is cash, time is money' is the title of a song by the Cologne rock group, BAP. This maxim of the market economy should also apply to individual travel and should include the *entire time* that is taken up by travel. It is interesting to look at the different amounts of travel time taken by the different car models. And since the society we are dealing with here is a class society, let us group the models sociologically into classes, as in Table 13.1.[54]

In Table 13.1, overleaf, car models are divided into five classes. The two lower classes include small cars of a type no longer produced by the car industry (Fiat Panda, 2CV) as well as the smallest VW model, the Polo, equivalent to the Fiat Uno or the Renault R5. Cars in this class have an average speed over one year of 40 km/h (column 2). The monthly average costs, for these smaller models, of garage, parking, motorway fees, etc. is 80 DM (column 7). The VW Golf is the medium-range car in this classification; its equivalents would be the Ford Escort and the Opel Kadett LS (Vauxhall Cavalier). For the Golf, the estimated average speed is 50 km/h, while the monthly costs for garage, parking, etc. is estimated at 100 DM. The two top classes include the Golf GTI (equivalent to the small Mercedes, the Audi 100, the Vauxhall Omega and the BMW, third series) and, in the very top range, the BMW 750i (equivalent to the Mercedes 500 SE, the Jaguar XJ 4.0 and the Porsche Carrera). The average speed estimated for the Golf GTI class is 55 km/h, and for the BMW 750i, 60 km/h. These estimates are valid only when the cars are used regularly to travel longer distances, for instance, on business trips. In the case of the more expensive cars, we have estimated the costs for parking, garage, etc. at 125 DM per month.

'Speed' refers to the distance covered in a specific amount of time, or the time needed to cover a specific distance. In the case of public transport, the time used to cover a particular distance is the time from departure to arrival; this may also include the time taken to reach and return from, for instance, the train station or the bus stop.

Table 13.1 Average Speed, Operation Costs and cost per km of Five Classes of Cars

1 Model	2 Speed average in one year km/h	3 Time in car (15,000 km) hours	4 Time inc. 50 hrs repairs hours	5 Speed over total time km/h	6 Operation costs yearly (ADAC) DM	7 Extra costs (parking etc.) DM	8 Total costs for one year DM	9 Cost per km DM
Fiat Panda (1)	40	375	425	35	4260	960	5220	0.35
VW Polo (2)	40	375	425	35	4860	960	5820	0.39
VW CL1.6 (3)	50	300	350	43	5472	1200	6672	0.45
VW Golf (4)	55	272	325	46	7476	1200	8676	0.58
BMW 750i (5)	60	250	300	50	20148	1500	21648	1.44

(1) Also Citroen 2CV, Lada Nova, Daihatsu Cuore, Suzuki Swift, Mini Cooper
(2) Also Fiat Uno 70, Renault R5, Citroen AX, Ford Fiesta C1.1, Lada Samara, Nissan Micra, Toyota Starlet, Vauxhall Nova (3) Also Citroen BX Classic, Fiat Tipo 400, Ford Escort C 1.4, Daihatsu Charade TX 1.3, Mazda LX1 4i, Mitsubishi Colt GL 1.3, Vauxhall Cavalier, Peugeor XLD Diesel, Renault R19 TR, Seat Ibiza XL 1.5, Toyota Corol (4) Also VW Passat CL 1.8, Renault R25 TX, Vauxhall Omega GL 2.0i, Mitsubishi Space Wagon, Mercedes 190, Mazda 626 GLX 2.2, Ford Scorpio GL 2.0i, Fiat Croma, BMW 318i, Audi 100, Saab 900i (5) Also Jaguar XJ 4.0, Porsche Carrera 2, Austin Range Rover, Mercedes 500

In the case of motorised individual transport, since the means of transport is the property of the person travelling, we would also have to include an additional factor which would take into account the time spent on filling the tank, car maintenance, small repairs, and so on. These are things that individual car owners have to spend time on. Our estimate of this additional factor, for all classes of cars, is 50 hours per year (or 54 minutes per week, 8 minutes per day). This is probably a very conservative estimate, especially if we include the Sunday car wash.

We have assumed a yearly average travel of 15,000 km. This is the figure used by the ADAC (the German equivalent of the AA or the RAC). Because of the large number of households now owning two cars, this figure has since fallen to 11,500 km. Similar figures apply to Britain. The figure of 15,000 km is still valid for the US. If the estimated yearly distance travelled is reduced for Western Europe, then the other estimates turn out to be even less favourable for car travel, since the life of the car remains essentially the same and the costs per kilometre increase.

The amount of time spent *in* the car, added to the time spent in its maintenance, gives us an average overall speed (column 5). On the basis of this estimate, however, the average speed difference between the cheaper and more expensive models is reduced; the range is no longer 40 to 60 km/h but 35 to 50 km/h.

The differences in operation costs (columns 6 to 9), however, remain considerable. Column 6 gives the annual operation costs for certain named models; these are the ADAC estimates for 1990 models. The figures include expenditure on tax, insurance, the fuel necessary to travel 15,000 km in one year, repairs and depreciation (i.e. the amount that must be put aside yearly in order to purchase a new car after four years, taking into account the value of the car when traded in against a new model). These estimates are conservative ones.

The difference in operation costs between, for instance the Fiat Panda or Mini Cooper (4,260 DM yearly) and the most expensive models (20,148 DM yearly) is very big indeed; the top models are five times more expensive to operate than the cheaper models. If we add to these operation costs the additional expenditure on garages, parking, etc. then we arrive at the actual costs per kilometre for each class of model. The cost per kilometre of the Fiat Panda or Mini Cooper in 1990 was 0.35 DM (£0.14); for the 'normal' VW Golf or Vauxhall Cavalier it was 0.45 DM (£0.19); for the expensive BMW or Jaguar it was 1.44 DM (£0.60). These estimates of average speed and costs of individual transport completely contradict the widespread belief, held especially by car drivers, that car travel is fast and cheap.

The cost comparison with rail travel is interesting here. The cost per kilometre of travelling on German railways at the same time (1991) was 0.21 DM for second class and 0.35 DM for first class accommodation. At the same time the average British Rail fare was £0.10 per mile. Even when we take into account the statistic that each car carries on average 1.2 people, the cost advantage is still with rail, even when compared with the cheapest car models, the Fiat Panda or Mini.

For drivers who buy their cars second-hand, the cost estimates are more favourable but not qualitatively different. Savings on the purchase price are offset by extra costs for repairs and the lower re-selling or trade-in price. The reduction in costs that is possible with the purchase of a second-hand car is not greater than 30 per cent.[55] The cost per kilometre remains significantly higher than rail travel.

Mileage per Hour of Life-Time

If we accept the definition of speed given above, namely, the time needed to travel a certain distance, then the estimates in Table 13.1 must be seen as incomplete and inadequate. The philosopher Ivan Illich has argued that, in the case of individual transport, we also have to take into account the time needed to earn the necessary money to purchase and operate a car. If time is money, then money is also time. According to Illich's notion of 'mileage per hour of life-time', the transport budget of an individual car owner has to include the time spent *in* the car; the time spent *for* the car; and the time spent *earning the necessary money for the purchase and maintenance* of the car. According to Illich:

The typical American male devotes more than 1,600 hours a year to his car. He sits in it while it goes and while it stands idling. He parks it and searches for it. He earns the money to put down on it and to meet the monthly instalments. He works to pay for petrol, tolls, insurance, taxes and tickets. He spends four of his sixteen waking hours on the road or gathering his resources for it.[56]

It is the third aspect, earning the money for purchase and maintenance, that adds a new dimension to our reckoning. The operation costs of the car are already included in the estimates of Table 13.1. What still needs to be estimated is the time necessary to earn the money needed to own and operate a car. This will give us a new 'mileage per hour of life-time' for car travel.

In estimating the time needed to earn the purchase and operation costs of a car, it would be unrealistic to assume a single income level. The Porsche driver spends more per kilometre but also probably earns more per hour than the Mini driver. The estimates in Table 13.2 [57] therefore are based on five income levels more or less corresponding to the five classes of car models. In the first income class are those who earn a net hourly wage of 19 DM or a net monthly income of 1,900 DM ($1,350). In the highest income bracket are those who have an hourly income of 50 DM, a monthly net income of 7,500 DM ($5,360.00).

Table 13.2, overleaf, has the same five classes of car models as Table 13.1. Columns 1 and 2 contain the estimates from columns 8 and 4 of the previous table, the total annual costs and the time spent in and for the car. Columns 3 to 7 contain the amount of time expended each year, in the different income classes, to earn the money needed to cover these costs. Columns 8 to 12 then provide the estimates for the total amount of time needed (in the car, for the car and for the purchase and maintenance of the car) by adding the respective hours given in columns 3 to 7. On this base, we arrive at the subsequent average speed of private road transport.

The concept 'kilometres per hour' is being used here in a quite literal sense. The total number of hours that the individual has to devote to transport is set against the distance travelled over a given period. The average speeds reached in

Table 13.2 Average Speed on the Basis of Total Time Expended (Transport Time and Work Time)

Model*	1	2	3	4	5	6
Fiat Panda	5220	425	435	348	261	209
VW Polo	5820	425	485	388	291	233
VW Golf	6672	350	556	445	334	267
Golf GTI	8676	325	723	578	434	347
BMW750i	21648	300	1804	1443	1082	866

Model*	7	8	9	10	11	12
Fiat Panda	104	860/17	773/19	686/22	634/24	529/28
VW Polo	116	910/17	813/18	716/21	658/23	541/28
VW Golf	133	906/17	795/19	684/22	617/24	483/31
Golf GTI	174	1048/14	903/17	759/20	672/22	499/30
BMW750i	432	2104/7	1743/9	1382/11	1166/13	732/21

Key: 1 = Total costs (DM) as in Table 13.1 col.8. 2 = Time in/for the car as in Table 13.1 col. 4.
3,4,5,6,7 = Time needed (in hours for whole year) to earn total expenditure arranged in 5 income classes with net hourly and monthly incomes in DM. 8,9,10,11,12 = Time (in hours per year and kilometres per hour) spent in the car, for the car (repairs, etc.) and to earn the money necessary to purchase and operate the car / average speed according to class of income.
Income classes: 3,8 = 12/1900; 4,9 = 15/2400; 5,10 = 20/3200; 6,11 = 25/4000; 7,12 = 50/7500
* Including other cars in same class as in Table 13.1.

this way vary from 7 km/h for the owner of a Porsche who is in the lowest income bracket to 31 km/h for the owner of a normal Golf with a monthly income of 6,400 DM. These two cases may appear extreme but one must recall that homo automobilis loves extremes, and the low earner who spends most of his income on an expensive upper-class car, and achieves an average speed of 10 km/h, really exists, as does the top earner who invests in a simple Golf and achieves the maximum average of 31 km/h.

The more realistic combinations would probably be the following: a person with a monthly income of 1,900 DM buys a Mini Cooper or Metro; another, with a monthly income of 2,400 DM ($1,360; £1,000) is the proud owner of a VW Polo; a person in the third income bracket will probably purchase a Golf or Vauxhall Cavalier; one would need an income of around 4,000 DM ($2,860; £1,670) to buy the Golf GTI or the 'small' Mercedes, while only top earners could manage a Porsche or Jaguar. In other words, the five classes of cars roughly correspond to the five levels of income.

The margin between the lowest and highest amount of time expended annually on the car is actually quite small: from 860 hours for the low-income Fiat Panda owner to 732 hours for the top income BMW owner. The result is a levelling out of the average speed (the bold figures in columns 8 to 12): the average speed is 17 km/h for the Fiat Panda, 18 km/h for the VW Polo, 22 km/h for the Golf, 22 km/h for the Golf GTI, and 21 km/h for the super-fast Porsche Carrera or Jaguar.[58]

The result is quite amazing: the real average speed achieved by the car society, around 20 km/h, is comparable to that achieved by a very fit cyclist (where the average speed of the cyclist is estimated in the same manner).

Children, the Elderly and the Disabled

The speed fetishism of the car society is in crass contrast not only to the real average speed ('mileage per hour of life-time') but also to what the car society imposes on the weak and the slow. The stronger are faster or can acquire the means to be faster while the weak become slower and more at risk.

The number of the weak is also increasing. In the last two decades of this century, there has been an important change in the structure of car ownership, a consequence of the declining birth rate and greater longevity in our society. The age structure pyramid is being turned on its head; there are now more senior citizens than youth. In 1976, in West Germany, less than 18 per cent of licensed drivers were over 65; in 1994, it is 35 per cent. In the year 2000, according to a study carried out by Uniroyal, over half of licensed drivers will be 65 or over. The study also points to the growing dangers linked to a higher rate of night blindness and a much slower reaction time.[59] The risk of accidents will increase significantly. According to a study published in 1989 by the German daily, *Süddeutsche Zeitung*, the risk of road accident increases with age. It is at its highest among young men during the first month after they get their driving licence. It then declines steadily until drivers reach the age of 55. 'From the age of 55 the risk of accident increases gradually and, for drivers between 70 and 74, is as high as for drivers between 18 and 20.'[60] The risk is extremely high among drivers over 75. Senior citizens behind the wheel can not cope with the aggressive and often anarchic driving habits of the modern car society.

The car lobby is aware of these changes and of the consequent threat to their own interests. The previously mentioned study carried out by the tyre company, Uniroyal, was not aimed at developing models of public transport that would correspond to the needs of a society with such a changing age structure. On the contrary, it is people who have to adapt to the needs of the car companies. The study proposes vision tests for the elderly, better street lighting and road signs, and the redesign of crossings and junctions to take into account the declining abilities of the elderly. With the increasing age of the population, the dangers increase not only for elderly car drivers but also for the elderly who are not car owners.

Similar problems exist for the disabled. In a society in which the car dominates and public transport is structured in such a way that it does not take their needs into account, the disabled are largely excluded from every form of mobility. According to official statistics for Germany, around 12 per cent of the population is disabled in such a way that public transport is impossible or difficult for them to use. The statistics are similar for other European countries.

Transport measures to help the disabled are very modest in most European countries. Here are some examples from Germany:

> The president of the German Federal Association of the Disabled, Dr. Hans Aegenent, resigned his post yesterday, at a fringe meeting organised on the occasion of the International Car Show in Hamburg, in protest against the failure of the public transport authorities to do anything for the disabled. 'The mobility needs of the disabled are not taken seriously', he said.'[61]

Three years later, in 1991, the German super train, the ICE, was unveiled. With a lot of publicity, the train made its first journey at the beginning of June 1991, but then came in for a lot of criticism when it ran into technical difficulties. Protests by the disabled, such as the following, appeared only in the small print:

> The German Federal Association of the Disabled claimed that the Bundesbahn, in spite of very heavy investment in the super train, had made no provision for helping the disabled to get on and off the train. The new flagship of the German railways had failed to solve the technical problem of access for wheelchairs.

When the disabled demonstrated in the Frankfurt railway station, the rail authorities claimed that their personnel were always willing to help a disabled person in a wheelchair. But when asked who would be responsible in the event of an accident during the dangerous manoeuvre of loading and unloading a wheelchair, the spokesperson for the railway company refused to answer.[62] The German ICE came in for a lot of hostility when it was taken on a public relations excursion to the US, where there exists anti-discrimination legislation and a strong disabled lobby. This may be one of the reasons why the German ICE has not been a success in the US.

The belief that the strong and fast are becoming stronger

and faster, while the weak are becoming weaker and less mobile is further confirmed in the case of children. The threat to children has dramatically increased with the growth of traffic. Walking and cycling are more restricted and more dangerous. The closure of small schools and the centralisation of education has meant an increase in school busing and an increase in the child's dependence on the bus. School busing also means a further restriction on the free time available to children for creative activities, play and games. The brutality of the car society towards the weak in Germany is emphasised in a report by Wolfgang Schubert in the daily, *Frankfurter Rundschau*:

> In 1975, 23 per cent of all children in Kindergarden walked alone to and from school. Now it is 11 per cent. The number of six-year olds that were accompanied by an adult to school rose from 10 per cent in 1975 to 31 per cent in 1984.[63]

The transport-policy expert, Professor Helmut Holzapfel, has pointed out that in the pre-car epoch children had access to a significantly larger geographical life-space and that the car is being used in the modern car society in order to extend that life-space which the car itself has restricted:

> At the turn of the century it was common for children to be independently active in an area up to three or four kilometres from home. Today, children are driven to their ballet or sports class in order to compensate for the restrictions on their mobility. Direct experience of nature is one thing; to see the world through a car window while strapped into the back seat is something else. Previously, the child itself had to conquer the world; today, the most important thing the child has to learn in order to survive is not to cross the road.[64]

Children brought up in this way will, at an early age, feel the need to own their own car as a way of making up for this restrictedness and dependence.

14

Alienation, Aggression
and Patriarchy

As terror spread among California commuters, officials were desperately casting about for a way to restore peace. California Assemblyman, Paul Zeltner, announced he would introduce legislation requiring a minimum three-year prison sentence and permanent revocation of the driver's licence of any person caught shooting from a car.

Time magazine,
17 August 1987

It is not just the historical and economic factors described in Parts I and II that led to and help maintain the dominance of the car in the industrialised countries. There must be more to it if car models such as the Mercedes, Golf GTI or Rover roll on wheels which, without tyres, can cost 5,000 DM, or when these wheels, with their special tyres, can cost the equivalent of a new Lada Samara, Seat Ibiza or Hyundai Pony. There must be more at stake if traffic conditions are considered normal in which

> more than five million cars travel daily on the 840 kilometre highway around Los Angeles. In the morning and evening rush hour, the traffic flows on only 90 km of the network. The rest of the 750 km of asphalt freedom is stuck in a hopeless traffic jam. The average speed here is around 30 km/h or even less. Experienced commuters use the jam to shave, read the newspaper, or have breakfast. Some shrewd entrepreneurs have recently been offering teach-yourself foreign language cassettes.[65]

This raises questions of individual and social psychology which we have not dealt with so far. In the critical literature devoted to the car, particularly in the 1960s, these questions were often in the forefront. Studies of this period offered many explanations for the phenomenon of mass motorisation: the car as substitute satisfaction, as an answer to the frustrations of consumer society, as instrument of aggression, street traffic as the continuation of war or class conflict by other means, the car as a symbol of potency. These explanatory models, as simplistic as any one of them may seem on their own, form an important part of a comprehensive theory of mass motorisation. The present chapter will deal with three aspects of such a comprehensive theory:

1. the relation between the capitalist labour process and the car society;

2. the daily aggression in traffic as the expression of unsatisfied elementary social needs;

3. the reproduction and reinforcement of patriarchal relations of power by the car society.

Capitalist Production, Alienation and the Car as Substitute Satisfaction

The car society reproduces an elementary phenomenon of the capitalist mode of production: the de-personalisation and reification of human relationships. The alienation of the producers (wage earners) in the labour process is reproduced in the organisation of transport.

A key difference between the pre-capitalist and capitalist mode of production is the universalisation of alienation to the great majority of the population – those dependent on wage labour. This development is structurally determined. Unlike the peasant or craftsperson, the wage earner no longer has direct access to the instruments or means of production; these appear to the wage earner now as the 'property' of an employer. Likewise, the wage earners no longer directly control their own labour, but are forced to *sell* it and thus define themselves as 'employees'. In this manner, what were previously seen as relations *among persons* now appear as relations *among things*. On the one hand, there is an increase in the division of labour in modern industrial society and thus in the mutual dependence of people on one another; on the other hand, the human being appears increasingly as an isolated person, as an atomised citizen and wage earner. The products of the labour process appears to the wage earners as alien objects, since they have to sell their labour and receive in return, not the products of their labour, but money. 'Thus the productivity of his labour, his labour in general, real labour, comes to confront the worker as an alien power. Capital, inversely, realises itself through the appropriation of alien labour.'[66]

These relations of power, which Marx saw as fundamental to capitalist society, remain hidden from the wage earners; they exist 'behind the backs of the producers'. It is not the appropriation of alien labour which appears as the foundation for the increasing power of capital, but a mystical cooperation of 'capital, labour and natural resources'. The wage earners build trade unions and political parties in their struggle against capitalist exploitation and also as a means of creating a counter-culture to the alienation of the capitalist production process. But if these class structures and organisations are undermined or destroyed, as they were under fascism, then the workers also relate to each other in an alienated manner, even as competitors (in the case of mass unemployment). Alienation affects not only the relation of the wage earners to the products of their labour but also their relation to all those who live and work in the same conditions. What we then find is not solidarity but 'the struggle of one against all', the climber mentality, the stress on real or artificial differences among those who live through the sale of their labour (unskilled manual worker, skilled worker, white collar worker, official, foreign worker, etc).

In capitalist society, the great majority of the population is excluded from access to the decisive means of production and from any real influence on the rules of the game, but the car society offers this social majority access to at least a means of transport. While the labour process – the interchange between humans and nature – is experienced by the wage earners as alienation, the escape to a weekend in the country in one's own car is indeed a form of interchange with nature. The ideology of the 'small escape' is important in a society in which the market economy has its invisible grip on all the major aspects of social life. This ideology can, in fact, even be used as an argument against public transport, as in the case of one of the first car enthusiasts, Otto Bierbaum, who praised the car in the following terms in 1902: 'We don't want to drive past all these beautiful spots at which the timetable hasn't arranged a stop. We want to really travel again, as free men, free to decide, in the free air.'[67] Henry Ford made a similar argument at the same time in his advertising:

It is your say, too, when it comes to speed. You can – if you choose – loiter lingeringly through shady avenues or you can press down on the foot-lever until all the scenery looks alike and you have to keep your eyes skinned to count the milestones as they pass.

It is interesting that, in this first advertising, the Ford Company made the link between the car and nature:

Built also for the good of your health – to carry you 'jarlessly' over any kind of half decent roads, to refresh your brain with the luxury of much 'out-doorness' and your lungs with the 'tonic of tonics' – the right kind of atmosphere.[68]

Students of the history of Western Europe after the Second World War, the period in which mass motorisation really got under way, meet again and again the same motif: the individual trip to the countryside, the picnic in the field, the attraction of the resorts and cafés: 'In these cafés, the restless driver waits for attention from the over-worked personnel and ends up with beer and food that he would have rejected out of hand were he at home.'[69] Spending the night in a motel became a stylised thing to do:

We left London after a luxurious dinner to arrive at Norman Cross in time at a motel. In the older type of hotel one is faced with the problem as to whether it is safe to leave one's luggage in the car overnight. ... In the motel one merely drives straight into the garage beneath one's temporary flat and the entire process of a single night's stay is simplified.[70]

The British magazine, *Country Life*, during the period from the 1950s to the 1970s, consistently equated love of nature with love for the car. This was, of course, not unrelated to the fact that most of the advertisements in this gentry-style magazine were from car and tyre manufacturers. There are annual special editions of this magazine devoted to the Motor Show and to Scotland. In these Scottish issues, no mention is made of the fact that most of the rail links in that country are threatened with closure. New road building through the beautiful Scottish countryside is welcomed, however, with enthusiasm:

> The resulting rapid increase in motoring induced the Scottish authorities to look more closely into their romantic road system with the object of improving it sufficiently to cope with the promising tourist traffic. ... But it left gaps in the projected coastline road system which meant miles of inland travelling to return to the sea. ... However, I have no doubt that all these gaps will be closed. Its completion will mean that the touring motorist will be able to drive from Kyle of Lochalsh to Loch Durnass in the far north, and thence to Tongue, either within sight of the Atlantic and its sea lochs, or at least close enough to allow their inspection on foot.[71]

These individual outings into the countryside at the weekend and during the holidays, or even the pleasant relaxation to be had from admiring the 'virtual reality' of the countryside in nature shows and holiday advertising, are offered as an answer to the problems of alienation. In fact, what we are being offered is a new form of alienation. A representative poll of German car drivers in 1995 showed that, for the majority of drivers, the means has become the end. What makes the majority of motorists take to the highways and roads at weekends and during holidays is the fear that they might otherwise be missing something. Only one in five actually wants to spend some time 'in the countryside'. Of greater importance are 'the need for a change' (26 per cent), 'getting away from the day-to-day routine' (23 per cent), and 'the pleasure in discovering something new' (20 per cent). Driving the car brought with it, for most of the drivers questioned, a 'sense of freedom'.[72]

The claim of the car society is that people in this uniform modern industrial society or in the new service industry society can express their individuality through their choice of car model. If the great majority of the population is unable to develop or to express its creativity in the world of work, if there is no real chance of rising above one's present situation, and if the power of capital has made most people, as wage earners, equal, then the car society, with its different combinations of horse power and chrome, allows the individual, for a price, to rise above the masses. According to the Volkswagen boss, Toni Schmücker: 'The people want to be different, in one way or another, for instance, through their car. The possibility of individual expression of character within definite norms belongs to the basis of our nature as free beings.'[73] The leading figures of the car society are well aware of the ideological function of the car. William Mitchell, manager of General Motors in Detroit: 'The car has to arouse desire; it can't be a mere means of transport. ... Otherwise people will spend their money on such things as swimming pools, boats, hi-fi sets, education, or trips to Europe ... .'[74] Of course, people are doing these things anyway; alongside the car, these commodities became prestige items during the 1980s. The car is still number one, however, the main *ersatz* satisfaction in an alienated society.

The differentiation which, according to Schmücker, the car makes possible, is not the 'individual expression' of creative activities that the wage earners have lost in the labour process. The alienation and reification of human relations are reproduced in the sphere of transport. According to the sociologist, Helmut Schelsky:

In car travel, people do not relate to each other as persons in a human encounter, but rather as people behind the mask of an apparatus, namely, the car. ... In this encounter, the individuals remain anonymous ... [they] are not forced to relate as one person to another, face to face, but as strangers ... .[75]

Bourgeois sociology tends to reduce the different forms of human behaviour to instinct and tends to neglect the specific social conditions which at least co-determine these behavioural forms. Schelsky's description of car drivers hiding behind the iron mask of their cars reminds one of the medieval knightly tournaments, those life and death adventures in armour in a wild medieval landscape. The car too can be made to fit into this image of raw nature and the struggle for survival to which the individual can escape from the uniformities of day-to-day existence. The 1991 car race from Munich to Marrakesh is one such example. This was a rally not for professionals but for the ordinary guzzler. The promotional literature for the event promised '3,000 kilometres through the wild landscape of Morocco' in which the teams would be 'vigorously tested'. The struggle with heat, deserts and mountains promised to be a 'once in a lifetime experience'.[76]

But the era of the 'free ride for the free citizen' has become all too familiar not just with the joys of racing through the countryside but above all with the traffic jam. The flashing headlights of the impatient overtaker in the outside lane is just one of the milder forms of aggression familiar to the modern driver. It takes on more menacing forms in the daily traffic jam, in the struggle of one against all. Astride a massive horse power, behind an armour of tin and steel, the modern cavalier of the motorway throws down the challenge to the anonymous opponent. But it is the car, and not the driver, that is the real combatant in this battle. The traffic counsellor, the new professional of the car society, has developed the correct psychological approach for the situation. Drivers about to lose their cool in the heat of the long tailback cannot be persuaded to desist from their journey by means of appeals to the state of their physical health. The approach has to be a different one: 'We know that you can make it but your car is about to give up the ghost. Haven't you noticed that the transmission has already begun to smoke?' According to one such professional counsellor, writing in the German weekly, *Stern*: 'To prevent something from happening to the holy car, every driver is willing to give it a rest.'[77]

War on the Streets

The car society means war on the streets for all its citizens,
whether car drivers or not. 1979 in the US saw the beginning of a new kind of traffic death. Gasoline was rationed at
the time and two drivers who tried to jump the queue at the
pump were shot. A number of drivers who tried to siphon off
gasoline from parked cars met a similar fate.[78]

In Germany, the weekly *Bunte* reported in 1989 on a
sensational car chase over the Swiss border. The title of the
story was 'Savage Hunt on the Basel–Karlsruhe Autobahn'.
According to the report, when an Opel Senator with Swiss
licence plates tried to stop a German Mercedes travelling at
180 km/h, there was an accident. The German Mercedes
driver had failed to pay his motorway fees in Switzerland and
when the border guards attempted to impose a fine, he
stepped on the gas and was pursued by what the Swiss radio
described as a 'Swiss Patriot'.[79]

This kind of highway madness increased dramatically in
the industrialised countries during the 1980s. The American
weekly, *Time* magazine, complained in the summer of 1987
that 'no one has offered any clear diagnosis of the highway
madness'. It began in 1987 when a frustrated driver in a
traffic jam fired with a Colt at another driver. In the months
that followed, three more were killed in similar incidents and
seven were severely wounded. *Time* reported in the same
issue that 'in the previous week, there had been 19 cases
involving the use of guns in traffic situations'. The highways
of Southern California, it said, were becoming 'a zone of
terror'.[80] In 1994, in Philadelphia, a passenger in a car,
Eileen McGuigan was shot in the head and killed by an
angry driver in a traffic jam. The driver then made his
escape via a highway exit.[81]

In considering this subject of 'war on the streets', our
attention is directed naturally to the American Wild West,
where the car society had its beginnings. But similar acts of
aggression on the streets are also being reported in Europe.
Here are just a small selection of reports from everyday life
on Germany's roads: 'A shipping agent from Hamburg,
Henry R., unintentionally cut off a red Ford Escort. At the

next traffic light, the Escort driver stabbed him with a butcher's knife in the chest.'[82] In Geesthacht, in Germany, 'a Mercedes driver, attempting to overtake a rubbish truck, forced the truck to brake suddenly. Words were exchanged at the next traffic light. Then the son of the Mercedes driver threatened the truck driver with a knife.' There are numerous reports of the use of guns in traffic. According to one such report: 'A minibus driver, Manfred König, overtook a slow Mercedes 350 SE. The Mercedes driver then got in front again. Again, König overtook. The Mercedes driver then peppered the minibus with pistol shots.' Many reports also tell about drivers' aggression against pedestrians and cyclists: 'In Munich a Golf driver beat up a 29-year-old student. The student was crossing correctly at the green light so the driver, who wanted to turn left, had to brake. The driver went into a rage.'[83]

In Berlin, in 1994, a headline in the local press announced: 'War on Berlin's Streets – Driver Beats Up Pedestrian because he Crossed the Pedestrian Crossing too Slowly.'[84] In Passau, in Bavaria, the weekly, *Stern*, reported that 'a 48-year old traffic judge drove on the pavement in pursuit of an 11-year-old boy. The boy saved himself by jumping over a fence. The judge was annoyed by the noise of the children who were playing.'[85] In the Taunus area near Frankfurt, a pensioner had a long-standing dispute with a housing agent who regularly and illegally parked his Kadett Caravan in front of the pensioner's window. In February 1990, when the housing agent, late at night, again parked his Kadett in front of the pensioner's house, 'the pensioner stormed out of his house, revolver in his hand, and fired four shots'.[86]

In advertisements for new car models, the car itself is frequently compared to a weapon. The Golf GTI was explicitly described in this way by a report in the *Financial Times*, under the heading 'Gunship or Racing Car?'. The Opel Lotus Carlton is described in the same paper as 'machismo personified'. Changing to third gear and giving full acceleration is described as 'like a shot being fired from the barrel of a gun'.[87]

This aggression is openly acted out in drag racing and in the Monster Truck shows that have been common in the US since the mid-1980s and that are now being popularised in Europe.

According to a report in the German sports magazine, *Sport Bild*, 25 million Americans follow the Monster Truck competitions in which these 3,000 horse-power monsters, with two-metre high wheels, smash wrecks and other obstacles on the race track. In one such competition, in the Jack Murphy Stadium in San Diego, California, the Monster Trucks had such names as Big Foot and Grave Digger. According to the American psychologist, Joan Hammer: 'With all the traffic jams we find today, the normal car driver dreams of being able to wipe out every car that is in front.'[88]

Joyriding was also passed off as a show or a game when it made its first appearance in Britain in mid-1991. Youths in cities and in urban districts with high levels of unemployment steal cars and drive them at breakneck speed, often with fatal consequences for themselves and others. It was only after two uninvolved youths, Daniel Davies and Adele Thomson, were hit by a Mazda MX3 or, to be more precise, by young joyriders behind the wheel of a stolen car and 'sent flying through the air like pigeons' (Adele died shortly afterwards) that the British public began to describe this kind of car mania more appropriately as 'death riders'. The psycho-social background to these events – the crisis of late capitalism, the meaninglessness of much of the work that society has to offer, large-scale unemployment, especially among the youth, the escape from the emptiness of life that is offered by these 'death rides' – is not seriously dealt with.[89] In Liverpool and elsewhere, parents have organised themselves and protested vigorously against this particular form of car madness.

Joyriding soon spread to Germany, where youths in Hamburg stole cars and drove them to destruction. In 1992 and 1993, joyriding became a major problem in East Berlin. On certain weekdays, hundreds of youths gathered to race cars, many of them stolen. It was no accident that the areas of East Berlin where this happened were also the areas with the highest levels of unemployment. This form of car madness is also closely linked to ordinary criminality, especially in the case of 'crash and carry', in which youths in stolen cars crash them into shop windows and then loot the shop. This form of 'ram raiding', which began in Newcastle in Britain, has also spread to Germany.[90]

According to a report published in Switzerland: 'Since the invention of the car, around 25 million people have died as victims of road traffic. This is approximately the same number that died in the great plagues in Europe.'[91] Every year, according to an estimate of the World Health Organisation (WHO), a quarter of a million people are killed on the roads of the world. The effects are similar to the bombs dropped on Hiroshima and Nagasaki. In the states of the European Union, in the early 1990s, around 50,000 people were killed annually on the streets. In 1988, there were 8,213 traffic deaths in West Germany. In the mid-1990s, for the whole of united Germany, that number has risen to 10,000.

In West Germany, in the period between the establishment of the Federal Republic and 1995, around 600,000 people died in traffic accidents. The number of injured was 25 million, of whom 6 million were severely injured. It is easier to predict traffic deaths than GDP; we already know that in the decade to come 100,000 people will be killed on German roads and 1.5 million will be severely injured.

A sad feature of the car society is the fact that half of those people killed on the road are not drivers. In the period 1967 to 1977, 165,623 people died in traffic accidents in West Germany. Of these, 35,169 were over 65 and 17,614 were children below the age of 15. According to the official German statistics, one-third of traffic deaths involve pedestrians and cyclists. The conclusions to be drawn from these statistics are: firstly, around half of all the people killed on the roads were not driving or sitting in a car at the time of their death – a large proportion of them, around one-third, had never possessed a driving licence; secondly, it is the weak in our society – children, the elderly, cyclists, and pedestrians – who are the victims of car traffic.

J. Roberts came to a similar conclusion in his study of British transport:

... other than motorcycling, walking and cycling have the highest casualty rates per kilometre travelled. Indeed the fatality rate for walking is eighteen times higher than that for car travel. It can be seen too that motor traffic, especially cars and lorries, is associated with the great majority of pedestrian fatalities and, moreover, that it is these types of vehicle which are increasing in number at the fastest rates.

The car society not only does not widen mobility, it is particularly brutal towards those that it has condemned to immobility – the young, the old and the disabled. According to the German authors, Till Bastian and Harald Theml:

> As far as the threat to children on our streets is concerned, Germany is sadly in the number one position in Europe. The number of children killed each year on our streets declined slightly from 387 in 1987 to 359 in 1988 (largely as a result of the law on seat belts in the back seat); but the number of injured children rose in the same period by almost 2,000.[92]

Figure 14.1 provides the figures for an international comparison of the numbers of children killed on European roads in 1988.[93] The highest figures are for West Germany, with Britain in second place.

Transport academics recommend education in transport and road safety as a way of avoiding the large number of deaths among children and youth. The official German road safety body (*Deutsche Verkehrswacht*) believes that the only way to reduce accidents involving children is to advise parents not to let their children use bikes until they are eight years old. In other words, children should accept a significant restriction on their mobility in order not to be killed or injured by the mobility of adults. Child psychologists are very sceptical about the value of traffic education for children, especially in typical accident situations. What about pedestrian crossings? A study of children in traffic accidents in Stuttgart showed that 35 per cent of the children involved were hit while walking on zebra crossings or at traffic lights. A study of traffic deaths in Zurich in 1971 found that half of the people involved were hit while on pedestrian crossings.[94]

According to a report in the German weekly, *Wirtschaftswoche*, at the end of 1984: 'Of 1,000 observed adult road users, 900 did not take children into account. ...' They exceeded the speed limits in built-up areas and particularly in

```
         Italy —41
        Sweden ——50
        Greece ——54
        Poland ——55
         Spain ———70
     Yugoslavia ———77
        France ———97
  Czechoslovakia ———98
    East Germany ———99
        Denmark ———122
      Netherlands ———152
          Austria ———————203
      Switzerland ————————211
         Belgium ————————217
         Britain* ——————————263
    West Germany —————————311
```

Figure 14.1
Children under 15 killed or injured on the roads,
in 1988 as pedestrians or cyclists
(per 100,000 of this age group)
* includes Northern Ireland

those areas that called attention to the presence of children,
in the vicinity of schools and kindergardens.[95]

Since, in the world of cars, the driver is competent to
drive, even the general public tends to assume, in the case of
accidents involving children, that it is the children themselves that are to blame. In the city of Düren, for instance, a
study of road accidents in 1986 found that, in over half the
cases, even those involving children below the age of five,
the victims themselves were considered responsible.[96]

The toy industry prepares the child to accept the motorised world to come as something natural. In the German city
of Regensburg, 'W. Fritz, a car dealer, is displaying the smallest car in the world. This mini-car is powered by a petrol-
driven lawn mower engine, three horsepower. ... It drives 30
km/h and is for children between the ages of 8 and 14. The
cost is 1,850 DM.'[97] Just as toy guns prepare the child to
accept war as a natural part of the adult world, the toy car

introduces the child to the car society. In the case of the Regensburg mini-car, one has to remember that a collision with an object at 30 km/h is the equivalent of falling from a height of four metres.

The brutality of the car society and the above mentioned accident statistics suggest a comparison with the world of 'ordinary' criminality. In 1982, in Germany, the number of people killed in road accidents was 12 times the number killed as a result of murder or manslaughter. The number of murders was 935 but the number of road deaths was 11,608.[98] It must be said, at this point, that this high number of traffic victims is not the necessary price for the freedom of mobility. These deaths were the result of a *specific form* of transport. They are taken for granted in the daily life of the car society. But they would be totally unacceptable were they to occur in any other form of transport, for instance, the railways. 'If 40 German jumbo jets in a year, on their Atlantic flight, were to crash and sink into the sea, with all passengers lost, world history would stand still. But this is precisely the number of people who die every year on our streets.'[99]

The Car Society and Patriarchy

'I suspect that when this century ends, the battle of the sexes concerning driving will also finish.' This was Sylvia Baker, writing in the magazine *The Lady* in 1991.[100] This is also the official line of the car lobby, according to which there are no gender differences in the car society. The statistics and the reality of daily travel point, however, to a different conclusion.

The annual statistics published by the German transport ministry also provide information on the gender structure of driving licences. If we look only at class 3 licences (private cars) then the picture corresponds to that promoted by the car companies: 48.2 per cent of eligible German men have a driving licence, while the figure for women is 48 per cent. Hence the conclusion of the *Süddeutsche Zeitung*: 'According to the most recent figures, 14.5 million of the roughly 34 million licensed drivers are women.'[101]

If we look, however, at the other classes of driving licence that also permit the licensee to drive a private car, then we get a different picture. When all licence categories are included, then 79.8 per cent of eligible men and 50.5 per cent of eligible women have a driving licence. Expressed in a different way, 3.3 million German men over the age of 16 (32.7 per cent) do not have a driving licence; the figure for German women in the same age group is 11.8 million (47.7 per cent).[102]

Possession of a driving licence, however, does not necessarily mean possession of a car. We are justified in assuming that the proportion of men who have a licence but no car is smaller than the proportion of women. In most households where there is 'only' one car, and both partners have a driving licence, then it is the man, as a rule, who uses the car on a daily basis. The woman, in such cases, will tend to use the car only on particular occasions: weekend shopping, driving home from the pub and from parties, or helping out with the driving on the annual holiday trip.

This pattern is further confirmed by the statistics for average car occupancy, which is 1.2 persons, and by the standard seating arrangement for the family car: man at the control column, woman as support unit in the front passenger seat, whining children squeezed into the back seat – the typical image of the weekend outing. The German statistics on access to a car show that 47.1 per cent of men over 18 have 'continuous' access to a car, in other words, access on a daily basis. For women the figure is 29 per cent. Among the 6 million people living in Germany who do not have a German passport, i.e. immigrant workers, the comparable figures are 33.1 per cent for men, 10.2 per cent for women. When we look at local public transport, we find the mirror image of these proportions. Here it is women who constitute the majority. Women, children and immigrants make up around four-fifths of the users of local public transport in most cities.[103]

Property has a central place in our society and this is also expressed in the pattern of car ownership. In Germany, in 1988, 5.5 million women were registered car owners; this is less than one-quarter (22.6 per cent) of the total number of cars registered. The patriarchal nature of the car society expresses itself also in the structure of property.[104]

The creation of artificial traffic, which, in the present analysis, is seen as the basis of the car society, is also, to a large extent, an expression of the patriarchal power structure of society: urban planning and residential structures are unfriendly to women. At a transport conference organised as a Citizens' Initiative in the German city of Kassel in 1985, a workshop on 'Women and Transport' made a report from which the following are extracts:

At least since the Second World War, when the destruction of so many cities offered an ideal situation for planners, the structures of urban housing and transport that were planned and built were based on the conceptions of the 1930s, the so-called segregated city ... .

These constructed male fantasies also contained the mechanisms of oppression, the reinforcement of a gender-specific division of labour ... . The precise function of rooms was predetermined, there was no space for women, no useable open spaces or gardens near where people lived, no social control over the streets. Our fear is built into the streets that are too wide, the underground parking, the empty inner cities and commercial areas. The pavements (sidewalks) are too narrow for friendly conversation and it is forbidden to walk on the grass. The retreat to one's private life, to one's own three rooms with kitchen and bath, is preprogrammed. The streets have completely lost their role as an important public space, as a social space.[105]

The specific function and structures of the car society have only in recent years become a subject of public debate. But as soon as it becomes an issue, we find that it is not just the Left and feminists who are concerned; it is a matter of profound interest to the whole of society. A newspaper in the German city of Cologne, the *Kölner Stadtanzeiger*, in 1990, invited responses to the question: 'How do women experience Cologne?' The response was quite large and the paper summarised the responses in an article in May 1990, the title of which was 'Only Fear on the Streets'. Here are some of the responses that the paper received from women. Many were concerned with violence on the streets: 'Why do we women always have to give way in order to protect our-selves? It's the men who are the guilty ones.' The biggest concern expressed was about underground stations. Women were afraid in the dark or poorly lit underground tunnels. There were some stations that women never stopped at, pre-ferring to get off a station earlier or later. In the words of one woman: 'It's the cars that should be sent underground, not us.' Many women had stopped going to the cinema or theatre in the evenings because of the fears about getting home. One elderly woman was 'afraid that my husband might die before me. Then I would never be able to leave the house.' The steps and escalators in underground stations were seen as a special problem by older people and mothers with prams. According to the newspaper article that sum-marised the responses: 'Many women see multi-storey car parks as unfriendly and threatening and they avoid them when they can. ... Many wanted more benches so they could sit and watch things without having to go into a café.'[106]

Car advertisements, especially those for car accessories, are clearly based on the assumption that the car society is male dominated. In no other industrial branch is the woman so openly and aggressively used as a sex object. Europe's biggest car accessory dealer is D&W. In Germany it has outlets in 200 cities. Its catalogue mixes images of hubcaps and spoilers with pictures of naked or almost naked women. A survey of D&W customers showed that 82 per cent of them used the catalogue and bought D&W products precisely because of this mixture of sex and cars. Favourite texts in ads for cars and accessories are 'Love at first sight', 'How do I find my dream rim?'.[107]

The more expensive the car, the more sexy has to be the appeal. An expensive sports car will not sell if it does not have an attractive woman displayed on its bonnet. The edi-tors of car magazines are well aware of the link between speed and male sexuality, more particularly, between the speed limit and the limits placed on the male sexual urge. One German car magazine wrote about the General Motors sports car, the Corvette, as follows:

Driving the Corvette on American highways is like spend-ing Christmas Eve with Miss Germany in a convent school:

thank you for touching with your eyes only. Shit! You know
what it would be like. You feel what you're missing. But
your desires are nipped in the bud by the powers that be.
You suffer this tortuous 55 m/h (the US speed limit), know-
ing that you could do 140. You exercise restraint, you
accept grudgingly the law of the slow majority.[108]

'A woman at the wheel' – that is a cry of horror and
abuse in the male-dominated car society. And this is in spite
of the fact that, as the statistics show, women cause fewer
accidents and women constitute only 7.9 per cent of drivers
who lose their driving licence. Of course, the car industry
has discovered that women are an important section of the
market. General Motors advertised one of its new models,
the City J, with an eye to the female market: 'What is it
about the City J that it wins the hearts of so many women?
It's quite simple: it is trustworthy and uncomplicated, can be
easily led and doesn't have bad moods. And at the end of the
month there's always enough left for a pretty blouse.'[109]
In 1990, Mercedes-Benz ran an advertising campaign in
which the image was of a woman wearing a hat and posing
on the bonnet of a Mercedes. The headline was: 'The typical
Mercedes driver wears a hat.' The text read:

If you look at who drives a Mercedes, you'll find that
many of our drivers are women. Last year alone, 22,700
women bought a new Mercedes. Which only shows that
German women are not only becoming more successful,
but they are also enjoying their success.[110]

What the advertisement does not tell us is that these 22,700
women are just 8 per cent of new Mercedes buyers; 92 per
cent are still men.
The previously mentioned traffic jam counsellors have
also made their contribution to our understanding of the
gender aspect of the car society. A husband, caught in a
traffic jam with his wife or wife and children, will never
leave the motorway and try another route to their destination. The reason, according to the traffic counsellors: 'Then
the husband would have to rely on his wife to read the road
map. But choosing the route is a man's job.' The traffic jam

is, in any case, nothing new for the family man; he experiences it every day on his way to work: 'The motorway tailback gives the family man the opportunity to let his loved ones experience what he has to put up with every day to earn a living for all of them.'[111]

In 1985, Austrian radio did a programme on going for a holiday in your car – the trip itself and all the necessary preparations. From the programme and from the phone-ins, what became clear was that it was the woman's task to make all the logistic preparations for the trip (clothes, food, packing, maps, etc.), while it was the man who was responsible for 'the trip itself'. One particular interviewee, a Frau Berger from Vienna, explained that she made a detailed list every year of the necessary items and even how to pack them in the car. But what happens, she was asked, when the man at the wheel gets in a bad mood or gets angry, in a traffic jam, for instance. Frau Berger answered: 'Then I've got the joke list. Oh yes, during the weeks before the trip, I collect jokes and write them down. When the situation becomes critical, I read him one of the jokes.'[112]

Ten years later, nothing has changed. Before the 1995 summer holiday period, the *Süddeutsche Zeitung*, one of Germany's leading daily papers, prepared its readers for the annual trip:

> Whining children, the silent father with his foot on the gas pedal, the mother doing her best to maintain harmony: the car trip is one of those endurance test for the family. The tight space, the heat, and the strain produced by the unfamiliar surroundings – it is no wonder that, as the results of a survey have shown, nine out of ten couples quarrel in their car.

The article ended with some tips for motoring tourists, among them:

> She's driving too slow for him; he makes comments such as 'it would be faster on foot'. Solution: if he doesn't stop complaining, then just get out of the car and let him continue on his own. No matter who is at the wheel, the rule remains: the driver decides, the co-driver remains

silent. That way, you avoid emotional land mines – and your holiday can get off to a perfect start.[113]

On 3 August 1985 there was a remarkable edition of the sports show, *Aktuelles Sportstudio*, on Germany's second channel, the ZDF. A number of those fearless men who drive the world's fastest cars and who are paid to carry adverts for the world's big corporations had been invited to appear on the show. Suddenly, and somewhat surprisingly, a man in a wheelchair joined the studio guests – the ex-car racer, Regazzoni, paralysed from the waist down as a result of a racing accident. As a naive viewer, I assumed that this was to be the 'critical' or 'thought-provoking' part of the show. But quite the opposite was the case. Regazzoni 'regretted nothing' and 'would do it all over again'. Today he is running a racing school for other victims of the sport. He has built special racing cars in which the accelerator is attached to the steering wheel so that even a paraplegic can shift into sixth gear at a speed of 200 km/h. We were informed by the host of the show that Regazzoni is carrying on a brave fight in Italy against a restrictive law which does not permit physically handicapped people to drive any car above a certain rpm. 'He is a model for us all,' he said, to prolonged applause from the studio audience.[114]

Among the studio guests was the Formula One racer, Manfred Winkelhock, who had a contract with the magazine, *Penthouse*, and who was to race on the Nürburgring the following day. Winkelhock was asked to compare the old Nürburgring, which was extremely dangerous, had cost many lives and had been boycotted for a time by Formula One racers, with the newly constructed and less dangerous race course. As was to be expected, the Swabian racer complained that the new Nürburgring was 'boring' and he missed the old one. This confession was rewarded with loud applause from both the host and the studio audience.

One week later, the virtues applauded by ZDF were to cost Manfred Winkelhock his life: participating in a 1,000-km race in Canada, on a course which has an image among Formula One racers similar to that of Nürburg, Winkelhock hit a concrete wall while travelling at 200 km/h. The media tend to overlook the link between the way they present the 'sport' of car racing and the deaths of drivers like Winkelhock in 1985 or Ayrton Senna in 1994. They prefer to draw attention to 'human error' or 'inadequate provision of first-aid'. The *Süddeutsche Zeitung* took up this theme but was resigned to the view that nothing would change:

> If anyone were to ask the only sensible question, how long this kind of organised suicide should be allowed to continue – they would be drowned out by the noise of the next race. Car racing is male, it is exciting, and it is business, business, business – and it is the risk that makes it attractive. Since the end of the war, as many as 78 Grand Prix drivers have been burned, crushed, at any rate killed in the exercise of this sport, and this is why so many fans crowd into every new race, because they know it will soon be 80, and eventually 100.[115]

Notes

Part I

1. In 1987, in the first edition of this book, for instance, I wrote that, although 'the industrial revolution began in England in 1780', the building of 'a rail network dates from the year 1835' (p. 34). I was also unaware, at the time, of the significance of the canals.
2. Jonathan Sale, 'Back on the Straight and Narrow', *Country Life*, no. 31, 1993.
3. Philip Bagwell, *The Transport Revolution from 1770*, London, 1974, p. 17.
4. R. Freethy and C. Woods, *Discovering the Leeds to Liverpool Canal*, (without place or date of publication), p. 4.
5. Ibid., p. 9
6. Bagwell, *The Transport Revolution*, p. 16.
7. B. Brecht, *Gesammelte Werke*, vol. 9, Frankfurt, 1967, p. 656.
8. W. Durand and A. Durand, *Kulturgeschichte der Menschheit*, vol. 17, Munich, 1981, p. 313.
9. Bagwell, *The Transport Revolution*, p. 33; previous quote from M. Clark, *Leeds and Liverpool Canal. A History and Guide*, (Aston, 1990, p. 31.
10. Bagwell, *The Transport Revolution*, pp. 33–4. By 1938 there were only just over 600 children living in the narrow boats. In so far as the canals fulfilled a decisive role in the transport revolution they did so at the expense of the canal boat people whose living conditions were more cramped and insanitary than those of the inhabitants of the back-to-back houses of the factory towns.
11. Clark, *Leeds and Liverpool Canal*, p. 139.
12. Bagwell, *The Transport Revolution*, p. 32.
13. *Deutsche Geschichte*, vol. 3, Berlin, 1989, p. 258.

14. E. Rehbein et al. (eds), *Einbaum, Dampflok, Düsenklip-per*, Leipzig/Jena/Berlin, 1969, p. 153.

15. Rehbein, *Einbaum*, p. 157.

16. Bagwell, *The Transport Revolution*, p. 32.

17. Freethy and Woods, p. 9. Previous quotation from N.T. Fryer, 'A Canal with a Future', *Country Life*, 2 May 1963, p. 1004. The examples from the US are to be found in Gustavus Myers, *History of the Great American Fortunes*, 3 vols, Chicago, 1910. The second and third volumes have the sub-title 'Great Fortunes from Railroads'. The information on how the Vanderbilt fortune was built is in vol. II, Chapters 3–8.

18. 'Richard Trevithick was born in the heart of the tin-mining area, the son of the manager of the Dolcoath mine and, in his early twenties, was himself the manager of a mine near Penzance. In 1800 he moved to Camborne where on 28 December in the following year he tried out a steam road carriage he had designed and built ... [He] attracted the attention of Samuel Homfray, proprietor of the Penydern colliery, near Merthyr Tydfil in Wales, who invited Trevithick to design a locomotive specifically for the 93/4-mile long railway which ran from Penydern to Abercynon. Both there and at Torrington Square near Euston, where he ran the locomotive Catch-me-who-Can round a circular track in 1808, the Cornish engineer demonstrated the practicability of the steam locomotive.' Bagwell, *The Transport Revolution*, p. 90.

19. Rodney Dale, *Early Railways*, London, 1994, p. 23.

20. Wolfgang Schivelbusch, *Geschichte der Eisenbahnreise – zur Industrialisierung von Raum und Zeit im 19. Jahrhundert*, Munich/Vienna, 1977, p. 11.

21. Dale, *Early Railways*, p. 29.

22. The quotation and the information in this paragraph are from Dee Brown, *Hear That Lonesome Whistle Blow*, London, 1977, pp. 20–3.

23. *Allgemeine Geschichte*, p. 258.

24. Karl Marx, *Capital*, vol. 1, Harmondsworth, 1978, p. 506.

25. The table is from H. Witte, 'Lebensadern der Wirtschaft – Die Ökonomischen Auswirkungen des Eisenbahnbaus',

in *Zug der Zeit – Zeit der Züge. Deutsche Eisenbahn 1835–1985*, West Berlin, 1985, p. 173.

26. V.I. Lenin, 'Imperialism, the Highest Stage of Capitalism', in *Selected Works*, London, 1969, p. 240.

27. Schivelbusch, *Geschichte der Eisenbahnreise*, p. 43.

28. 'Friedrich List', in *Staatslexikon*, published in 1837. List's major work on the railways was first published in 1833: *Über ein sächsisches Eisenbahn-System als Grundlage eines allgemeinen deutschen Eisenbahn-System*. The Friedrich List Institute of Transport in Dresden, in the GDR, devoted itself to promoting and developing the ideas of List. This Institute came under new leadership as a result of unification and, as early as the summer of 1990, began to promote the car.

29. Figures in Table 2.2 are from R. Fremdling, 'Industrialisierung und Eisenbahn', in *Zug der Zeit*, pp. 129–31.

30. According to *Bevölkerung und Wirtschaft 1872–1972*, published by the Statistical Office, Wiesbaden, 1972, p. 247.

31. Werner Sombart, *Die deutsche Volkswirtschaft im neunzehnten Jahrhundert und am Anfang des zwanzigsten Jahrhunderts*, 7th edn, Berlin, 1927, pp. 240ff.

32. Ibid., p. 242.

33. G. Sammet, 'Das Klassensystem der Beweglichkeit', in special supplement to *Nürnberger Nachrichten*, 10 May 1985.

34. Dorothee Klinksiek, 'Die Eisenbahnbauarbeiter in der Frühzeit des Eisenbahnbaus in Bayern', in *Zug der Zeit*, p. 252.

35. Peter Herzog, *Die stählerne Strasse, Roman der Eisenbahn*, Bonn, 1955, p. 326.

36. Cf. Dick Roberts, *American Railroads*, New York, 1980, p. 53.

37. Paul A. Baran and Paul M. Sweezy, *Monopoly Capital*, New York, 1966, pp. 220ff.

38. Fremdling, 'Industrialisierung und Eisenbahn', in *Zug der Zeit*, p. 126.

39. Ibid., p. 132.

40. Ibid., p. 133.

41. The quote from Engels is from a letter to Marx, 5 September 1869, in *Marx Engels Briefwechsel*, vol. 1,

Berlin/GDR, 1950, p. 140. Information on Strousberg from Manfred Ohlsen, *Der Eisenbahnkönig Bethel Henry Strousberg – eine preussische Gründerkarriere*, East Berlin, 1987, pp. 132ff.; R. Fremdling, 'Pioniere – Portraits deutscher Lokomotivhersteller', in *Zug der Zeit*, vol. 1, pp. 140ff.

42. Sombart, *Die deutsche Volkswirtschaft*, p. 243.

43. Schivelbusch, *Geschichte der Eisenbahnreise*, p. 43.

44. Max J. Coturnix, 'Der Kampf um das Mass', *Die Schöne Welt*, no. 3, 1985. The Russian gauge of 1534 millimetres (five feet) was used by the Austrian, Franz Anton Gerstner, in constructing the Petersburg to Tsarskoye Selo line, and is still in use today. In Australia there were four different gauges which were standardised to the normal gauge in the twentieth century. For instance, the Adelade to Port Pirie line was standardised only in 1984. (See Fritz Stöckl, *Die grossen Eisenbahnrouten der Welt*, Hamburg, 1985, p. 444. It is often maintained that the Spanish and Portuguese railways run on the same gauge, but this is not true. The Spanish gauge is 1674 millimetres while the Portuguese one is 1665 millimetres, nine millimetres narrower. Only a small number of specially equipped trains are able to run on both lines. (See Brian Hollingsworth, *Railways of the World*, New York, 1979.)

45. Schivelbusch, *Geschichte der Eisenbahnreise*, p. 44.

46. Rossberg, *Geschichte der Eisenbahn*, Künzelsau, 1977, p. 90.

47. Ibid., p. 67.

48. Ibid., p. 103.

49. 'US-Eisenbahnen. Ein ruhmloses Ende?', in the German weekly, *Wirtschaftswoche*, 14 June 1985.

50. Joseph A. Schumpeter, *Business Cycles*, vol. 1, New York, 1939, p. 346.

51. In French, Italian and Spanish, the joint stock company is appropriately named 'anonymous' company.

52. Karl Marx, *Capital*, vol. 3, London, 1972, pp. 436–8.

53. H. Bodenschatz, 'Eisenbahn und Städtebau', *Stadt*, published by Neue Heimat, no. 2, 1985.

54. Myers, *History of the Great American Fortunes*, vol. II, pp. 77ff.

55. Ohlsen, *Der Eisenbahnkönig*; see also J. Bochart, 'Der Mann der zuviel wollte', *Süddeutsche Zeitung*, 25 August 1985.
56. Ulrich Küntzel, *Die Finanzen grösser Männer* , Frankfurt/Berlin/Vienna, 1984, p. 447.
57. Nicholas Faith, *The World the Railways Made*, London, 1990, pp. 24–5; The report in the House of Lords mentioned in the following paragraph is quoted by Marx in *Capital*, vol. 3, pp. 408ff.
58. Schumpeter, *Business Cycles*, p. 344.
59. See Ohlsen, *Der Eisenbahnkönig*, p. 77.
60. Rossberg, *Geschichte der Eisenbahn*, p. 155.
61. Robert Fitch, 'The Love machine: Sex and Scandal in the Penn Central', in *Ramparts*, Berkeley, California, March 1972.
62. Marx, *Capital*, vol. 2, Harmondsworth, p. 260.
63. Schumpeter, *Business Cycles*, pp. 406ff.
64. Myers, *History of the Great American Fortunes*, vol. 3, pp. 126ff.
65. See Roberts, *American Railroads*, pp. 34 and 22.
66. Constantin Pecqueur, *Economie Sociale*, Paris, 1839, pp. 335–8, quoted in Schivelbusch, *Geschichte der Eisenbahnreise*, pp. 67ff.
67. Supplement to *Nürnberger Nachrichten*, 10 May 1985.
68. Sombart, *Die deutsche Volkswirtschaft*, pp. 244ff.
69. A leading judge by the name of Poinsot was murdered. See Schivelbusch, *Geschichte der Eisenbahnreise*, p. 77.
70. Quoted from Harmann Glaser, 'Das Transitorische', *Nürnberger Nachrichten*, 15 September 1982, p. 71.
71. Bagwell, *The Transport Revolution*, p. 108.
72. Ibid., p. 109.
73. Quoted in D. N. Smith, *The Railway and its Passengers. A Social History*, North Pomfret, Vermont, 1988, p. 17.
74. Ibid., p. 12.
75. Bagwell, *The Transport Revolution*, pp. 109–10.
76. Ibid., p. 110.
77. *Wirtschaftswoche*, 1 June 1984.
78. Ibid.
79. Schivelbusch, *Geschichte der Eisenbahnreise*, p. 98.
80. Rehbein, *Einbaum*, p. 386.
81. Rossberg, *Geschichte der Eisenbahn*, p. 386.

82. Schivelbusch, *Geschichte der Eisenbahnreise*, p. 96.

83. See Rossberg, *Geschichte der Eisenbahn*, p. 151; also Herzog, *Die stählerne Strasse*, p. 52.

84. Schivelbusch, *Geschichte der Eisenbahnreise*, p. 103. See a similar report on the Trans-Siberian Railway in Rossberg, *Geschichte der Eisenbahn*, p. 365.

85. Myers, *History of the Great American Fortunes*, vol. II, pp. 132ff.

86. Rossberg, *Geschichte der Eisenbahn*, p. 153; Herzog, *Die stählerne Strasse*, pp. 260ff.

87. The bogie was widely used in Europe after the First World War.

88. Myers, *History of the Great American Fortunes*, vol. II, p. 76.

89. J.R. Daughen and P. Binzen, *The Wreck of the Penn Central*, Boston/Toronto, 1971, p. 35; see also, Myers, *History of the Great American Fortunes*, vol. II, p. 214, for an account of the same incident.

90. Friedrich Engels, 'Der 24 Juni', in Marx Engels Werke, vol. 5, Berlin, 1959, pp. 123ff.

91. M. Junkelmann, 'Die Eisenbahn im Krieg', in *Zug der Zeit*, p. 237.

92. From Moltke's military correspondence, quoted in ibid., p. 238.

93. F. Sonnenberger, 'Kolonisierung heisst transportieren – Europa und der Begin der Eisenbahnzeitalters in Afrika', in *Zug der Zeit*, p. 228.

94. Horst Drechsler, *Aufstände in Südwestafrika*, Berlin, 1984, pp. 47–140.

95. Walter Rodney, *Afrika – Die Geschichte einer Unterentwicklung*, Berlin, 1975, pp. 180ff. and 196.

96. E. Galeano, *Die offenen Adern Lateinamerikas*, Wuppertal, 1973, p. 227.

97. See the account of Lenin's train journey in Edmund Wilson, *To the Finland Station*, London, 1960, pp. 466ff.

98. For an account of Trotsky's tactic of rapid movement on 'internal lines', see Isaac Deutscher, *The Prophet Armed*, Oxford University Press, 1970, pp. 432ff.

Part II

1. Sombart, *Die deutsche Volkswirtschaft*, p. 239.
2. *Allgemeine Geschichte der Technik von den Aufängen bis 1870*, Leipzig, 1981, p. 259.
3. Herzog, *Die stählerne Strasse*, p. 46.
4. Rehbein, *Einbaum*, p. 107.
5. Ibid., p. 112.
6. Ilya Ehrenburg, *The Life of the Automobile*, London, 1985, p. 17.
7. Henry Ford, *My Life and Work*, Chicago, 1910, p. 73.
8. Ibid., p. 103.
9. Marx, *Capital*, vol. 1, p. 548.
10. Ford, *My Life and Work*, pp. 105–6.
11. Ehrenburg, *The Life of the Automobile*, p. 17.
12. Information on the early military uses of the automobile is to be found in 'Autos an die Front – Krieg auf vier Rädern', *Geschichte mit Pfiff*, Nürnberg, no. 1, 1986.
13. According to Baran and Sweezy, *Monopoly Capital*, p. 227.
14. Ibid.
15. Hollingsworth, *Railways of the World*, p. 139.
16. Dick Roberts, *The American Railroads*, New York, 1980, p. 53.
17. Figures from Schumpeter, *Business Cycles*, vol.2, p. 1,024.
18. A. Kock, 'Auf dem Highway Number One durch die Karibik', *Welt am Sonntag*, 16 September 1990.
19. For an account of the major capital groups in the US in the nineteenth and early twentieth centuries see Myers, *History of the Great American Fortunes*.
20. This should refer to state revenue.
21. Data from Ulrich Küntzel, *Der Nordamerikanische Imperialismus*, Darmstadt & Neuwied, 1974,) pp. 42ff. and 49ff.
22. F. Lundberg, *America's 60 Families*, New York, 1938, pp. 63ff.
23. Roberts, *The American Railroads*, p. 53.
24. B.C. Snell, *American Ground Transport. A Proposal for Restructuring the Automobile, Truck, Bus, and Rail*

*Industries, presented to the Subcommittee on Antitrust
and Monopoly of the Committee on the Judiciary,
United States Senate*, 26 February 1974, Washington,
1974.

25. Snell, *American Ground Transport*, p. 18. Previous infor-
mation from Robert Lacey, *Ford, Eine amerikanische
Dynastie*, Düsseldorf/Vienna/New York, 1987, p. 245;
Albert Speer, *Erinnerungen*, Frankfurt/M, 1969, p. 357;
Daniel Yergin, *The Prize. The Epic Quest for Oil, Money,
and Power*, New York, 1991, Ch. 17.

26. Markus Völkel, 'Einigkeit und Freiheit', in *Zug der Zeit*,
p. 226.

27. The figures are from *Bevölkerung und Wirtschaft
1872–1972*, published by the Statistical Office in Wiesbaden, pp. 203ff.

28. *Bevölkerung und Wirtschaft*, pp. 203 ff.: my own estimates.

29. Ibid.; *Süddeutsche Zeitung*, 14 May 1985: my own estimates.

30. Lichtenstein, *Mit der Reichsbahn in den Tod – Massen-
transporte in den Holocaust*, Cologne, 1985, p. 12.

31. Lichtenstein, *Mit der Reichsbahn*, p. 12; P. Hilberg,
Sonderzüge nach Auschwitz, Mainz, 1981.

32. G. Aly and S. Heim, *Vordenker der Vernichtung. Auschwitz und die deutschen Pläne für eine europäische Ord-
nung*, Frankfurt/M, 1993, pp. 436ff.

33. A. Ganzenmüller, quoted in H. Schwartz, 'Das Räder-
werk des Todes', in *Zug der Zeit*, vol. 2, p. 689.

34. R. Doleschal and R. Dombois, *Wohin läuft VW?*, Hamburg, 1982, p. 20.

35. Rehbein, *Einbaum*, p. 237.

36. The first Hitler quote, from his speech at the automo-
bile exhibition in 1934, is from Doleschal and Dombois,
Wohin läuft VW?, p. 23. The second quote is from
Hanno Loewy, 'Reichsautobahn – Pyramiden des Dritten
Reichs', *Links*, June 1983.

37. Press quotations from Hans Dollinger, *Die totale Autogesellschaft*, Munich, 1972, p. 131.

38. This was the requirement of the Ministry of Transport,
quoted from Doleschal and Dombois, *Wohin läuft VW?*,
p. 23.

39. OMGUS – *Ermittlungen gegen die Deutsche Bank*, published by the US Military Government for Germany, 1946–7; republished by Franz Greno, Nördlingen, 1985, p. 116.

40. R. R. Rossberg, 'Neubeginn in Trümmern', in *Zug der Zeit*, p. 742.

41. From U. Häusler, D. Haase and G. Lange, *Schienen statt Strassen*, Würzburg, 1983, pp. 53ff; E. Haar, S. Merten and F. Prechtl (eds), *Vorfahrt für Arbeitnehmer*, Cologne, 1983, pp. 163ff.; Rossberg, *Geschichte der Eisenbahn*, p. 60; *Verkehr in Zahlen*, published by the German transport ministry, Bonn, 1994; my own estimates.

42. R. Rossberg, *Geschichte der Eisenbahn*, p. 60.

43. Haar, Merten and Prechtl, *Vorfahrt für Arbeitnehmer*, p. 163.

44. Source: *Aktionsprogramm der ÖTV für den öffentlichen Personennahverkehr*, Stuttgart, 1983, p. 29; Häusler, Haase and Lange, *Schienen statt Strassen*; my own estimates.

45. Source: *Bevölkerung und Wirtschaft 1872-1972*, pp. 204ff.; *Lange Reihen zur Wirtschaftsentwicklung*, pp. 100ff.; *Verkehr in Zahlen*, 1994.

46. Figures from: *Lange Reihen zur Wirtschaftsentwicklung*, pp. 102ff.; differences from 100 per cent: other social layers.

47. See V. Ronge and G. Schmieg, *Restriktionen politischer Planung*, Frankfurt/M, 1973, p. 264; V. Ronge and G. Schmieg, *Projekt Klassenanalyse. Det Staat in der BRD*, Hamburg/Berlin, 1977, pp. 171ff.

48. Figures from the annual statistical publications of West and East Germany.

49. Figures from *Beitrag zur Entwicklung des Personenverkehrs – DDR 2000*, published by the Hochschule für Verkehrswesen 'Friedrich List', September 1989, p. 18.

50. Ibid. pp. 7ff.

51. Werner Gross et al., *Komplexe Modernisierungs- und Erneuerungsstrategien im Eisenbahnverkehr*, Part 3, Dresden, 1989, p. 12.

52. *Leistung in Zahlen*, published by the German Economics Ministry (BMWI), Bonn, 1984, p. 21.

53. *Guardian* 'Weekend', 6 August 1994.

54. 'Return Train', *The Economist*, 24 August 1985.

55. *European Conference of Ministers of Transport, Trends in the Transport Sector 1970–1989*, Paris, 1990.

56. Ibid.

57. The 12 corporations are as follows (the numbers in brackets are the number of units produced in 1981): 1. General Motors/Opel (6.2m); 2. Toyota (3.2m); 3. Ford (3.7m); 4. Nissan/Datsun (3.1m); 5. VW/Audi (2.2m); 6. Renault (1.8m); 7. Peugeot (1.6m); 8. Fiat (1.2m); 9. Toyo Kogyo/Mazda (1.1m); 10. Mitsubishi (1.1m); 11. Honda (1.0m); 12. Chrysler (1.0m).

58. According to *Le Monde*, 3 July 1979.

59. Figures according to the *Statistisches Jahrbuch 1984*, p. 97.

60. John Griffiths, 'Car Output', *Financial Times*, 23 December 1994.

61. Data and estimates from: 'The Global 1000', *Business Week*, 13 July 1992, and from *Wirtschaftswoche*, 24 December 1992.

62. Data from 'Die Grössten im Überblick', *Wirtschaftswoche*, 24 December 1992.

63. Information on London from T. C. Parker and Michael Robins, *A History of London Transport*, vol. 1, London, 1963, p. 66; information on Berlin from Winfried Wolf, *Berlin – Weltstadt ohne Auto? Eine Verkehrsgeschichte 1848–2015*, Cologne, 1994, p. 33; see also Wally Seccombe, *Weathering the Storm*, London, 1993, pp. 132ff.

64. The health of the poor was not of interest until they were needed for war. At the end of the nineteenth century, the German war ministry discovered that only 28 per cent of eligible young men in Berlin were fit to serve in the army; among young men from the rural areas, the figure was 64 per cent. Information from: Werner Hegemann, *Das steinerne Berlin. Geschichte der größten Mietskaserne der Welt*, Braunschweig/Wiesbaden, 1992, p. 288; previous quotation from H. von Treischke, *Der Sozialismus und seine Gönner*, Berlin, 1874. On the housing shortage in Berlin at the time, Treischke wrote: 'Everyone is responsible for their own

actions; no one is so poor that, in their cramped room, they can't hear the voice of their god.'

65. Bernhard Strowitzki, *U-Bahn London*, Berlin, 1994, p. 44. The previous information on the development of London during this period is also from Strowitzki.

66. Quoted in F. Geist and K. Küvers, *Das Berliner Miet-shaus*, vol. 2, 1862–1945, Munich, 1984, p. 150; also Wolf, Berlin, pp. 25ff.

67. Quoted in Dieter Radicke, 'Öffentlicher Verkehr und Stadterweiterung – Berlin 1800–1875', in Fehl/Rodriguez, *Stadterweiterungen 1800-1875, Von den Anfängen des modernen Städtebaus*, Hamburg, 1983, p. 349.

68. The figures for London are from Parker and Robins, *A History of London Transport*, pp. 196 and 263; figures for Berlin from Wolf, *Berlin*, p. 33.

69. Quoted in Wolf, Berlin, pp. 38ff.

70. Estimates based on figures from Parker and Robins, *A History of London Transport*; Wolf, Berlin; J. Joyce, *London's Tram*, London, 1920.

71. The term 'Underground' (German: 'U-Bahn') is used here to refer to the whole system, even though only a portion of it actually runs below ground: in London, only 40 per cent of the 400-km tube is below ground (160 km).

72. Figures for Berlin from Wolf, *Berlin*, p. 247 (derived, in turn, from the official statistics of the Berlin transport authority, the BVG).

73. The figures in the table are from *Die BVG und ihr Betrieb*, published by the BVG, Berlin, 1934.

74. The amount of energy used by the escalators in the Frankfurt underground is higher than the amount used by the underground itself. Since the London tube is even deeper below ground, the proportion of electricity consumed by the escalators is probably even higher.

75. Hegemann, *Das steinerne Berlin*, p. 312.

76. According to Michael Busse, *Autodämmerung*, Frankfurt/M, 1980.

77. T. C. Parker, *A History of London Transport*, vol. 2, London, 1974, p. 191.

78. H. J. Dyos and D. H. Aldercroft, British Transport. *An Economic Survey from the Seventeenth to the Twenti-eth Century*, Harmondsworth, 1969, pp. 149–50.

79. Information in this section mainly from B. Strowitzki, *U-Bahn London.*

80. Dieter Apel, *Verkehrskonzepte in europäischen Städten,* Berlin, 1992, p. 96. The figures, at the same time, for Hamburg (300) and Munich (210) were lower.

81. W. Hegemann, *Das steinerne Berlin,* p. 311.

82. 'Despite their slowness and their inconveniently situated central termini [outside the centre of London], the tramways gained traffic at as fast a rate as the omnibuses' (Parker and Robins, *A History of London Transport,* p. 263).

83. These two events are described in greater detail in Wolf, *Berlin,* pp. 55ff.

84. For greater detail see Wolf, *Berlin,* pp. 95ff.

85. Already in 1949, a sub-committee of the US Senate reported that: 'by 1949 ... General Motors had been involved in the replacement of more than 100 electric transit systems with GM buses in 45 cities including New York, Philadelphia, Baltimore, St. Louis, Oakland, Salt Lake City, and Los Angeles'. Quoted in Roberts, *American Railroads,* p. 53. In 1974, Bradford Snell prepared a report for the US Senate which showed in detail how Ford, GM, Chrysler, and the tyre corporation, Firestone, had conspired to replace the rail systems in the cities: *American Ground Transport – A Proposal for Restructuring the Automobile, Truck, Bus, and Rail Industries,* by Bradford Snell, presented to the Sub-Committee on Antitrust and Monopoly of the Committee of the Judiciary, United States Senate, Washington, 1974.

86. Figures from *Berliner Zeitung,* 23 December 1993.

87. In all of Berlin in 1994 the number of journeys on public transport per inhabitant was 344; in 1929 it was 449.

88. Quoted in Parker, *A History of London Transport,* vol. 2, p. 13.

89. Figure from *Mobilität und Klima – Wege zu einer klimaverträglichen Verkehrspolitik,* published by the German Parliament's Commission of Enquiry into the Protection of the Earth's Atmosphere, Bonn, 1994, p. 117.

90. Ibid., p. 118.

Part III

1. Figures for united Germany (1991): in a total population of 79.6 million, there are 41.6 million driving licences (52 per cent). Among people over 18 years old (60.5 million), 31.1 million have continuous access to a car. A further 6 million have 'occasional access'. In the whole population over 18, 51 per cent have continuous access to a car and 10 per cent have occasional access. As a proportion of the total population, 39 per cent have daily access to a car and 8 per cent have occasional access. The statistics are from *Verkehr in Zahlen*, 1994, pp. 125ff.

2. André Gorz, *Ökologie und Politik*, Hamburg, 1977, p. 89.

3. Robert Fedden, 'The Lure of Skiing at St. Moritz', *Country Life*, 5 November 1964, p. 1,217.

4. *Der Spiegel*, no. 19, 1980.

5. Alexander Mitscherlich, *Thesen zur Zukunft der Stadt*, Frankfurt, 1971, p. 62.

6. Cf. Le Corbusier, *Concerning Town Planning*, London, 1947, pp. 57ff. Le Corbusier's book was first published in France in 1945.

7. From Hans Dollinger, *Die totale Autogesellschaft*, p. 26.

8. Cf. A. Mitscherlich, 'Thesen zum Städtebau' and 'Die Stadt der Zukunft, two lectures held in 1965 and 1967 and published at the time as well as in the collection, *Thesen zur Zukunft der Stadt*, Frankfurt, M, 1971.

9. S. Cautacuzino, 'American Solutions to Office Planning', *Country Life*, 20 October 1966, pp. 984ff.

10. Strowitzki, *U-Bahn London*, p. 48; figures for Germany: in 1970, Germany had 3,588 km of tram lines, in 1990, 1,309 km. From *Verkehr in Zahlen 1994*, p. 84.

11. D. Appleyard and M. Lintell, 'The Environmental Quality of City Streets: the Residents' Viewpoint', *Journal of the American Institute of Planners*, no. 38, 1972, pp. 84ff.

12. Quoted in Dollinger, *Die totale Autogesellschaft*, p. 27.

13. Mitscherlich, *Thesen zur Zukunft der Stadt*, pp. 67ff.

14. Le Corbusier, *Concerning Town Planning*, p. 59.

15. Ibid., pp. 74–6.
16. Ibid., p. 88.
17. Walter Schwagenscheidt, *Ein Mensch wandert durch die Stadt*, Bad Godesberg, 1957, pp. 10 and 21.
18. Fritz Jaspert, *Vom Städtebau der Welt*, West Berlin, 1961, p. 363.
19. Le Corbusier, *Towards a New Architecture*, London, 1947, pp. 278–80.
20. Wolf Linder, Ulrich Maurer and Hubert Resch, *Erzwungene Mobilität*, Cologne and Frankfurt/M, 1975, pp. 39 and 43.
21. Busse, *Autodämmerung*, p. 127.
22. Stella Margetson, in *Country Life*, 14 November 1963, p. 1,259.
23. 'Fussänger – und Fahrradverkehr in der Bundesrepublik Deutschland', *DIW-Wochenbericht*, no. 39, 1981.
24. Rainer Hopf, Heilwig Rieke and Ulrich Voigt, *Analyse und Projektion der Personenverkehrsnachfrage in der Bundesrepublik Deutschland bis zum Jahr 2000*, published by Deutsches Institut für Wirtschaftsforschung (DIW), 1982, p. 113.
25. *Guardian*, 28 July 1994.
26. Jörg Linser, *Unser Auto – eine geplante Fehlkonstruktion*, Frankfurt/M, 1978, p. 27.
27. Brian Sewell, 'The big car has become a gross codpiece driven by overgrown adolescents', *Financial Times*, 1995; figures on petrol consumption from *Verkehr in Zahlen 1994*.
28. Jörg Linser, *Unser Auto*, p. 67.
29. Ibid., p. 15.
30. Ibid., pp. 97, 63 and 101ff.
31. R. Chimelli, 'Renommiermodelle als Pfadfinder für eine schnelle Zukunft?', *Süddeutsche Zeitung*, 3 October 1988.
32. Sewell, 'The big car'.
33. *Handelsblatt*, 13 October 1984; *Wirtschaftswoche*, no. 17, 1985.
34. *Bild*, 4 May 1985.
35. Linser, *Unser Auto*, p. 123.
36. *Wetterauer Zeitung*, 19 May 1984.
37. *Handelsblatt*, 12 October 1984.

38. Data from Bruno Liebaug, ... *und man fährt trotzdem weiter*, Niederkassel, 1981, pp. 15ff. Previous figures for the Nazi state from Till Bastian and Harald Theml, *Unsere wahnsinnige Liebe zum Auto*, Weinheim and Basel, 1990, p. 52.

39. According to *Auto-Zeitung*, 9 August 1985.

40. The statistics are already weighted according to the frequency of different models on German roads.

41. *Der Spiegel*, no. 29, 1985.

42. Data from Peter Klinkenberg, 'Beim Stickoxid nur ein geringes Einsparungspotential', *Frankfurter Rundschau*, 9 October 1984.

43. 'Japan – riesiger Vorsprung bei Katalysator Autos', *Der Spiegel*, no. 34, 1984.

44. F. Gröteke, 'Nur im Traum zu erreichen', *Die Zeit*, 15 March 1985.

45. Bastian and Theml, *Unsere wahnsinnige Liebe*, p. 105.

46. *Wegweiser der Apotheke*, no. 1, 1990.

47. Advertisement in *Country Life*, July 1958.

48. Fiat's advertisement for the Fiat Panda backfired when the model was described as 'remaining voluntarily below the recommended speed limit of 130 kph'.

49. *Frankfurter Rundschau*, 22 September 1989.

50. 'Kult mit Keksdosen', *Der Spiegel*, no. 10, 1990.

51. *Der Spiegel*, no. 10, 1990.

52. 'Operation Lauf der Autobahn', *Stern*, no. 24, 1989.

53. Linser, *Unser Auto*, pp. 129ff.

54. From ADAC *Motorwelt*, no. 4, 1990.

55. The *Öko-Magazin* did a study that compared new and used cars. The used car was 29 per cent cheaper, (*Öko-Magazin*, no. 32, 1985). Figures for British Rail are from *British Railways Board Annual Report and Accounts 1994–95*, p. 68.

56. Ivan Illich, *Energy and Equity*, London, 1974, pp. 30–1.

57. My own calculation on the basis of the statistics given in Table 19.

58. An example of how the amount of time needed to cover costs is estimated for a Golf owner with a net hourly wage of 20 DM: operational costs 6,672 DM, divided by 20 DM per hour, gives us 334 hours (col. 5). Time needed in/for car in column 2 added = 684 hours as the total number

of hours in the year for the car (col. 10). 15,000 km in the year divided by 684 gives us 22 km/h.

59. The Uniroyal study is reported in *Süddeutsche Zeitung*, 8 February 1985.
60. *Süddeutsche Zeitung*, 7 November 1989.
61. *Hamburger Abendblatt*, 2 June 1988.
62. *Süddeutsche Zeitung*, 29 May 1991.
63. *Frankfurter Rundschau*, 7 May 1991.
64. Helmut Holzapfel, in *Freytag*, 15 March 1991.
65. Peter Kraus, 'Blech und Blut, *Penthouse*, no. 3, 1989.
66. Karl Marx, *Grundrisse*: London, 1973, p. 307.
67. Quoted in *Spuren Suchen*, published by the Körber Foundation, no. 4, 1990, p. 11.
68. Ford, *My Life and Work*, p. 55.
69. 'Vier Räder und die Esskultur', *Geschichte mit Pfiff*, no. 1, 1986, p. 40.
70. J. Eason Gibson, 'From London to the Highlands', *Country Life*, 8 September 1966.
71. W. A. Poucher, 'The New Highland Coast Road', *Country Life*, 20 October 1966.
72. *Frankfurter Rundschau*, 13 June 1995.
73. Quoted in Busse, *Autodämmerung*, p. 2.
74. *Der Spiegel*, 16 August 1991.
75. Quoted in Dollinger, *Die totale Autogesellschaft*, pp. 103ff.
76. According to *Penthouse*, no. 1, 1991.
77. 'Die Lust am Stau', *Stern*, no. 24, 1984.
78. Cf. Busse, *Die Autodämmerung*, p. 7.
79. *Bunte*, 14 February 1985.
80. 'Highway to Homicide', *Time*, 17 August 1987.
81. *Express* (Cologne), 13 January 1994.
82. *Tageszeitung*, Hamburg, 16 November 1990.
83. *Stern*, no. 4, 1989, *Neue Revue*, no. 13, 1988.
84. *BZ* (Berlin), 8 November 1994.
85. *Stern*, no. 44, 1990.
86. *Bild*, 22 February 1990.
87. Stuart Marshall, 'Gunship or Racing Car?', *Financial Times*, 10 November 1990.
88. Clemens Hagen, 'Die Monster kommen', *Sport Bild*, 27 June 1990.
89. 'Death Riders – A Tragedy in Toxteth', *Sunday Times*, 3 November 1991.

90. *Stern*, nos. 33 and 41, 1991.

91. *Umwelt, Verkehr, Umkehr* (Herzogenbuchsee, 1983), p. 19.

92. Bastian and Theml, *Unsere wahnsinnige Liebe*, pp. 50 and 88; The previous quote is from J. Roberts et al. (eds), *Travel Sickness. The Need for a Sustainable Transport Policy in Britain*, London, 1992, p. 221.

93. According to *Stadt für Kinder*, published by the Hesse ministry for development, Wiesbaden, 1991.

94. Inge Peter-Habermann, *Kinder müssen Verunglücken. Von der Aussichtslosigkeit, bei uns Kinder vor Autos zu schützen*, Reinbeck, 1979, quoted in Liebaug, p. 30.

95. *Wirtschaftswoche*, 21 September 1984.

96. According to D. Apel, B. Kollek and M. Lehmbrock, *Stadtverkehrsplanung, Teil 4: Verkehrssicherheit im Städtevergleich*, published by the Deutsche Institut für Urbanistik (difu), Berlin, 1988.

97. *Regensburger Woche*, 30 September 1982, quoted here from *Verkehrte Kinder?*, published by the Fussgänger-schutzverein (Society for the Protection of Pedestrians), Berlin, 1991.

98. *Statistisches Jahrbuch 1984*, p. 345.

99. Otl Aicher, *Kritik am Auto – Schwierige Verteidigung des Autos gegen seine Anbeter*, Munich, 1985.

100. Sylvia Baker, 'Lady Drivers take to the Road', *The Lady*, 12–18 February 1991, p. 351.

101. 'Frauen fahren den Männern davon', *Süddeutsche Zeitung*, 8 November 1988.

102. *Verkehr in Zahlen 1990*, p. 119; the figures are for 1985.

103. Ibid., p. 120; figures for 1985.

104. 'Frauen fahren den Männern davon', *Süddeutsche Zeitung*, 8 November 1988; 'Immer mehr Frauen halten sich jetzt einen Wagen', *Süddeutsche Zeitung*, 3 September 1987.

105. Quoted from the conference records.

106. *Kölner Stadtanzeiger*, 26–7 May 1990.

107. *Die Zeit. Magazin*, no. 22, 1995.

108. *Autowelt*, no. 4, 1984.

109. In Liebaug, p. 101.

110. *In Welt am Sonntag*, 25 November 1990.

111. 'Lust am Stau', *Stern*, no. 24, 1984.
112. Österreich 3, programme on 19 June 1985, 14.50 h.
113. *Süddeutsche Zeitung*, 14 June 1995.
114. Regazzoni's book, *Der Unzerstörbare* [*The Indestructible*], Germany, 1985, is written in a similar vein.
115. *Süddeutsche Zeitung*, 14 August 1985.

Index

Index by Auriol Griffith-Jones